Looking at the Broad Picture

Looking at the Broad Picture: Smarter Software Development for Irish Companies

By

Marty Sanders

Edited by

Ita Richardson and Mícheál Ó hAodha

CAMBRIDGE
SCHOLARS

PUBLISHING

Looking at the Broad Picture:
Smarter Software Development for Irish Companies,
by Marty Sanders

This book first published 2011

Cambridge Scholars Publishing

12 Back Chapman Street, Newcastle upon Tyne, NE6 2XX, UK

British Library Cataloguing in Publication Data
A catalogue record for this book is available from the British Library

ISBN (10): 1-4438-2397-X, ISBN (13): 978-1-4438-2397-5

TABLE OF CONTENTS

LIST OF FIGURES

LIST OF TABLES

PREFACE

The development and maintenance of computer software continue to be surrounded by mystery. Even simple software is still very complex. Dr. Chris Horn, co-founder of Iona Technologies and President of Engineers Ireland, described it this way:

> The English translation of Tolstoy's *War and Peace* has about 43,000 lines. The full release of Debian version 4 for Linux [operating system] has about 283 million lines of code, which is thus about 6,500 times as big as *War and Peace* (Horn 2009).

Working with software is a solitary effort for one or a thousand individuals. What you see on the outside screen or in a printed report does not necessarily reflect what is going on inside. Bugs can lurk inside a system for years before surfacing when the triggering set of conditions finally occurs in the right sequence. How do you know what is going on? What is happening in the guts of the system? Where can things go wrong?

This book evolved from research into what long-term benefits some companies derived from changing the way they manage software development and maintenance. They did it to help answer some of these questions. In order to do that research, a model had to be developed which could be used in multiple types and sizes of companies to create a series of company profiles. These then could be compared to evaluate similarities and differences in company experiences.

The model developed was based on components from three sources. Therefore it is called the Multi-Model Assessment Instrument (MMAI) and it turned out to be very useful on its own merits. Models and standards abound; they usually have one of two formats: they look at many parts of the software process in great detail, or they look at a few parts of the software process, also in great detail. Using either type of model can be useful, particularly in a procurement, contracting or partnership situation. But a model like the MMAI may be more useful for an organisation at the very beginning of trying to understand how it manages software now and how it could do better. The MMAI covers a broad spectrum of issues at a basic level for a good overview of strengths and weaknesses.

Read the book, particularly the profiles of companies interviewed. See if you think using the MMAI could help your organisation understand its software development and/or maintenance practices better.

ACKNOWLEDGEMENTS

To give credit to all the people, groups and companies who made this possible would create a new document with many chapters going all the way back to thanking my first instructor in FORTRAN at Purdue University in June 1961. This book documents a history I lived as well as the current research and I thank the many people who made it all possible.

For this particular exercise in frustration, I have my advisor, Dr. Ita Richardson, to thank. She has suffered with me through sloughs of despair to bring us through to the other side.

This research was partially supported by Science Foundation Ireland grant 03/CE2/I303_1 to Lero - the Irish Software Engineering Research Centre (www.lero.ie). It is hard to overstate the value of support from Lero personnel, ranging from Professor Kevin Ryan through my graduate student companions and the administrative staff who have been there to help in diverse ways. Dr. Jim Buckley, Dr. Norah Power, Professor Eamonn Murphy and Professor Brian Fitzgerald all had helpful comments and suggestions during the research and Jim's thoughtful review of an earlier paper and detailed comments were particularly useful.

My husband, Joc, is approaching sainthood.

CHAPTER ONE

INTRODUCTION

1.1 Introduction to the research

Software problems have existed since the earliest days (O'Connell 1994, Pulford *et al.,* 1996). These problems have been met with many different solutions, including improved processes, other software methods, standards and improved skills as shown in Figure 1-1. Sometimes these solutions have been implemented sequentially, sometimes concurrently.

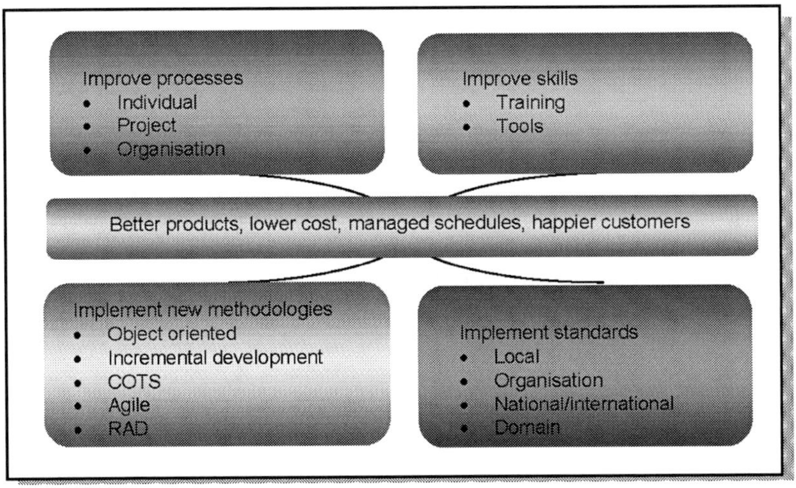

Figure 1-1 Software problem solutions over time

This volume reviews a range of software problems and solutions and explores how general patterns evolved as tools and the development experience have improved. The concept of software process improvement (SPI) has grown since it was originally proposed (Humphrey 1990) to become an environment where a range of SPI standards and models exist.

These have been used to help companies manage software development and maintenance more effectively, to provide an opportunity for recognition, to demonstrate capabilities and to deliver the products and services required.

The research presented was designed to:

1) Evaluate the commonalities and differences in selected standards and models
2) Adopt or develop an assessment model which could be used in companies that incorporated these different standards and processes for improvement
3) Use the chosen assessment model to evaluate the current status of companies which participated in SPI programmes sponsored by the European Commission from 1994 through to 1999; applying this model enabled improved validation of the usefulness of the model, and also determined a likely answer to the question, "Was SPI assistance useful in helping these companies improve their software processes?"

1.2 Structure of this book

Chapter two describes the software environment, starting with the general culture of software development and maintenance that makes it so difficult to manage. Specific problems including late deliveries, cost overruns on software projects and poor quality software, are all described, as are some of the solutions which were developed to improve these issues. General solutions, including various standards and models, were developed to change the entire culture of an organisation. This was followed by the idea of software process improvement—better processes lead to better products. Certification of an organisation's capability to provide the required goods and services has been driven and enabled by the evolution of all the major SPI standards, thereby leading to extended globalisation of the software market.

Chapter three describes SPI events in Ireland between 1994-1999, and the historical research undertaken in relation to them. Some short-term benefits of SPI as described in various reports and case studies are presented and programme differences outlined.

Chapter four looks at successes and failures in SPI from researchers in different locations and types of environments.

Chapter five outlines the environment for this research and the methodology followed.

In Chapter six, the development of a chosen model for cultural assessment, the Multi-Model Assessment Instrument (MMAI), is described.

Chapter seven shows profiles of the companies interviewed for this research, describing both their culture and improvement experiences.

Chapter eight presents the actual data collection and analysis. Extraction of the collated data and the correlations of data which are of particular interest are also discussed. Comparisons are made between the results of SPI in the literature and results from this research.

Chapter nine is a summary, with conclusions about the usefulness of the MMAI, company improvements and the objectives which were met. There is a review of the research process and its limitations, the contributions facilitated by this research, the post-research environment and some plans for the future.

The appendix shows the interview guide used to gather information.

CHAPTER TWO

THE SOFTWARE ENVIRONMENT

2.1 The culture of software development and maintenance

Software project management can be difficult due to the inherent nature of the product. The most common software-related problems identified include intangibility, complexity and volatility of requirements (Jurison 1999). A lack of understanding concerning the relationships between technology, people, the organisational culture and the general business environment all contribute to project failures (Mitev 2000). Personal/political reasons may also make people hope that a project fails (Rost 2004). Software managers are frequently not business people and vice-versa.

2.2 Problems in software development

2.2.1 Introduction

The losses from software failures can be expensive. Out of the many examples a few stand out. In Ireland, the Health Service Executive and other government departments spent over $190M on computer systems which overpaid staff, had security issues and other continuing problems including suspension before completion for some systems (Coulter 2005, Donnellan and Reid 2005, McGee 2008, Horn 2009). In the UK, J Sainsbury PLC abandoned its supply-chain management system after deployment for a loss of nearly $600M (Charette 2005). McDonald's Corporation cancelled the Innovate information-purchasing system after $170M was spent (Charette 2005). The literature is full of examples of money spent for little or no return (Flowers 1996, Labanyi 2005, Reid 2005, Horn 2009) to name a few.

2.2.2 Specific problems and solutions

Many reasons for these types of failures that have been identified include: late deliveries and cost overruns, poor software quality, inadequate value management and lack of support. For each of these problems, potential solutions are presented.

2.2.2.1 Late deliveries and cost overruns

Projects that overrun schedules and budgets, as described by Brooks (1975, reprinted in 1995) are improved through better project estimation and/or project management processes. Risk mitigation for a company is also sometimes expanded to include risk management techniques specific to software systems.

Project estimation

Description

Good project estimation consists of understanding the tasks which need to be done and the time it takes to do them. Where this knowledge is absent, projects tend to overrun their schedules and budgets and software products are inadequate or incorrect. For example, one of the principal mistakes made in project estimation was noted by Brooks (1995) as long ago as 1975: project duration does not depend linearly on staff-numbers and adding more people will not necessarily shorten the duration of a project.

Benefits

Good project estimation is important because it provides essential input to pricing, planning and budgeting processes and therefore ensures that everyone has a clear understanding of the price to be paid for a specific product or service.

Problems

Inconsistency in estimation may be a result of not using formal estimation models and a lack of training in using them (Grimstad and Jørgensen 2007, Gruschke and Jørgensen 2007). Schedule and resource estimation, planning to meet business goals and bidding for contracts can be confused with one another since they all have different goals. A single method of estimation is probably inadequate and inaccurate but this is frequently the way it is done, nevertheless (Jørgensen 2005). Technical people are asked to contribute to the estimation process but frequently in business terms that they would normally not use (Putnam *et al.* 2005). Estimation frequently does not take into account team sizes or the impact of schedules, costs and quality constraints (Putnam *et al.* 2005). Of course estimation is no better than the knowledge of the estimators. Software requirements always change (Jones 2008). Changing requirements, a vague project description, or other issues can make estimation a very difficult task (Roetzheim 2005). An experienced member of one team said that on all projects more than 50% of the effort was a consequence of unexpected events (Jørgensen 2005).

Project management

Description

Regardless of their size, all projects exhibit certain common characteristics that distinguish them from other types of work. Projects are temporary, undertaken to provide a specific product or service, have a finite schedule, clear outputs and goals, a specific leader, a schedule and particular resource requirements (Clements *et al.* 2005, Jurison 1999). Projects are also carried out by teams (Jurison 1999).

The role of project management is expanding. The decreasing costs of equipment and communication, the increased costs of people and potential failures, the increased complexity of software, and the increased availability and capability of tools have led to profound changes in project management. Distributed project management is used to support the development of large, complex systems in many sectors (Nidiffer and Dolan 2005), one of these being global software development (GSD) as initiated in more than one country.

GSD contains challenges for project management that may already have existed at some level in other distributed development enterprises but have become more visible with GSD. Amongst these challenges is the need for better planning, the enhanced management of people, more efficient organisational structures, risk management, infrastructural processes, conflict management and more supportive team structures and organisations (Ebert 2006, Casey and Richardson 2006).

Decision support systems are evolving to accurately estimate dynamic project behaviour (Donzelli 2006). More specialised tools are being developed to marry the organisational chart with the precedence diagram for the dynamic re-assignment of resources or the assignation of additional capabilities which may be needed at certain times in the project (Rifkin 2000).

Benefits

Good project management enables one to reach the project objectives within time and in accordance with estimated cost and performance. These three variables are the critical project dimensions which require continual project management attention. More recently, managers have added a fourth constraint: good client relations. To manage the above constraints two additional factors are essential: visibility and commitment (Jurison 1999).

Problems

Good project management is difficult. People have different skills and personalities, with productivity studies showing substantial differences between individual developers. No single methodology can be applied to every project (Howard 2001). This means that the project manager needs good management skills and flexibility in how to apply them. Project management with GSD has its own set of problems, including: lack of shared values, poor understanding of requirements, inadequate management of shared artefacts, unclear work assignments and ownership, insufficient communication, inadequate management strategies, unknown legal requirements, a high employee turnover rate or cultural and linguistic difficulties (Ebert 2006, Casey and Richardson 2006, Sarma and van der Hoek 2006, Hsieh 2006).

One study examines the factors for success or failure. These include: problems with the project manager and the overall management of the team; poor information gathering, a lack of understanding for the management of requirements and/or changing requirements. Optimistic or inaccurate scheduling and poor estimation are also amongst the factors contributing to project failure (Verner and Evanco 2005).

Risk management

Description

The risk management process as described by Conrow (2005) is outlined in Figure 2-1.

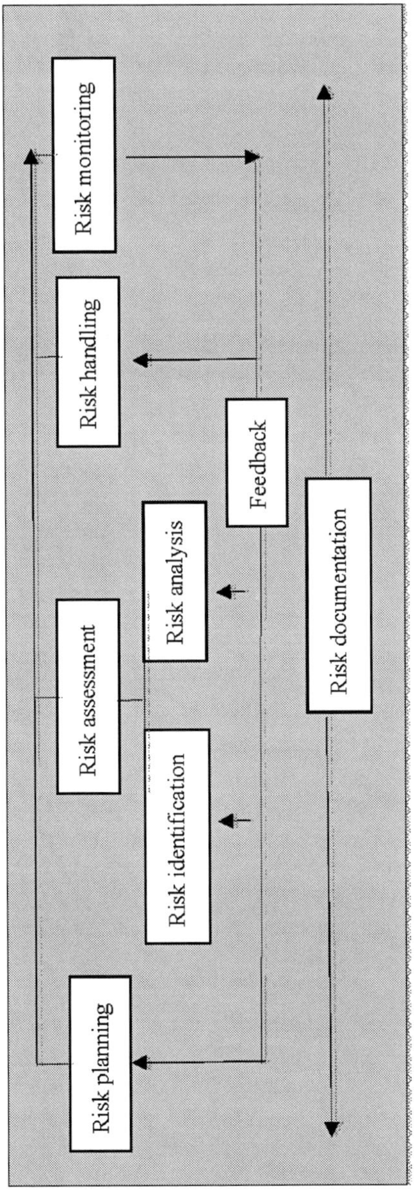

Figure 2-1 Risk management process

Succinctly, risk can be defined as a potential problem, event, hazard, threat, or situation with undesirable consequences (Hantos 2005).

Three major factors which influence project risk are: project size, project structure and experience with technology. The larger the project, the less structured it is and the less experienced the team are with the technology of the project, the greater the attendant risk. To counteract this, during the planning phase, the project manager needs to perform a realistic assessment of risks and develop a plan for controlling these same risks (Jurison 1999).

Benefits

In one sense, risk management is the most important activity for any company. If a company is not managing risk, what are its chances of even staying in business? In another sense, risk management is the umbrella under which everything else fits. A good risk management strategy should identify whether better project management, configuration management, project estimation, or other improvements are needed. Unfortunately, risk management seems to be both poorly understood and seldom practiced.

Problems

It is necessary to analyse the most significant risk drivers such as potential difficulties with schedule, technology, funding, integration, etc. Then develop risk scenarios so as to determine those events or trigger points which warn of any imminent risk (Holt 2005). However, it is not always so easy to determine what these risk drivers are, particularly on a new type of project.

For example, a risk assessment tool was used in the examination of 720 projects by senior IT managers in 60 large companies. Some of the findings were a surprise to the researchers because the top risk driver was one which is often neglected by management (use of inappropriate technology), while the least influential risk driver (requirements volatility) was one which managers often complain about the most. Six key risk drivers were identified, along with their relative importance to software project risk, and this, in turn, led to the introduction of a one-minute risk assessment tool that can be applied to improving software practice (Tiwana and Keil 2004).

Regardless of individual risks, risk has to be addressed from a system perspective in order to prevent: costly delays, increased stress for team members, development of a lesser product or even project failure (Holt 2005). For systems which incorporate large systems themselves, additional issues need to be understood, including such questions as multiple stakeholders, long life cycles, integration risk as a result of complexity, and other issues which may or may not be important within smaller systems (Conrow 2005).

Another example is the special environment that is object-oriented software development, a process which carries its own set of risks. Boehm's top ten risks were re-evaluated in an object-oriented sense and shortfalls in external components, architecture, performance and quality were identified as being far more important than in other environments (Hantos 2005).

The conclusion reached here is that every organisation and project should be evaluated for the special risks associated with its unique attributes, rather than attempting to follow one set of recommendations for the entire software environment.

2.2.2.2 Poor software quality

Poor quality software has been rectified at several levels by learning to gather and manage requirements better, by testing quality within the software itself, and the use of quality management tactics.

Requirements elicitation and management

Description

To "elicit" means to draw forth, to bring out something's latent potential, (Brown 1993). So requirements elicitation is simply the gathering of requirements. As is expressed more broadly in ISO TR 15504 (1998) requirements elicitation means: *to gather, process and track evolving customer needs and requirements throughout the life of the software product and/or service so as to establish a requirements baseline that serves as the basis for defining the required software work products.* Requirements are elicited through interviews, questions, observations and various other techniques; no matter which process is used, some level of structure is preferred (Dieste *et al.* 2008).

One definition of requirements management is from the CMM, Paulk *et al.* (1993) *Requirements management is used to establish a common understanding between the customer and the software project of the customer's requirements that will be addressed by the software project.* Activities include the following: the software engineering group reviews the allocated requirements before they are incorporated into the software project; the software engineering group uses the allocated requirements as the basis for its software plans, work products, and activities; changes to the allocated requirements are duly reviewed and incorporated into the software project.

High quality requirements of any type are adequate, unambiguous, consistent and verifiable (Glinz 2008). Functional requirements are those which define what the product *does*; these form most of the requirements as defined by the customer. Non-functional requirements are those that define *how* the product does the task; this includes quality, performance and maintenance requirements. Technical requirements are those requirements which define how the system is built—hardware, language, interfaces to other systems, etc. (Dekkers 2005). Requirements come from many sources including customers, users, other members of the organisation and other constraints due to hardware or system limitations.

Benefits

Requirements specifications define what the software is required to do. With well-managed requirements, developers can design the correct software, testers can test the software and compare the results with the requirements and programmers can write the correct code (ISEB 2002). Good requirements elicitation and management are necessary for good design and implementation, although it is not a guarantee of success on every occasion.

A computer system is designed and based on the requirements the developers have been given. Therefore, the more clearly the requirements are understood and expressed, the more likely the system will meet the customer's needs.

Problems

Project estimation is a formidable task from the beginning—especially before and during the requirement discovery process. Poor requirements lead to poor estimates and poor schedules. An estimate is only as good as its least reliable input variable (Dekkers 2005). One of the most common and best-known problems in project estimation is the failure to deal with requirements, which are about a complex real world and not simply a computer system (Jackson 2004). Part of that current complex real world is GSD, where the requirements have to be tasked and managed across cultural, time-zone and organisational boundaries (Damian 2006). Additionally, there are usually more requirements than can be implemented with the time and resources available (Karlsson and Ryan 1997). A successful process will incorporate a risk-based, value-oriented strategy in order to prioritise the requirements and mitigate the risks (Glinz 2008, Feather *et al.* 2008).

Requirements change, particularly during long projects. If the changes are not documented and well-managed, systems will be designed and developed according to the wrong requirements. Additionally, it is difficult to avoid defects in functional requirements. After a major failure, it is usually easy to see where more attention and care were needed, but this is not so obvious while the system is being developed (Jackson 2004). More specific problems may include: users cannot express their requirements unambiguously, users cannot express their requirements completely or developers do not fully understand the business (ISEB 2002).

Testing

Description

A test is a controlled exercise involving an object under test, a definition of the environment, a definition of the inputs, a definition of expected outputs or results. When a test is performed you get an actual output or result and a determination as to whether the result is correct. Common stages of testing are: component or unit testing, link testing (integration testing of a few components), functional and non-functional system testing, integration testing of major subsystems and the whole system, and user acceptance testing. Regression testing tests the rest of the system which has not been intentionally changed to ensure it still works correctly (ISEB 2002).

Benefits

A human being can make an error which introduces a fault to a program, thereby causing possible failure of the software. Testing helps find the faults before they translate into failures. Successful testing can save significant effort and increase product quality, thereby lowering maintenance costs (Juristo *et al.* 2006).

Problems

Component or unit testing is normally done by the developer but is constrained by what the developer knows regarding testing. For example, frequently developers do not consider full structural coverage (Runeson 2006). Despite obvious benefits, testing practices in industry generally are not as sophisticated or effective as they should be (Juristo *et al.* 2006). The level of effort required for testing has to be adjusted to the size of the job and the organisation, although it is often difficult to know the scope (Menzies and Cukic 2000).

Also, testing can be a very expensive way to find potential problems, if that is the sole method employed.

Quality management

Description

Quality management has taken many forms over the years, but two particularly stand out. ISO 9001 is a quality management standard used throughout the world. Total Quality Management (TQM) was used in Japan in the 1970s and became popular in the US during the 1980s (Dellana and Wiebe 1992). Four essentials of TQM are: top management's direct involvement in the delivery of quality, customer orientation, company-wide participation in quality, and the use of systematic methods to resolve quality problems (Bagchi 1997). Both TQM and ISO 9001 are designed to change the culture, attitude and organisation of a company that seeks to provide customers with quality products and services which satisfy their needs (Lee and Roberts 1997). Both require management commitment to quality and changes throughout the organisation to support this attitude. Activities are included which increase the level of confidence in quality from customer focus in designing the business processes down to software tests and inspections as added to the software life cycle.

Benefits

TQM is a management philosophy that seeks to integrate functions and focus on meeting customer needs. ISO 9001 is also focused on meeting customer needs but with specific processes defined. The premise is that high quality leads to high productivity and shorter schedules (Jones 2008).

Problems

Quality, like beauty, is in the eyes of the beholder. Developing a notion of quality that everyone understands, whether or not they agree with it, has proven difficult. For example, TQM has as a basic tenet that all processes are continually improved through process improvement and statistical process control (Biehl 2004). Not everyone sees the same benefit or the same cost through the implementation of TQM, however. The business owner is trying to strike a cost/benefit balance that will enable the business to make a profit and provide products and services the customer(s) will buy and use. Different customers are likely to have different ideas of what quality is. The users may have a different idea about how the system operates and whether it has quality or usability. TQM requires non-stop effort from everyone in the company. However, this practice can sometimes prove dehumanising since it is dominated by corporate and business interests (Bagchi 1997, Lee and Roberts 1997).

Six Sigma has grown out of the TQM environment (Biehl 2004) and has as a goal to build self-correcting mechanisms into the system. Therefore, software failures should not occur and the customer should not see any defective software. However, all of this costs time and money and may not be appropriate for some software environments.

Another issue concerning quality measures is their effectiveness. Formal design and code inspections are said to be more than 65% effective in finding bugs or defects while testing finds about 30% of the bugs that actually exist (Jones 2008). Therefore, through the use of more accurate requirements and better design, quality measures need to be implemented from the very beginning of the software project. This is all the more important given that if these percentages are correct, inspections and testing will not by themselves find all of the problems anyway. The cost-to-benefit ratio also always has to be considered, particularly in a smaller company. Historically, fixing software bugs is the most expensive software activity (Jones 2008).

Fixing software bugs means time and resources have to be allocated for a new cycle of code and implementation, a documentation update, testing of several types and, in some cases, the recall or reissue of software. Therefore, it is a very expensive proposition.

2.2.2.3 Inadequate value management

Description

Concern that activities were not providing appropriate value for the effort expended on them has led to various value management activities. The term "return on investment" (ROI) can be used to mean profits, competitive advantage or simply "something good" (Erdogmus *et al.* 2004). At its simplest, value management can mean increased quality of products, accuracy of plans and budgets with reduced cost of software projects (Fetzer 2002). Optimal release cycle duration (the scope of the product/project vs. the time it took), optimal project staffing levels and the effects of uncertainty on staff, customers and the market place (Little 2004) are also considered in value management.

Benefits

A case study by Boehm and Huang (2003) merged earned value management with a business value model. The goal here is to make sure that not only are the tasks completed within budget, but that the business goals are met in addition to the technical goals. This is depicted graphically in Figure 2-2.

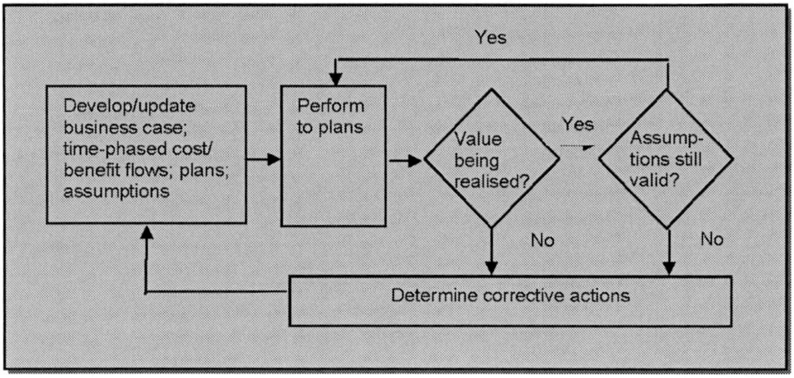

Figure 2-2 Value-realisation feedback process (Boehm and Huang 2003)

The quantitative element of this analysis includes the effects on the organisation's profit-and-loss "bottom line", either in terms of additional profit streams or cost savings. The benefits analysis should also include a qualitative evaluation of benefits including customer satisfaction, company reputation, and supply-chain controllability (Boehm and Huang 2003).

Problems

It is not always easy to follow the trail from technical improvement to business improvement. This is one of the reasons that improvement initiatives are frequently not tied to any business orientation. Management commitment and understanding is frequently lacking because of this (Debou and Kuntzmann-Combelles 2000). The links between IT investment and profitability are not always clear (Dedrick *et al.* 2003, Gerlach *et al.* 2002), let alone the links between other improvements and profitability. Productivity is not easy to calculate and the reasons for increases or decreases are not always easy to understand (Groth 2004).

The ROI calculation of "benefits-cost/cost" organises the costs and benefits into a formula, but strategic analysis to determine the business value of software management techniques has also to take into account both time and risk. Time costs money and a lower risk project is probably more attractive than a higher risk one. Some kind of common denominator is needed to make decisions about what makes business sense and what does not, however. One way of looking at things is the net (present) value, which looks at all of the costs. The value of money in the bank earning interest vs. the cost of inflation in a long project is one example. Valuation can be made on the risk vs. reward for a particular project (Erdogmus *et al.* 2004, Fetzer 2002). Calculation of productivity, the value of the work being done and the best options to take are difficult to ascertain in software engineering. The credibility of the model and the results of using it depend on the data, definitions and assumptions (Premraj *et al.* 2004).

Additionally, personal motives may be important. Executives are motivated by compensation and bonuses and these are frequently based on current profits and not future benefits. This might prove a driver for short-term benefits but not extend the value-for-money that may require more long-term investment (McGibbon 1999).

2.2.2.4 Lack of support activities

Measurement and training are described as separate activities which can improve all of the aforementioned areas.

Measurement

Description

A measurable attribute is a distinguishable property or characteristic of a particular software entity. A base measure is the measure of a single attribute defined by a specified measurement method. A measurement method is a logical sequence of operations, described generically and used in quantifying an attribute with respect to a specified scale. Measurement can be subjective involving human judgement or rating, or objective as based on numerical rules (McGarry *et al.* 2002, ISO/IEC 15939). Common measurements taken include: quantity of function (lines of code, function points are examples), schedule (planned and actual), headcount applied in relation to time or defects (Card 1991).

Benefits

Measurement can support effective communication using objective information; enable the tracking of project objectives; assist in identifying and correcting problems at an early stage; provide important information for making key trade-off decisions within the constraints of cost, schedule, capability, technical quality and performance; and provide a rationale for the decisions made (McGarry *et al.* 2002, Herron and Garmus 2005).

Without careful measurements, continuous progress is unlikely (Jones 2008). Measurement can also provide clear targets for improvement.

Problems

Common mistakes in measurement include: "overkill" with too much data; measurement that tells people what they want to hear; measures that lead to inconclusive data analysis and picking measures that reinforce the wrong processes (McGarry *et al.* 2002)

According to Grable *et al.* (1999), in one big organisation a number of small projects tried to use measurement but failed. The data collected was inconsistent, unreliable and incomplete. Then a grand "master plan" for measurement was put in place, albeit that poor cooperation and completeness/accuracy problems plagued the collection effort. Observations about the early efforts included the following:

- Project engineers did collect data of some kind but resisted doing anything with it;
- The simple presentation of data was appreciated and used by management;
- Measurement did bring improvement, at least initially;
- The act of using cost models produced good estimates even where there were no grounds for validation;
- People were concerned that data would be used against individuals;
- Project leaders were concerned about the time their projects took and that their projects would look bad against other projects; and it was difficult to get consistent measurements.

The response to these observations was to develop a simplified measurement programme and address the management issues head-on (Grable *et al.* 1999).

Measurement will fail without support from highest management, training on analysis of data, up-front investment in time and tools, validation of the data, periodic calibration of the cost model, statistical confidence in the data and regular feedback (Grable *et al.* 1999). The key to the acceptance of measurement in small organisations is to keep it simple, tailor it to each organisation and ensure that it produces valuable information. This means the severe pruning of more general checklists and guidelines which may have been designed for larger organisations (Kautz 1999).

Training

Description

Training in an employment context means teaching the skills and abilities uniquely needed by the organisation. Training could be required for any of the subjects discussed in this volume. Training for employability includes variability in subject and presentation to suit the needs of the organisation and its trainees, linkage between business goals and training output, career development benefits for the trainees and organisational efforts which enable the trainee to use the new skills to everyone's benefit (Nilson 1998).

Benefits

Organisations increasingly recognise that formal training is critical not only to the success of the software professionals but to the company's competitive position in the marketplace. A key objective of training programmes is to help participants develop mental models into which they can place learned concepts (Devaraj and Babu 2004). The quality of the mental models is judged by how well the models represent the market reality. Organisational-wide models reflect the general understanding of a business, its vision, operational purpose, the environment in which it operates and its corporate culture and values (Chen *et al.* 2003). An integrated training and consulting method has been used successfully to instil lasting change. The combination of team-based learning and applying the new learning to a real-world situation helps improve performance (Hutchings *et al.* 1993).

Problems

Training has to reflect the way the student processes information. Linear processing is the step-by-step approach and global processing takes in the bigger picture. Some people respond to visual stimulation, some to verbal. Other intelligences have to be considered when determining the format and content of training. If not, the benefits will be limited (Vidakovich 2000).

Frequently, courses do not take into consideration the work situations of the students, and in the case of public training, the trainer does not usually fully understand those work situations. Although technical knowledge may be successfully gained in the classroom, the degree to which it is applied on return and integrated into one's group varies (Hutchings *et al.* 1993). While individual training may be informative and raise awareness of the issues, it is seldom the key to lasting change within an organisation. In 1995, more than $5 billion was spent by U.S.

companies on end-user training. However, there was little evidence of verifiable returns or of effective results as a consequence (Nelson *et al.* 1995). The effect of training on a trainee's job performance is rarely measured (Mahapatra and Lai 2005).

2.2.2.5 Conclusions about specific solutions and support

Berry (2008) has some interesting observations on silver bullets, those individual developments that we assume will solve software problems.

1. Once we put anything in writing—from a formal specification to executable code—it becomes much more difficult to change and we are not inclined to do it at all regardless of what tools or methodologies are available.
2. Once change starts to happen (and it will), the difficulty increases. This may be in the changing of documentation or code where the developers do not want to (carefully) track each change and its effects but they choose instead to make a quick patch, a move which increases system brittleness.
3. Silver bullets do come along, but once they have solved that particular problem, they are not silver any more; one example is GUI builders. They encouraged people to examine the user interface in a way they never had before, since the problems were too great to solve in making interactive interfaces. Once a library of easily-usable tools appeared, the unsolvable became solvable and taken for granted.

Specific solutions to problems and support activities can all be valuable solutions, whether used alone or in conjunction with the more general solutions described in the following sections. Most organisations profit by some combination of solutions.

2.2.3 General solutions to software problems

While each of these activities in their own way could be effective in helping to solve software problems, organisations started looking at more general solutions which provided cultural change within the environment for developing and maintaining software. General solutions to change an organisation's culture include lean programming techniques of various types and the use of open source software. Standards and models are used to gain certification that is at an accepted level of quality in terms of both process and product. Why are there differences in these general solutions?

> "With more than 13,000 projects examined, it can be stated categorically that there is no single method of development that is universally deployed or even universally useful." (Jones 2008)

This comment was made after looking at the relationship between the size of a program vs. the software processes to be used, but there are also other considerations, some of which are described in the next sections.

Lean programming

Description

Agile, extreme programming (XP), crystal development, adaptive software development, feature driven development, rapid application development (RAD)—including dynamic systems development method (DSDM) and incremental funding method (IFM)—scrum software and other slimmed down methodologies stress and improve communication among project members, reduce paperwork, and increase customer involvement. Testing is carried out throughout the project life-cycle. Teamwork and cooperation are paramount for success. All support iterative incremental development of small packages (Rising and Janoff 2000, Howard 2002, Drobka *et al.* 2004, Lindvall *et al.* 2004, McMahon 2005, Sliger 2004, Jones 2008).

The founders of many of the most popular agile methods created The Agile Manifesto with some of these beliefs in mind:

- Individuals and interactions mean more than processes and tools;
- Working software is the principal measure of success and more important than documentation;
- Close and daily contact, face-to-face conversation, between developers and clients is necessary;
- Small self-organising teams give the best results;
- Quality is critical, so early and continuous testing is important (McMahon 2005, Jones 2008).

These value statements apply to any of the lean programming techniques, as the unique features of the lean methods approach include the decomposition of the application into separate iterations, the daily face-to-face contact with one or more user representatives, daily sessions to discuss the backlog of work left to be accomplished and any other problems that might slow down progress (Jones 2008).

Benefits

According to proponents, XP is an agile, iterative development process which creates focused, efficient software development that heavily emphasises customer involvement (Drobka *et al.* 2004, McMahon 2005). This means slimming down the processes altogether and working closely with customers at every step. Agile proponents would agree that paperwork is the second most expensive software activity historically, as stated by Jones (2008).

One view of agile or XP is that it is unique because it provides constant feedback to the developers. Dynamic quality assurance and modern quality principles are built into the process using on-site customer presence, pair programming, continuous integration and testing, and individual responsibility for quality (Howard 2002, Huo *et al.* 2004). However, there are also examples of agile being used in distributed environments with less of the customer presence than is customarily acknowledged as required; such examples have been successful with globally-applied, continuous build and integration, and verification tests (Paasivaara and Lassenius 2006).

One report on four large corporations (ABB, Daimer-Chrysler, Motorola, Nokia) which belong to a consortium, the Software Experience Center, was designed to investigate various different aspects of software development. It discussed the results of 15 pilot projects which involved XP in these large organisations, either using XP as is, choosing selected practices and incorporating them into their regular processes, or using XP terms to refer to the practices they already used. Business drivers for these experiments are common to nearly all software developers, such as the drive for increased flexibility, improved productivity and quality, and eliminating unneeded or time-consuming work. All pilot projects the XP study covered had similar positive experiences. The subjective and objective measures indicate that these projects succeeded in terms of increased agility and made improvements to one or more of the following attributes: customer satisfaction, quality, productivity and cost. In addition, most developers involved in the projects had positive experiences; team morale increased and introducing the practices did not prove costly. The report's authors then spoke about some of the situations unique to large organisations, situations which probably would not be a problem for most Irish companies. Points they noted above should apply to anyone using XP (Lindvall *et al.* 2004). Another project manager decided that the formal processes and schedules, meeting notes, issue logs, action items and other formal trappings of project management were not best for all projects. This manager observed that traditional project management methods such as those promoted in the CMM, seemed to work best with the largest and most complex projects (building a bridge, launching a space probe, designing new aircraft), or when staff were dispersed at different geographic locations (Sliger 2004). Indeed, this is what the CMM was designed for in the first place.

In traditional requirements-design-implementation models, too many systems were delivered that met the user requirements at the time of design, but did not meet changed requirements when the system was delivered months or years later. RAD and other lean programming aims to reduce the time between determining requirements and implementing them, reducing the likelihood that they will change in the interim period (Howard 2002).

The Incremental Funding Method (IFM) version of RAD maximises returns by delivering functionality in "chunks" of customer-valued features, carefully sequenced so as to optimise the project's net present value (NPV). Instead of focusing exclusively on controlling risk and cost, IFM also addresses "time to value" (that is, the rate at which value is returned to the customer). It can work in conjunction with any iterative software process. IFM decomposes the system to be developed into units of functionality known as minimum marketable features—small, self-contained features that can be delivered quickly and that provide market value to the customer. The concept is carried further by decomposing a large project into mini-projects; IFM increases the likelihood of success for large-scale development efforts where management can be difficult (Denne and Cleland-Huang 2004).

Many of the new programming styles offer something in exchange for a change in work habits, and (sometimes) in exchange for a cultural change, too (Rifkin 2001). In summary, lean programming offers the opportunity to work more closely with customers and with one another than some of the more formal processes or models. With much more emphasis now placed on developing software rather than developing plans and documentation, it offers almost instant improvements to developers and has the potential to be very satisfying to managers who like to spend their time liaising with their customers instead of with paper.

Problems

Pair programming requires large blocks of time. One solution is to set aside large blocks of time in developer's schedules, and dedicate these to pair programming. Managers must choose pairs carefully to balance both personalities and experience (Drobka *et al.* 2004).

Cross-team communication can be difficult since the lean programming techniques are set up to support a small team on a single project. It requires sufficient people to create the right number of teams. It requires developers and customers who are committed to and understand lean principles and processes. And of course, not all types of applications are appropriate for lean programming (Lindvall *et al.* 2004, O'Sullivan and Fitzpatrick 2004).

There are elements of concern about implementing agile processes in traditional development organisations. The differences between current development processes and the diametrically opposed agile methods may seem to be irreconcilable. Different life cycles and the necessity to deal with legacy systems may make it difficult to make the transition to agile. Strategies to overcome these difficulties include serious preparation and work on new processes and responsibilities. Problems may sometimes be more a question of perception than "real" technical or management issues, although changes do need to be made (Boehm and Turner 2005).

All the processes outlined here are on a continuum of software development methodologies rather than being discrete pockets of completely different thinking. One distinction between agile methods and rapid application development is the pair programming associated with agile methods.

Open Source Software

Description

Open Source Software (OSS) components are available from extensive libraries to be integrated into complete systems at the company site. Most of these components are free and make software available that would normally be far beyond the reach of individual developers.

OSS consists of downloading reusable components from the web or other sources which can then be assembled into a finished or nearly-finished system—this has become a major factor in today's software industry. Beaumont Hospital in Dublin, for example, wanted to get the best possible return for the taxpayer's money by using several components of OSS (Fitzgerald and Kenny 2004).

Benefits

A benefit from the developer's point of view is that they have access to visible source code which they can use to make derivatives relatively easily. The resulting products benefit in two ways: the reused open source code will often be of higher quality than the customer-developed code's first incarnation, the functionality that the reused element offers will often be far more complete than what the bespoke development would afford. Products can easily incorporate a standardised, sophisticated open source element to satisfy requirements that, in the past, a customer-built, small-scale sub-optimal implementation would have fulfilled (Spinellis and Szyperski 2004).

Other positive aspects can include the diffusion of best practices by open source developers to the rest of the open source community including: version control, peer reviews, issue tracking, release engineering and regression testing. As was pointed out by Richard Stallman in his keynote address at ICSE 2004, the effects of software ownership have meant that there is only a small body of software as literature (Stallman 2004). OSS counteracts this with increased visibility with regard to aspects of the software and its development. Most open source programs have been:

- Documented, published and reviewed in source code form;
- Discussed, internalised, generalised and paraphrased;
- Used for solving real problems, and often in conjunction with other programmes.

OSS currently affects development in numerous small ways, but could in the long run lead to a paradigm shift in the way we develop software (Spinellis and Szyperski 2004).

Problems

Many of the reuse options using OSS can isolate reused code from its original authors and maintainers, leading to divergent evolution paths or a fossilised code base. The effort of upgrading reused source code elements may mean large-scale duplication of effort. Reuse in source code form can also result in poor overall design and interfaces when programmers hack together the adopted code into a working implementation instead of using or designing modular interfaces. Published interfaces of open source components often change in ways that are not backward-compatible and rapid innovation in open source projects coupled with the lack of financial pressure from an existing customer base tend to make such changes more prevalent than on proprietary products. Quality varies widely from shoddy to industrial-strength and no standardised processes and metrics exist for assessing the quality of a given element (Spinellis and Szyperski 2004).

A quality definition has been proposed for OSS, however, one which suggests four primary factors to be considered by any OSS developer: high-quality software must be reliable, maintainable, easy-to-operate and must meet the functionality expectations of its domain (Jensen *et al.* 2004).

Summary of general solutions

Each of these methodologies is used today, but some organisations have adopted standards and models that can provide certification or some other sort of recognition that gives customers confidence in an understood level of service and product quality.

2.2.4 Standards and models for certification

Description

Watts Humphrey (1990, first published in 1989) wrote *Managing the Software Process*, where for the first time a wide-ranging and public argument was put forward to the effect that if software processes are better, the software products they create are likely to be better. This led to the concept of Software Process Improvement (SPI) whereby a framework for the most important software processes is established and (then) each individual software process is improved to help advance the whole development/maintenance environment. One of the drivers for SPI is the desire for the independent assessment of how companies are developing software and to provide confidence in their ability to develop software for different projects in the future. This can lead to the certification of process capabilities, rather than earlier types of certifications that said defined procedures were being followed.

Benefits

Certification to any standard is designed to give customers an improved level of confidence in the quality of services and products to be delivered. In some cases, certification to a specific standard or model is required by a contract request for proposal.

Data is now becoming available that makes it possible to investigate the premise that the quality of a software system is governed by the quality of the process used to develop and maintain it. Benefits that have been claimed for software process improvement include:

- Increased control, predictability and effectiveness of the process ;
- Increased product quality;
- Increased productivity;
- Improved staff morale;
- Improved customer satisfaction;

- Greater ability to meet budget;
- Improvement in on-tine deliverables and project completion;
- Decreased defects, costs, reworks, test times (Hunter and Thayer 2001, Richardson 1999).

The most recognized return-on-investment drivers include the value to users, the cost of development, maintenance upgrades, customer supports and the risks of project failure, budget overrun, and revenue shortfall (Messerschmitt and Szyperski 2004).

For example, Advanced Information Services, Inc (AIS) wrote a technical report noting improvements which they were able to quantify. They are a global software contracting company with a development group in India (albeit not a particularly large one) comprising 20-35 people in the development group at any one time. In 1999 when the report was written, AIS had been assessed to have certain capabilities. AIS reports average schedule deviations (planned vs. actual) improved from 112% to 5%; Average effort deviations (person-hours planned vs. actual) improved from 87% to 4% with a measurable gain in productivity as rework decreased. Most important of all, the SPI programmes led to a change in culture and personal attitudes—SPI became a way of life for everyone (Ferguson *et al.* 1999).

Payoffs from SPI are claimed by organisations such as NASA Systems Engineering Laboratory, IBM Federal Systems Company (which then became part of Loral and later Lockheed Martin) Space Shuttle Programme, Hewlett Packard Corporation, Raytheon Equipment Division Software Systems Laboratory (now RES) (Krasner 2001). Every organisation has its own environment to deal with and its figures are set within this context. All the benefits described in the above paragraphs have been noted by individual organisations as well as the increased reuse of software components, the better management of time for shortened delivery schedules and more predictable schedule outcomes.

Problems

The use of standards and models requires investment in time and effort and (particularly) in smaller companies, this can be difficult to sell to both managers and employees. In addition, standards can suffer from mixed interpretation, a fact which directly impacts the value of certification (Voas and Laplante 2007). SPI has become popular with some because they believe the benefits will outweigh the costs. However, one of the most difficult issues can be to answer the following questions:

- How does one define benefits of SPI?
- How does one determine if a company is successful, judged by a "universal" standard that can apply to all organisations being evaluated?
- How does one evaluate the "true" return on investment (ROI) or business value, recognising that most firms are unlikely to have kept detailed data on exactly how their time and money has been spent?

A survey by Dedrick *et al.* (2003) analysed whether there was any empirical evidence of improved economic performance when information technology (IT) was introduced. The survey was wide-ranging and looked at studies documented in a dozen peer-reviewed scholarly journals. They were looking at the basic investment in IT. The issues and concerns often expressed about SPI are mirrored in the outcomes of this survey.

1. Costs of SPI have to include some more obvious activities such as training, but also the costs of any business process reengineering and other more subtle changes that take place as part of the improvements.
2. Productivity may be affected less by the presence or absence of a particular process or practice, such as Total Quality Management or one of the software standards, than by manner of implementation of the process or practice. Particularly important is employee involvement in decision-making.
3. A firm's financial performance is determined by a wider-range of strategic and competitive factors rather than simply the state of software management.
4. Most firm-level research has been based on large firms. It is more difficult to get financial data on small firms which are usually privately-owned.
5. Accurate recording of the benefits of SPI requires accurate measurement; therefore it may be extremely difficult to get any quantitative measures.

Since a company which starts an improvement programme probably has little or no data of what its initial status is, the measurement of benefits can be difficult.

Standards and globalisation

Globalisation and standards are advancing together through software and other business economies. According to Altman (2006) "International standards have become, at the same time, the price of admission to the global economy and the glue holding it together. Adherence to the standards is a condition of entry to the World Trade Organisation. And as the global economy grows, so do they." Altman was not speaking directly about software standards here, but their usage around the world has to be at least, partly due to the need for subcontractors and partners to "follow the sun" and take advantage of the lower costs in developing countries. At a different level, and bearing in mind the changing project management environment noted in section 2.2.2.1, standards can enable the adoption of particular project management practices (Garcia 2005).

Main standards used for software

Three principal standards are in use for SPI: ISO 9001, ISO/IEC 15504 and the Capability Maturity Model (CMM), which has evolved to become the CMM Integrated (CMMI). Table 2-1 shows the strengths and weaknesses of each of these standards (Richardson 1999); it is still valid even though each standard has changed somewhat in the last 10 years.

	Strengths	Weaknesses
CMM	• Improves software process • Specific set of guidelines	• Assessment is expensive • Lack of improvement model • Tailoring required for small companies • No credit for higher levels • One-dimensional
ISO 9001	• Market-driven • Internationally recognised • Recognised outside software community • Improves software process	• Not designed for software • Results in cumbersome procedures • Lack of improvement model • One-dimensional
ISO 15504	• Developed from existing models and experiences • Credit for higher levels • Specific set of guidelines	• Expensive assessment • Lack of improvement model • One-dimensional

Table 2-1 Summary of software process models

However, rather than focus on process improvement models when choosing a model, an organisation should focus on its problems (Kimmerly 2005). Each of the standards and models used in the research is summarised in the following sections.

2.2.4.1 ISO 9001 : 1994

Description

ISO 9001 was designed for manufacturing but is a Quality Management System which was adapted for software and used effectively by even small software companies (Demirörs *et al.* 1998). ISO 9000-3 was the guide to software used to interpret ISO 9001 in a software context[1].

ISO 9001 : 1994, Quality systems, model for quality assurance in design/ development, production and installation has 20 clauses or areas of concern which span the entire organisation, including such functions as purchasing and training. (TickIT 1992). In addition, there are clauses which can be applied directly to software, such as design and document control. A useful way of understanding the different clauses of the standard is (Sanders 1997):

First steps at level of overall management

4.1 Management responsibility
4.2 Quality system

Second steps taken site-wide

4.5 Document and data control
4.8 Product identification and traceability
4.12 Inspection and test status
4.13 Control of nonconforming product
4.14 Corrective and preventive action
4.16 Control of quality records
4.17 Internal quality audits
4.18 Training

---

[1] Different authors use the terms ISO 9000 and ISO 9001 when what they actually mean is ISO 9001 : 1994, which is part of the family of standards, ISO 9000 : 1994. ISO 9003 was only for final inspection and testing. ISO 9002 added production, installation and other services. ISO 9001 added design and development. The newer version, ISO 9001 : 2000 supersedes the ISO 9000 : 1994 family of standards.

More detailed actions which may need to be developed independently to satisfy specific customers, contracts or projects

4.3 Contract review
4.4 Design control
4.6 Purchasing
4.7 Control of customer-supplied product
4.9 Process control
4.10 Inspection and testing
4.11 Control of inspection, measuring and test equipment
4.15 Handling storage, packaging, preservation and delivery
4.19 Servicing
4.20 Statistical techniques

Benefits

ISO 9001 was the first internationally accepted standard to provide a certification for a particular level of control and quality management. Certification has no levels of activity or capability but it is nevertheless widely used and considered meaningful within the business community. ISO 9001 is not always thought of as the definitive roadmap in SPI. But it does have some basic concepts which can be seen when looking at the standard. These are shown in Table 2-2.

Basic concepts	**Results**
Focusing on the customer	Increased revenue and market share
Choosing effective leaders	Motivation towards achieving organisational goals
Involving people	Fostering innovation, creativity and accountability
Understanding processes	Systematically defining the activities necessary to obtain a desired result
Valuing a systems approach	Structuring a system to achieve the organisation's objectives in the most effective and efficient way
Looking for continual improvement	Making continual improvement of products, processes and systems as objective for every individual in the organisation
Exercising good judgement	Informed decisions
Recognising common cause	Increased ability to create value for both parties

Table 2-2 Possible benefits from ISO 9001 : 2000

Problems

ISO 9001, like any standard, requires resources and time to implement. Small companies, in particular, can have difficulty knowing how to adapt it to be cost-effective. The quality of an ISO certification may be more dependent on the rigor of the auditor than on any assessment in accordance with the other standards. This may be because no auditing processes or guidelines are incorporated as an integral part of the standard.

Evolution of the standard

ISO 9001 : 2000 is more process-oriented than the earlier version. Management responsibility was limited in an earlier version to developing a quality policy and to ensuring that it is used and applied within the organisation. The new version has words such as "creating and maintaining awareness of the importance", "performing management reviews" and "ensuring the availability of resources". This change in language and in areas of emphasis permeates the newer version of the standard. Dreyfus *et al.* (2004) note that ISO 9001 can enhance a company's ability to implement effective TQM (although this enhancement may be only marginal using ISO 9001 : 1994). The original study took place in the mid-1990s, but empirical findings lend support to the transformation towards a more process-oriented ISO 9001 : 2000.

2.2.4.2 Capability Maturity Model (CMM)

Description

The CMM originated at the Software Engineering Institute in the United States. It has since become a de facto standard for developing key elements of an effective software process. The CMM describes an evolutionary path for software development from an immature process (Level 1) to a more disciplined process as based on quantitative feedback at the organisational level (Level 5) (Ferguson and Sheard 1998) as described in Table 2-3.

Benefits

"What the CMM provided was a solid framework of activities, much better rigour in the areas of quality control and change management, and much better measurement of progress, quality and productivity than was previously the norm." (Jones 2008). What the CMM also did was provide relatively clear understanding about the capability to do a job. For example, organisations might attain CMM Level 2 by different paths but it provides a level of confidence that the basic skills and processes are in place to manage a software project successfully.

Maturity level	Focus	Key process areas
Level 1 Initial	Heroes	No key process areas
Level 2 Repeatable	Project management	• Requirements management • Software project planning • Software project tracking and oversight • Software subcontract management • Software quality assurance • Software configuration management
Level 3 Defined	Engineering process	• Organisation process focus • Organisation process definition • Peer reviews • Training programme • Intergroup co-ordination • Software product engineering • Integrated software management
Level 4 Managed	Product and process quality	• Software quality management • Quantitative process management
Level 5 Optimising	Continuous improvement	• Process change management • Technology change management • Defect prevention

Table 2-3 CMM maturity levels and key process areas (Ferguson and Sheard 1998)

Capability levels are defined in Table 2-4 (Paulk 1999).

Maturity level	Description of software CMM maturity levels
Level 1 Initial	The software process is characterised as ad hoc, and occasionally even chaotic. Few processes are defined, and success depends on individual effort and heroics.
Level 2 Repeatable	Basic project management processes are established to track cost, schedule and functionality. The necessary process discipline is in place to repeat earlier successes on projects with similar applications.
Level 3 Defined	The software process for both management and engineering activities is documented, standardised and integrated into a standard software process for the organisation. All projects use an approved, tailored version of the organisation's standard software process for developing and maintaining software.
Level 4 Managed	Detailed measures of the software process and product quality are collected. Both the software process and products are quantitatively understood and controlled.
Level 5 Optimising	Continuous process improvement is enabled by quantitative feedback from the process and from piloting innovative ideas and technologies.

Table 2-4 CMM level description (Paulk 1999)

Problems

Implementation of the CMM and its successor the CMMI on small projects or in small companies is the subject of several articles (Brodman and Johnson 1994, Cepeda *et al.* 2008, Brodnik *et al.* 2008). Experience from many companies has shown that the use of the CMM is very limited within the small development company sector and companies are continually tailoring the available methods to suit the small project or subsidiary. Lessons have been learned about the necessity to establish sponsorship and support from all stakeholders, develop infrastructure, build processes as small as possible while linking them to business needs, establish a life cycle of appraisal and improvement and get a quick win to build support (Cepeda *et al.* 2008, Brodnik *et al.* 2008). However, questions still exist whether this is the best way to manage small projects effectively (Jones 2008).

One researcher taught formal processes but saw on his own project that they were not always appropriate. His contention was that the best practices as described in the literature are tailored for huge, one-of-a-kind projects created for certain clients. He feels that many of these best practices require a minimum (critical) project size to be efficient (Rost 2005).

Evolution of the standard

Several Capability Maturity Models were developed as reference models of mature practices in a specified discipline, and used to assess a group's capability to perform that discipline. Examples were CMMs for software, systems engineering, and specific sectors such as the Federal Aviation Authority (Caputo and Hefner 2004, Ibrahim 2001). The software CMM was created to provide guidelines for improving the software process. The CMM Integration, or CMMI, was created to recast the existing CMMs into a common, integrated framework:

- Reduce differences in terminology, scope, structure and appraisals;
- Combine the best features of each model;
- Drive disciplines to be engineered and managed more similarly;
- Provide a standard structure for developers on new models to follow (Caputo and Hefner 2004).

A further goal included ensuring that the CMMI is consistent and compatible with the ISO/IEC 15504 Technical Report for Software Process Assessment. "The CMMI framework accommodates multiple disciplines and is flexible enough to support two different representations (staged and continuous). The components of both the staged and continuous representations are process areas, specific goals, specific practices, generic goals, generic practices, typical work products, sub-practices, notes, discipline amplifications, generic practice elaborations, and references". (Capability Maturity Model® Integration 2002).

The staged representation organises process areas into five maturity levels to support and guide process improvement. The staged representation groups process areas by maturity level, indicating which process areas to implement in order to achieve each maturity level, in the same manner as the older CMM did for the software. Components are slightly different as shown for Level 2 in Table 2-5.

CMM for software, 1993 (Paulk *et al.* 1993)	**CMMI for software, 2002 (Capability Maturity Model® Integration 2002)**
Requirements management	Requirements management
Software project planning	Project planning
Software project tracking and oversight	Project monitoring and control
Software subcontract management	Supplier agreement management
	Measurement and analysis[2]
Software quality assurance	Process and product quality assurance
Software configuration management	Configuration management

Table 2-5 CMM-SW vs. CMMI Level 2 process areas

2.2.4.3 ISO/IEC 15504/SPICE[3]

Description

The third standard commonly used in software development, ISO/IEC 15504/SPICE, was designed to be used in two ways: as a roadmap for organisational self-improvement and as an assessment guide for evaluating one organisation's capabilities against another, particularly in a procurement environment. Parts of SPICE are:

Part 1 Concepts and introductory guide
Part 2 A reference model for processes and process capability
Part 3 Performing an assessment
Part 4 Guide to performing an assessment
Part 5 An assessment mode and indicator guide
Part 6 Guide to qualification of assessors
Part 7 Guide for use in process improvement
Part 8 Guide for use in determining supplier process capability
Part 9 Vocabulary

[2] This is a common feature rather than a specific process in the CMM for software.

[3] The version of ISO/IEC most discussed in this volume is the Technical Report, which will hereafter be referred to as SPICE. The evolved formal standard is referred to as ISO/IEC 15504. Whatever refers to both versions is called ISO/IEC 15504/SPICE.

The categories contained in the SPICE Part 2 reference model are listed in Table 2-6.

ISO/IEC 15504/SPICE is not *binary* like ISO 9001 where one is either ISO 9001-certified or not. Neither is it *staged* like the CMM where one meets all requirements to be at Level 2, 3, 4, or 5 and each builds on the other. For example, in the case of the CMM, if one meets all requirements for Level 2 and 90% of the requirements for Level 3, one is still at Level 2. If one meets all the requirements for Level 3 and 90% of the requirements for Level 2, one is still at Level 1. Not until all the requirements for Level 2 are met can the organisation get to Level 3, although some organisations do both at the same time.

CUS Customer Supplier process category	**SUP Support process category**
CUS.1 Acquire software	SUP.1 Develop documentation
CUS.2 Manage customer needs	SUP.2 Perform configuration management
CUS.3 Supply software	SUP.3 Perform quality assurance
CUS.4 Operate software	SUP.4 Perform work product verification
CUS.5 Provide customer service	SUP.5 Perform work product validation
ENG Engineering process category	SUP.6 Perform joint reviews
ENG.1 Develop system requirements and design	SUP.7 Perform audits
ENG.2 Develop software requirements	SUP.8 Perform problem resolution
ENG.3 Develop software design	**ORG organisation process category**
ENG.4 Implement software design	ORG.1 Engineer the business
ENG.5 Integrate and test software	ORG.2 Define the process
ENG.6 Integrate and test system	ORG.3 Improve the process
ENG.7 Maintain system and software	ORG.4 Provide skilled human resources

MAN Management process category	ORG.5 Provide software engineering infrastructure
MAN.1 Manage the project	
MAN.2 Manage quality	
MAN.3 Manage risks	
MAN.4 Manage subcontractors	

Table 2-6 SPICE TR key process areas

ISO/IEC 15504/SPICE is described as *continuous*, meaning that the company can be at various capability levels for any of the key process areas listed above. Each process is evaluated separately and described by (Paulk 1999) as in Table 2-7.

Level	**Description**	**Capability level description**
0	Incomplete	There is general failure to attain the purpose of the process. There are little or no easily identifiable work products or outputs of the process.
1	Performed	The purpose of the process is generally achieved. The achievement may not be rigorously planned and tracked. There are identifiable work products for the process, and these testify to the achievement of the purpose.
2	Managed	The process delivers work products according to specified procedures and is planned and tracked. Work products conform to specified standards and requirements.
3	Established	The process is performed and managed using a defined process based on good software engineering principles. Individual implementations of the process use approved, tailored versions of standard, documented processes to achieve the process outcomes.
4	Predictable	The defined process is performed consistently in practice within defined control limits, to achieve its defined process goals.
5	Optimising	Performance of the process is optimised to meet current and future business needs, and the process achieves repeatability in meeting its defined business goals.

Table 2-7 SPICE capability levels

The assessment process itself is more extensive than the audit procedure for ISO 9001 if one evaluates full capability levels. Of course, this is both a benefit and a problem.

Benefits

SPICE has the benefit of being more comprehensive and flexible than either the CMM or ISO 9001 : 1994. It is not designed for any one type of organisation and can be used in many different environments.

Problems

SPICE is no different from the other standards in that it needs resources and time to implement. In addition, as a somewhat complex standard it can be difficult to learn.

Evolution of the standard

SPICE has evolved into ISO/IEC 15504 in terms of organisation and format rather than as relating to specific processes. The document structure has changed from nine parts to five, as shown in Table 2-8.

SPICE 1998	ISO/IEC 15504: 2004
Part 1, concepts and introductory guide	Part 1, concepts and vocabulary
Part 2, a reference model for processes and process capability	Part 2, requirements (normative)
Part 3, conducting assessments	Part 3, guidance on performing assessments
Part 4, guide to conducting assessments	Part 4, guidance on using assessment results
Part 5, an assessment model and indicator guidance	Part 5, an exemplar process model
Part 6, guide to competency of assessors	
Part 7, guide for use in process assessment	
Part 8, guide for use in determining supplier process capability	
Part 9, vocabulary	

Table 2-8 Evolution of ISO/IEC 15504/SPICE document structure

ISO/IEC 12207, amendment 1, is described as the compliant process reference model for the updated standard (Rout 2005)[4]. The main changes that occur from the ISO/IEC TR 15504 to ISO/IEC 15504 are:

- The name change from Software Process Assessment to Process Assessment;
- The restructuring of the standard from 9 parts to 5 parts;
- The inclusion of an exemplar assessment method;
- The removal of the Process Dimension which now resides in an annex to ISO/IEC ISO 12207 and is published as ISO/IEC 12207 AMD1 and AMD2;
- The introduction of the concept of Process Reference Models;
- The revision and alignment of the Capability Dimension with ISO 9001: 2000.

The major benefit of this change is that it expands the available scope of the standard substantially. Instead of being constrained solely to software life cycle processes, it now defines a common assessment approach that can be applied to any process. Two of the requirements for SPICE, "cover conformance of different process models" and are "supportive of existing standards ISO 9000, ISO 12207..." (Rout 2005) express the function for SPICE as a framework for other standards. This is described in the standard as follows:

> "The major benefits of a standardised approach to process assessment are that it will:
>
> - Provide a public, shared approach for process assessment;
> - Lead to a common understanding of the use of process assessment for process improvement and capability evaluation;
> - Facilitate capability evaluation in procurement;
> - Be controlled and regularly reviewed in the light of experience of use;
> - Be changed only by international consensus;
> - Encourage harmonisation of existing schemes.

[4] This is the ISO/IEC standard which defines steps in the software life cycle; this was not used in any of the training/consulting programmes and therefore not considered as a possible model for the assessments (ISO/IEC 12207 1995).

Process assessment as defined in SPICE is designed to provide a basis for a common approach to describing the results of process assessment, allowing for some degree of comparison of assessments based on different but compatible models and methods." (ISO TR 15504, Part 1, page vi 1998)

ISO/IEC 15504/SPICE can be described as a framework because the result of an assessment is a profile of maturity in different software processes, rather than a staged level of maturity as defined by the CMM or a binary yes or no certification for ISO 9001. Models can be developed that are compliant with ISO 9001, CMM/CMMI level 2, 3, 4 or 5, or any type of standard used in software. There is not a one-to-one comparison between ISO/IEC 15504/SPICE and any of these other standards; but neither ought there be inconsistencies or contradictions.

This means, for example, that an organisation that wishes to select a supplier or contractor is able to develop a "preferred" profile and compare it to profiles of different companies who might be certified or assessed to different standards. The closer the fit between the preferred profile and another, the more likely the potential supplier or contractor can meet the organisation's requirements.

2.2.4.4 Example using the standards in a framework

The next paragraphs present an example of the kind of analysis that might be done using each of the previously mentioned standards.

A department within the government's Humanity Relationships Executive (HRE) is interested in some new ways for personnel to access data from workstations scattered about the department. The department is interested in some different ways to present the data than the current system provides.

Some possibilities might include three-dimensional graphical images to highlight particular areas of concern, use of touch screens to bring up different kinds of information, or perhaps different ways of both accessing and presenting data through hand-held devices. Without knowing the particulars of what will be created, the department can create a profile of the strengths needed in the company to develop once-off throw-away prototypes which can be evaluated by all the stakeholders involved in using and paying for the new system. The capability needed for each process is evaluated separately as described by Paulk (1999) in Table 2-9.

SPICE process	*Importance for HRE job*
ENG.1.1, system requirements analysis and design process: to establish the system requirements and architecture, identifying which system requirements should be allocated to which elements of the system and to which releases	*0 - Not important at this stage for this prototype software*
ENG.1.2, software requirements analysis process: to establish the requirements of the software components of the system	*3 - Important because the company has to be able to analyse and manage the requirements of users (office personnel), providers (IT department personnel) and funding body (HRE)*
ENG.1.3, software design process: to define a design for the software that implements the requirements and can be tested against them	*4 - Very important since the HRE hopes several designs and options will be explored and be available for evaluation*
ENG.1.4, software construction process: to produce executable software units and to verify that they properly reflect the software design	*3 - Important since the design must be transferred to something that works at prototype level. Note that if operational code were being produced here, the required capability level might be higher*
ENG.1.5, software integration process: to combine the software units, producing integrated software items and to verify that the integrated software units properly reflect the software design	*2 – capability required at some level but not as important with development of disposable prototypes as with other, more permanent, types of software*
ENG.1.6, software testing process: to test the integrated software producing a product that will satisfy the software requirements	*1 – some capability required but little testing is expected at this stage*

ENG.1.7, system integration and testing process: to integrate the software component with other components, such as manual operations or hardware, producing a complete system that will satisfy the customers' expectations expressed in the system requirements	*0 – Not applicable at this stage*
ENG.2, system and software maintenance process: to manage modification, migration, and retirement of system components (such as hardware, software, manual operations, and network, if any) in response to customer requests.	*0 – Not applicable at this stage*

Table 2-9 HRE required processes (for example)

This definition of characteristics needed by the company selected to do the job might lead to a profile like Figure 2-3.

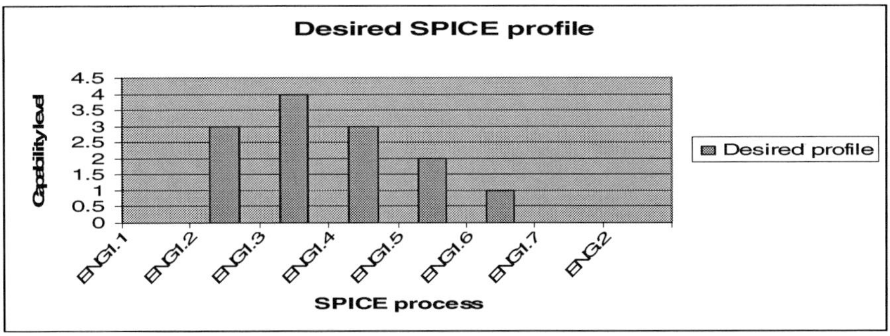

Figure 2-3 HRE desired SPICE profile

In this example, three vendors might apply for the job of developing this prototype software. Vendor A is a company with experience developing software components for games; these components are sent to the game company for integration with components developed by other companies. Vendor B is a strong systems engineering company that mostly integrates commercial-off-the-shelf components but does little component software development. Vendor C is a business software development company with one major product that is only upgraded and expanded. Comparison of SPICE assessment profiles provided by each vendor for the Engineering Process Category can be shown as in Figure 2-4.

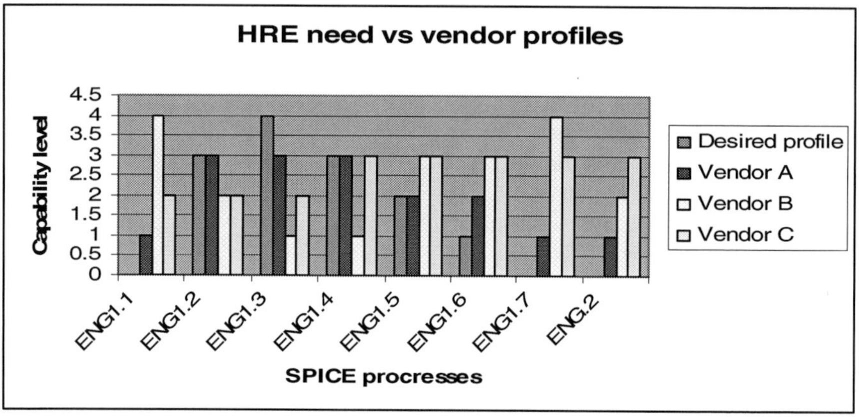

Figure 2-4 Comparison of desired and vendor profiles

The furthest left line, the desired profile of the HRE, is compared to the submitted profiles to find as close a match as possible. In this case, Vendor A is the closest match and would be the most likely to be selected as the winner in this part of the technical procurement process. Of course this is just one of many factors to be considered, but it can be an important one.

The reverse of this can be used to assess a group of companies who are developing a preferred profile or model of good practice for assessment purposes when the companies have had different experiences with standards and the use of effective software processes. If common areas can be identified that were taught to/used by all of the companies, regardless of which models they may have used previously, this is the model that can now be used for assessment in any number of new environments.

2.2.5 Harmonisation of the standards

Each of these standards can be audited or assessed by third parties for certification by a standards authority. In Ireland, only ISO 9001 is widely-recognised for this purpose. The first party establishes a quality management system which is consistent with the requirements of ISO :

9001 2000. Independent audits are then performed by a second party, either by a company which specialises in this or an arm of the National Standards Authority of Ireland (NSAI). An audit which exhibits conformity with the standard, albeit with possibly some areas needing minor improvement, allows the first party to be certified as ISO : 9001 2000 conformant.

In other areas of the world, assessments are commonly performed against the CMM/CMMI. This is the model developed (primarily) for US government contractors and their subcontractors who develop software. ISO/IEC 15504 is not as widely used for this purpose, although its usage is developing. Sectors, such as automotive and banking, are also developing versions suitable for each new domain.

However, the use of different standards may need to be harmonised (Caputo and Hefner 2004, Ferguson and Sheard 1998, Kitson 2005, Paulk 1994 and 1999, Richardson 2001, Rout and Tuffley 2007). This may be required because of partnership needs, transition periods or to match requirements for different customers. No two standards or version of the same standard is a one-to-one match. Indeed, there is no reason why they should be, since all standards were initially developed to satisfy different requirements.

Some effort has been made to harmonise the processes associated with these standards, although each was developed for a different purpose. No attempt has been made to do this at more than a high level (Kitson 2005, Rout and Tuffley 2007). A detailed comparison between the CMM and ISO 9001 (Paulk 1994) and between CMM and SPICE (Paulk 1999) showed both the similarities and the difficulties of matching up standards with one-to-one, one-to-many and other relationships (See Table 2-10).

CMM	SPICE	ISO 9001
RM		4.2, 4.3, 4.4.3, 4.4.6, 4.5.2, 4.19
PP	***CUS.2***	4.1.2.2, 4.2, 4.3, 4.4.2, 4.9.1, 4.9.2
PP	MAN.1	4.1.2.2, 4.2, 4.3, 4.4.2, 4.9.1, 4.9.2
PP	MAN .2	4.1.2.2, 4.2, 4.3, 4.4.2, 4.9.1, 4.9.2
PP	MAN.4	4.1.2.2, 4.2, 4.3, 4.4.2, 4.9.1, 4.9.2

Table 2-10 Harmonising CMM, ISO 9001 : 1994, SPICE

No attempt to validate such a model has been documented, as yet, in the literature.

Summary

The ISO/IEC 15504/SPICE assessor is evaluating each process to determine its capability level. The result of this is a profile, with capability levels as shown in the example. This is similar to the CMM although the different processes are not level-dependent. In the CMM, Requirements Management is at Level 2. However, to be at CMM Level 2, the organisation has to perform a requisite set of activities. SPICE "ENG.1 Development of system requirements and design" can be at Level 0 (incomplete), Level 1 (performed), all the way to Level 5 (optimising). Therefore it is possible to pick any process included in the standard and see the level at which the project or organisation is performing. This difference in the standards is shown graphically in Figure 2-5.

Any of these standards can be used to guide self-improvement by organisations. Each can be used as a model of good practice with emphasis on different areas of excellence. Each of these models has its advantages and the choice of which to use is mostly determined by the customer requirements. Each was developed for a different purpose by different organisations and any individual company wishing to standardise should evaluate carefully where the best benefits for the least cost are to be found.

In this book, software problems, specific solutions to address these problems and general solutions to change the culture of an organisation are all discussed. Amongst these general solutions are the major standards that were developed to address quality and management issues in different environments.

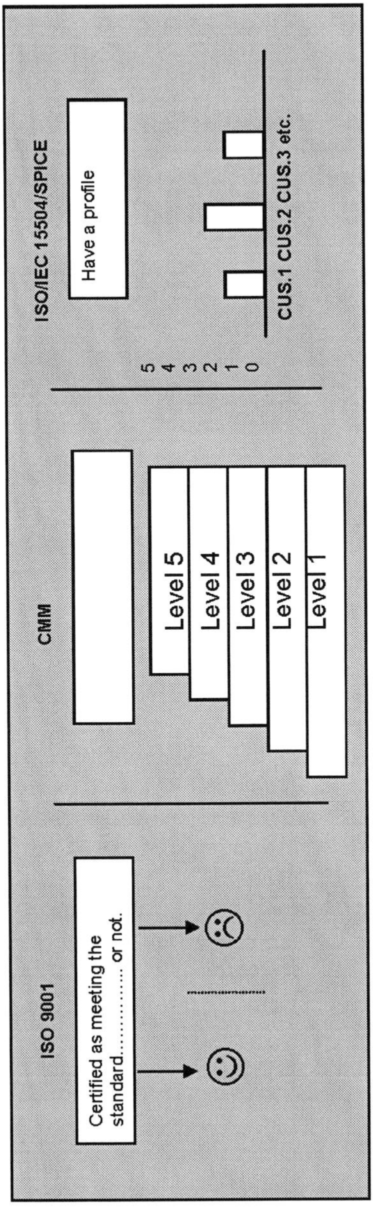

Figure 2-5 Comparison of standards

Research questions

The use of standards as the input model for assessing companies with different types of environments makes sense. Standards are developed by experts who have both academic research and good business experience. Although the major standards differ, many of their processes are similar in intent, if not in actual wording. Developing a model which contains the processes common to the major standards satisfies the need for harmonisation. Such a model can be validated by checking whether or not the work done in the SPI programmes of the 1990s was effective. This enables the answering of both research questions:

What actually happened after SPI assistance in Ireland?

How can one answer this question in companies with diverse environments?

The author was trained in and used both ISO 9001 and the CMM. She was one of the early developers of ISO/IEC 15504 and has been involved in training and consulting in all of these standards. Standards are not always easy to implement or follow but they have the advantage of providing a structured environment, one which can be assessed or audited and produces a known value (and possible certification) as a result.

Companies who took advantage of European Commission-sponsored programmes to help them learn to manage software better either worked with one of three standards (SPICE, CMM or ISO 9001 : 1994) or with focused improvements using the advice of an experienced consultant/ mentor to solve specific problems.

Consequently, one of the difficulties in comparing the results of SPI training and mentoring within these companies was to find a common ground for comparison. For example, an ISO 9001 audit of a company that was trained in ISO 9001 and had a steady evolution to ISO 9001 : 2000 is useful and reasonable. However, that type of audit is not appropriate for other companies who are not familiar with ISO 9001, its requirements or its language.

This development of an appropriate model, one which can be used to assess different types of environments—irrespective of the previous standard used—has not been documented before although Kitson (2005), Paulk (1994, 1999) and Rout and Tuffley (2007) have documented one-to-one comparisons. ISO/IEC 15504/SPICE is designed to be used in different environments but a full process assessment has many components that are not reflected in other standards. Thus there was a real need for a model that would be limited to but yet include processes common to all three standards. This drawing out of the actual equivalent processes from each of the major standards is unique to this research.

Before discussing the format of this model, the improvement programmes used and some general factors in success and failure of SPI are discussed in the next chapters.

CHAPTER THREE

SPI IN IRELAND, 1994-1999

3.1 Historical research

The European Commission (E.C.) sponsored the programmes discussed in this book from 1994 through 1999. European Software Process Improvement training Initiative (ESPITI) was the first, developed to raise awareness of the importance of software management in European companies. Lectures by software process experts, a forum where companies could meet and talk about their improvements and ISO 9001 for Small Companies Programme (ISCP) were all components of ESPITI. ISCP had two company cluster-training programmes that each extended for a year during 1995 and 1996. Company representatives attended training sessions and each company was assigned a mentor to help the company learn the requirements of the standard and how to implement it in the company. The TRans Ireland-Software Process Improvement Network (TRI-SPIN) provided mentoring for specific SPI initiatives from 1995-1996. Process Improvement Experiments (PIEs) provided mentoring for SPI initiatives from 1996 through 1999, with funding granted directly by the E.C. This was the largest programme, with proposals and grants for big improvement projects given throughout Europe. Small Company Action Training and Enabling (SCATE) was a cluster-training programme developed by the author and based on the CMM. It provided monthly training for 9 months and was taught by 3 companies to 52 organisations in 11 groups in 9 countries in 3 languages from 1997-1998. The last programme covered is Software Process Improvement in Regions of Europe (SPIRE); this was based on SPICE. It provided a mentor to help analyse areas for improvement using an SPICE-compliant assessment tool and regular visits of a mentor to guide and monitor improvement. SPIRE was deployed in 4 countries for ~60 organisations from 1997 through 1999.

All of these programmes except SCATE and Process Improvement Experiments (PIEs) were managed through the Centre for Software Engineering (CSE) at Dublin City University (DCU). SCATE was managed by Catalyst Software in Dublin (where the author was employed) and PIEs were managed individually by the E.C.

Description of each SPI programme

There was a mix of delivery: training only, training plus expert help in varying amounts and expert help for focused SPI projects only. There was also a mix of standards, or no standard but good practices, followed in the programmes. ESPITI training courses were designed independently by different people for a programme that was intended to spread quality management and SPI approaches among many organisations of different sizes across Western Europe. Different organisations came to public courses that had no continuity or relationship to one another. In Ireland, training was given in subjects ranging from specific activities such as risk management to discussion of standards like the CMM (Sanders 1996). Other awareness raising events and workshops were held throughout the project, some pan-European and some within Ireland.

Programmes such as ISCP (under the ESPITI umbrella) and SCATE were developed specifically for small companies although small departments in larger companies could participate in SCATE if no company-wide software process existed. Each of these followed an established model, ISO 9001 and the CMM respectively, for quality improvement. Both used cluster training of two people from each of up to 8-10 organisations who came to regular classes to learn the model.

ISCP participants had a mentor who made regular visits to review the client's progress both in developing an ISO 9001-compliant Quality Manual and Procedures, and implementing these processes and procedures in their software environment. The last step for each participant was a mock audit by the mentor of the client's Quality Manual and associated documentation, and the actual implementation of the processes thus defined.

SCATE had the same CMM training for all companies, but encouraged each company to have a small pilot, then longer baseline improvement project running simultaneously with the training so that what was learned in the classroom could be applied in the business immediately. SCATE training included CMM and other technical information. It also covered training in cultural and social issues, such as how to build effective teams, how to sell SPI to others and how to motivate yourself and others (Sanders 1997). It was the only one of the SPI programmes to address these issues in depth. Since few companies took advantage of the on-line support offered, SCATE is treated as training only for the purpose of this research.

TRI-SPIN organisations were selected on an individual basis, with every improvement project and mentoring event unique. Organisations of varying size and composition participated. There was no attempt to co-ordinate activities among organisations or mentors to direct anyone into using a particular model for improvement.

PIEs were managed directly through the E.C., although the CSE did have the SPI Forum for dissemination of information in various improvement projects, including PIEs. Later the E.C. wanted local management of any new initiatives. In order to stimulate, support and co-ordinate PIEs by means of experience exchange, dissemination and co-operative activities, the European Commission established a network of competent partners, the ESSI PIE Nodes (ESPINODEs). Eighteen ESPINODEs distributed throughout Europe and Israel[5] started their work in the spring of 1998, for a period of 24 months. (ESPINODE Executive Summary 2002) These ultimately were followed by SPIRE, which provided a mentor to work with each participant in a mini-PIE, very focused and of smaller duration than some of the earlier PIE contracts.

One new twist to SPIRE was the use of SPICE-conformant assessment instruments to assist company management to focus their improvement project and to capture standardised data about the company's process status *before* improvement, for later comparison with similar data *after* improvement (Sanders 1998).

These instruments were used at the beginning and the end of the projects to check how much improvement had actually been made. As with any assessment, objectivity can be difficult to maintain even when you are using a software programme that has no built-in bias.

Another SPIRE innovation was the use of staff attitude surveys because the attitudes of staff at all levels within an organisation can significantly affect the success or otherwise of any improvement initiatives (Sanders 1998). Eleven statements were given, with answers ranging from "strongly agree" to "strongly disagree". Some examples are:

- SPI is essential for the future success of the organisation.
- By applying SPI my organisation can significantly improve the quality of software supplied to customers.
- SPI is not cost-effective in my organisation's circumstances.
- Senior management in my organisation supports SPI activities by arranging sufficient resources for training.

---

[5] Israel was included as part of the European Economic Area although it is not part of the European Union.

The act of discussing these questions and asking why people answered as they did was an important introduction to the SPI project in each organisation.

Described short-term benefits from these programmes

In most of these programmes final reports were made to the E.C. Some companies wrote case studies. In reading these final reports it is important to understand that the writers are likely to have a bias towards success and the reports might be somewhat misleading for a lot of reasons:

- The person who wanted to do the improvement, or someone reporting to that person, is unlikely to say it was all a time-wasting mistake and a failure. This is probably the same person writing the report or case study.
- Improvement initiatives tend to occur simultaneously since companies cannot afford to wait and see if one works. Many of the ISO 9001 customers were already following their own industry standards or some other improvement processes. Many of the CMM customers for SCATE were already ISO 9001-certified and looking for more. Therefore, it can be difficult to attribute improved bottom line or productivity figures to only one cause.
- Data such as productivity, cost to produce systems, process improvement costs and related data are not only highly confidential, the meaning of the data varies from company to company. Everybody wants to read reports on industry trends or programme results but nobody really wants to contribute the hard data (Sheard and Miller 2000).
- The correct data can be very hard to gather unless a company is used to keeping that kind of statistics. The author worked with some companies on their project final reports and even accounting for the time spent on the SPI project alone was not easy.

With all of those constraints in mind, a sampling of improvements reported by some people who participated in the programmes, for example the project managers of the E.C. programmes, is presented in the next section.

ESPITI

In the standard training courses of ESPITI, it would be hard to know exactly what happened in each company that took a one-day course. There was a user survey reported by the CSE which presented some data on what the users thought (Scannell 1996). This includes participants in ISCP who may have more or *less* positive views because they had more training. Of those who answered:

93% said, "I personally benefited from the events I attended."
74% said, "I have already applied what I learned in my job."
81% said, "I expect to apply what I learned in the future."
95% said, "The events were well worth attending."

Kautz and Larsen (2003) revisited ESPITI to see how well it accomplished its goals in Norway, which had a similar set of seminars and activities to those in Ireland. Their conclusion was that although the events were appreciated, they did not generate the desired effect due to their diversity and general lack of focus.

ISCP

It was important that some simple metrics be used to help manage and tune the programme and to show evidence of real improvement. Stability of cluster was the first measurement: all but one company completed the programme. The company that dropped out did so firstly because of internal resource constraints, and secondly because of a lack of shared commitment by the management team. The second measure was attendance at group sessions. While attendance initially was high, nearing the middle of the programme there was a noticeable fall in numbers. When participants were questioned regarding falling numbers it was found to be due to pressure of work and lack of resources in a small company environment.

Following each session/workshop all participants completed a feedback form. Each of the sessions was graded on a scale of 0 to 5. A constant high score was obtained for both the sessions and for the course material.

At the completion of the cluster each participant was interviewed to obtain feedback to improve the cluster. All except one company stated they were planning to go for ISO certification by the end of the year. Of the companies audited, no major problems were found with items that they had in place. However the newness of the quality management system meant that that the employees of the companies audited may not have been fully aware of all the procedures.

From interviewing participants of the cluster it was found that the greatest benefit was the rise in quality awareness in the company. Companies also found it useful that the programme gave them the opportunity to query why their organisation operated in such a manner. Having documented procedures allowed processes to be carried out in a consistent manner, which most found useful.

When participants were questioned regarding what improvements they noticed since joining the cluster, the majority of respondents found that the small companies' programme improved the work-force performance. They also found that the programme contributed to the overall level of communication and increased staff morale. The companies claimed that the introduction of a Quality Management System (QMS) had made them more efficient. A cluster of companies working together and pursuing a common goal was a great success. When queried, all companies said that they derived great benefit from this. All companies stated that they would recommend both the cluster approach and the small companies programme to a peer company.

These are comments from the report for the first cluster (Corbett 1995). It does not designate which company gave which answers. A similar report for the second cluster was not available. The ISCP materials were licensed to companies in three other countries.

TRI-SPIN

After 20 months the TRI-SPIN project drew to a conclusion with the majority of its objectives achieved or surpassed. The project, as originally envisaged, was an amalgam of approaches to encourage the use of Software Process Improvement (SPI) within the software industry in Northern Ireland and the Republic of Ireland and to disseminate information on the results of good SPI experience. (Morrison 1996) The report goes on to note that there is no way to know whether the interest in SPI raised by those participating in TRI-SPIN initiatives will "stick" but it has been broadcast to sufficient people to suggest it will. Several of the TRI-SPIN companies wrote case studies describing their experiences. Table 3-1 is a summary of these benefits.

No companies	Benefit
	Improved:
2	Delivery times, project scheduling
1	Product quality
3	Culture and working practices
2	Quality control and assurance
1	Contractual agreements
1	Requirements specifications
2	Change control, configuration management
1	Project visibility
1	Tools and related procedures
3	Project management
3	Effectiveness of organisation, efficiency of software process
1	Testing
1	Peer reviews
3	Documentation, documented procedures and standards
3	Accomplished ISO 9001 certification

Table 3-1 Summary of benefits from TRI-SPIN case studies (TRI-SPIN 1996)

PIEs and other experiments in Ireland

These projects were much larger in scope than the improvement projects listed elsewhere and had much longer final reports, including more results and benefits. The subjects covered were varied, and in some cases quite extensive. Each report covers in detail the process of making improvements, what worked and what did not, and other information about the project. Process Improvement Experiments (PIEs) were meant to be experiments, providing a financial incentive to companies to try new tools and processes. Consequently, all projects had some aspects that were too far advanced to be practical or work as intended.

These complaints are listed in nearly all reports:

- The lengths of time between original proposal, grant, start of project and end of project were so great that the businesses had moved beyond the initial need for the improvement originally proposed

- The lengths of PIEs, typically 18-24 months, were too short to get a full measure of business benefit
- The complexity and primitive state of tools used in the experiment required far more effort than anticipated

However, all project reports listed some improvements; Table 3-2 lists a sample of the benefits described in the reports from the PIEs that took place in the Republic of Ireland.

Project	Benefits
ALCAST[6]	• Formal reviews, leading to increased defects being found at the early stages of development due a more formalized review process • Improved documents • System controls and test planning have moved significantly to earlier phases of the development lifecycle • Full test plans with built-in schedules and risk evaluations • Introduction of automated testing • Now straightforward to gather statistics on testing and software defects
AUTO-DOC	• Reduction in system revisits • Reduction in bugs reaching final phase • Reduced development resources • Improvement in the proximity of actual project costs to estimates • Increase in reusable code and use of reusable components • Electronic document management system implemented
JAVA-V&V	• Invaluable information both from our clients and our workforce obtained; it provides valuable benchmark data • Developed a series of procedures, standards, guidelines and knowledge preservation and quality assurance techniques • Evaluated series of JAVA tools and determined usefulness in different environments
MASLYD	• Developed automated source code analyser • Improved configuration management • Life cycle defined, cost estimation procedure developed leading to projects developed within cost and on schedule
PCS	• New configuration management system improves file management and general organisation, allowing new staff members to be introduced easily to ongoing projects

[6] ALCAST was in a pilot programme preceding the PIE projects, but managed in the same way

	• Reduction in the error rate led to a decrease in the costs of rework and increased customer satisfaction. • Improved organisation led to an increase in the level of customer satisfaction • Productivity improved • Training staff members has been a very worthwhile experience and has been one of the major causes of our productivity growth • Size of work force has increased (12→50) to meet the increase in business growth, due in large part to the improved customer satisfaction brought about by the new procedures and technology • Cost of rework caused by software defects and errors in configuration was reduced by 69% in the baseline project • The costs related to project configuration and administration were reduced by 52%
Phoenix	• A process to re-engineer legacy applications was established • Technical project team members acquired a high level of CASE expertise, enabling the application of modern tools to support systems development more effectively; this is helping to achieve a more cost-effective development environment
PITA	• Automated project easier to manage • Completely eliminated the typical re-work needed • Helped staff to modularise development of code
PROMM[7]	• Improved delivery rate • Results for both cost and schedule variance were positive; 78% improvement in Final Schedule Variance being the most significant • Estimation Model provided Project Managers with a framework for managing uncertainties within the project • Risks identified, quantified and controlled; total risk is translated into a potential budget/time scale variance and agreed with clients
SEPIE	• Cost model used for effort estimation changed • Requirements gathering requires 20% more effort but a more thorough and complete process • Effort in the testing phase reduced by 30% • Effort in handling release notes reduced by 70% • Effort in email handling reduced by 25%

Table 3-2 SPI benefits listed in PIE reports

[7] Interviewed as part of this research

SCATE

The information on SCATE results is more in quantity because it was different from the other programmes for two reasons:

1. It is the only programme where the real words of the students are recorded so as to represent the entire group of trainees in Ireland.
2. Since this was not a final report to a funding agency, but rather a presentation to peers who had also taken SCATE, the freshness and veracity of the feedback is less likely to be tempered by what the author of the presentation thought someone else wanted to hear.

SCATE was structured so that each CMM key process area (KPA) would have a representative, somebody who would pick it for implementation in a pilot project that could be implemented within a month or so. This was then to be replaced by a baseline project which would run concurrently with the SCATE training and focus on this same CMM KPA. The representative would do a SCATE presentation on the KPA, how it was implemented in the pilot project and in the longer baseline project. As can be seen in the comments below, this process had its difficulties. One of them was that most people wanted to specialise solely in Project Planning/Tracking and Oversight or Requirements Management.

A final conference was held in Brussels with each SCATE User Group (Belgium, Finland, France (2 groups). Greece, Ireland (2 groups) Luxembourg, Switzerland, The Netherlands (2 groups)) sending a representative to report on the combined results of participating in SCATE. Each group representative had inputs from all members of her/his training group and final approval from the members of the group. The following points are from the final presentation given by the Irish representative (Metzler 1998).

Starting points

- The companies differed from one another. One had no processes at all although most them had instigated some level of improvement. There was also a very mature company with a strong background and culture of repeatability including good process support.
- Most assumed they had already implemented most aspects of CMM Level 2. This is clearly reflected in the first set of assessment results, 1.5 out of 3, which were very optimistic.
- All companies had difficulties in identifying pilot projects. There were many reasons for this but the "bottom line" for all commercially-

driven companies was that there was no such thing as a completely suitable project.

- In terms of implementing changes, all attendees felt that it was only after giving a presentation on their selected area of interest that they really gained a clear understanding of what they were trying to achieve. Most probably attempted to change too much without adequate knowledge. Most of the group felt much better equipped to champion an improvement project after their presentation, which was supposed to be a presentation on what they had done as opposed to what they were going to do.
- Many underestimated the amount of change generated by SCATE. Changes were not necessarily focused on a specific project and many included cultural issues which were difficult to resolve, such as the problems some "champions" had about sharing knowledge with their work colleagues.

Implementation issues—cultural[8]

It is important to get "buy-in" from key people by having a clear vision of what form the improvement will take, what problems it will guard against and how measurement of the improvement will be collated and analysed. People should be reminded about the problems they have, problems that will be resolved. Most of the group suffered by trying to change too much, too soon.

Implementation issues—organisational

People need to understand how their work fits into the company business and the company champion needs to understand the roles of those involved in the process and what is required of them prior to implementation.

The mistakes

Areas thought to be solid were in need of improvement and improper assumptions were made about good processes. Improvements take time and because improvements are not tangible, it is necessary to be patient. Management buy-in must be visible. This is best achieved by showing the benefits of change through results.

---

[8] All of these points did not emerge within every company but it was agreed by all that these were major issues.

Lessons learned

Everyone experienced the same problems even if the types of businesses and organisations were quite different. Changes will not happen of their own accord and it is necessary to ensure that people are not over-burdened or constrained without justification. If you try to change many aspects of a person's routine, they will resist the change. Also, making many changes at a time greatly increases the opportunities for error. Never assume that something cannot be improved. Measurement is required. This is the one aspect of CMM where all members fell down. It is important to change by consensus or the wrong solution may be implemented. As experienced in certain organisations, champions can propose solutions and be unaware of the potential pitfalls. All members recognised the need for training for both the champion and the users.

Benefits of SCATE

SCATE participants had a broad idea of what CMM entailed. What SCATE provided was the direction required, and turned the theoretical ideas of CMM into practical steps to work towards Level 2. Even in an ideal world, companies would probably still want more time and management sponsorship.

SPIRE

As part of SPIRE, a SPICE-based assessment instrument was used to evaluate the processes included in SPICE with each client. Then the mentor worked with the client to decide what to improve as their SPIRE project. The processes assessed (Sanders 1998) were as follows:

Customer-supplier	Acquisition, supply, requirements elicitation, operation
Engineering	Development, system and software maintenance
Support	Documentation, configuration management, quality assurance, verification, validation, joint review, audit, problem resolution
Management	Management, project management, quality management, risk management
Organisation	Organisational alignment, improvement process, human resource management, infrastructure, measurement, reuse

These are not in complete alignment with SPICE, but were a compromise, focusing on the areas deemed to be most important for the clients selected for SPIRE. Improvements for individual companies included in this research are described in each company profile. (SPIRE Case Studies, September-December 1998). Table 3-3 lists a summary of these benefits.

No companies	Benefit
	Improved:
3	• Accuracy of time and money estimation
1	• Component based design
1	• Control and communication
2	• Customer support
1	• Documentation standards
1	• Efficiency in software development
3	• Life cycle process
1	• Problem resolution
1	• Project management
1	• Quality management
2	• Reviews
1	• Risk management
1	• Source code management
1	• Tool and associated procedure usage
All	• Understanding of importance of quality and SPI
	Decreased:
1	• Rework
2	• Defects

Table 3-3 Summary of benefits from SPIRE case studies

3.2 Programme differences

There were variations in the patterns of the programmes being researched:

- How was knowledge transferred; training, training and consulting, consulting?
- Focus of the knowledge transferred; was this important to an individual, a team or an organisation?

- Focus of the people to whom the knowledge was transferred; was this to the individual or a team?

Any of these variations could have affected the benefits gained from the programmes. However, there was a pattern to the order in which the programmes were offered. The E.C.-sponsored programmes were a long-term process of instilling good software practices into European companies. Looking at the timelines of the various programmes in Table 3-4, one can see by the arrows the learning curve of the programmes, how each event built on the ones before.

Training

- ESPITI events (1994-1996) were designed primarily to raise awareness in software companies. All but one of the events in Ireland was a once-off panel discussion, training session or workshop (ESPITI—The Complete European guide to the Initiative 1995). ESPITI was also designed to subsidise training so that even very small companies could take advantage of it. However, it soon became apparent that smaller companies need a more direct approach with more help, so other types of programmes were developed.
- ISCP [part of ESPITI] (1995-1996) was very focused training and consulting with the same objective for every organisation that took part in the cluster groups of companies—to develop a quality system that was compliant with ISO 9001 : 1994 and enabled the company to become ISO 9001 : 1994 certified after an audit by an external auditor.
- SCATE (1997-1998) was the same type of cluster training but using the CMM as a model, with each organisation developing its own local projects to apply what was learned in class.

Consulting

- TRI-SPIN (1995-1996) was the first of the Irish programmes which had mentoring consultants going into companies to solve individual problems, not using any particular standard or model.
- PIEs (1996-1999) were the same type of work with generally bigger projects and larger expected gains.
- SPIRE (1997-1999) was really a follow-on from the PIEs, to go back to smaller projects but this time with a particular standard, SPICE, used for assessments before and after improvements.

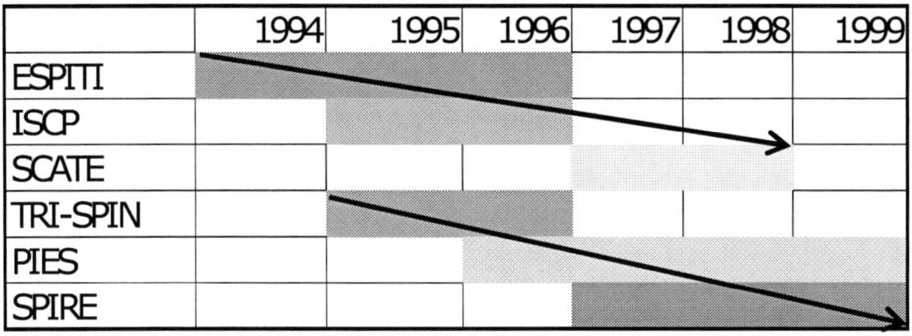

Table 3-4 Timelines for training and consulting programmes

From the initial awareness-raising training sessions, a facilitator of some kind was included in each of the programmes. These were called by different terms—mentor, tutor/trainer, consultant—but the role was always that of change agent. This role has been described by Hutchings *et al.* (1993) as assisting the student to immediately apply new learning to their real world situation, encouraging them and providing counsel and feedback. Part of the E.C. programme implementation was to look for these benefits of adding a facilitator (at different levels):

- Improved understanding and confidence on the part of the students as they implement new ways of working;
- Minimised risk of inappropriate application of faulty practices.

ISCP had more emphasis on the formal processes and regular interaction with a tutor/trainer, but SCATE had more emphasis on the process of implementation and people working together to accomplish it. It is probably worth noting what mentors and consultants actually did in these improvement programmes. As Brodman and Hannigan (2003) describe quite clearly, the role of an SPI consultant can have many aspects:

- Understand the organisation: culture, knowledge of SPI, current status of software processes, types of projects and workload, corporate and software goals and expectations, level of senior management support as determined through assessment or audit
- Determine optimum route for achieving goals: appropriate type of assessment or audit, how to guide, plan and track the SPI effort, what level of action plans and improvement projects, how much existing

documentation to use, what level of improvement is desirable and practical, what training needs to be provided when
- Aid organisation to reach its goals: guidance in understanding and improving the software processes, attendance at improvement team meetings, review of documents, tracking of activities and software products

These improvement programmes covered a broad spectrum of format and content as the European software community explored ways to make their products and services more competitive and acceptable in a global marketplace. Each programme had its strengths and weaknesses but all served to raise awareness of new ways of developing and maintaining software and increased understanding in how to apply these successfully in Europe.

CHAPTER FOUR

SPI SUCCESSES AND FAILURES

4.1 Introduction

For this research we looked at factors for success in SPI. Elsewhere in the literature, a great deal has been written about what is important to make SPI succeed, or conversely, what helps it to fail. This chapter lists the first example of SPI success factors (Humphrey 1990) and some interesting examples which may be of value in planning and implementing SPI.

4.2 Recognising success

Years in the software industry have taught the author that success in SPI is not always easy to define, measure or recognise. So the first issue for each organisation is to determine what defines success, what type of measurement will be used to determine if it exists, and how will people know when success occurs. Will success be simply implementation or improvement of a process or is a proven business benefit, such as increased productivity and/or revenue required?

Productivity issues are an example. It was claimed in October 2004 that productivity in the United States of America had decreased by 0.9% a year for the last five years and that software remains a very labour-intensive business. It is not like computer hardware, where overall performance and quality have continued to increase dramatically over time. Additionally, outsourcing has not appeared to raise productivity (Glen 2004 cited in Groth 2004).

Factors involved in determining success and increased productivity are not always clear. Many in the software business recognise that the traditional line-of-code/hour or even the more specific function points/hour might not really tell the story. Neither of these gives proper credit for reuse of software from libraries, use of standardised open source software, and most particularly, they are misleading in a maintenance environment where the skill and effort are as much in analysis as in actually writing code. So if we are not always clear on how to define productivity in software, and if improved productivity is one of the measures of SPI success, it starts to become clear how difficult it can be to really understand what improvements SPI brings to the organisation.

4.3 Some examples of factors for SPI success

However, while realising the existence of this problem is important, trying to solve it is beyond the scope of this book. What can be discussed here is more about the factors that have been identified as important for SPI success, particularly those that are unique to one source.

The six basic principles for software process change were developed by Humphrey (1990) as the first widely publicised factors for success in SPI:

1. Major changes to the software process must start at the top. Senior management leadership is required to launch the change effort and to provide continuing resources and priority.
2. Ultimately, everyone must be involved. Software engineering is a team effort, and anyone who does not participate in improvement will miss the benefits and may even inhibit progress.
3. Effective change requires a goal and knowledge of the current process. To use a map, you must know where you are.
4. Change is continuous. Software process improvement is not a one-shot effort; it involves continual learning and growth.
5. Software process changes will not be retained without conscious effort and periodic reinforcement.
6. Software process improvement requires investment. It takes planning, dedicated people, management time, and capital investment.

Table 4-1 shows the results of research on the critical success and failure factors for small and medium sized software development enterprises in Parquesoft, a software park in Columbia. It shows some factors commonly shown in the literature and some newly documented (Osorio *et al.* 2007). Some of these may be more likely in South American countries.

Success factors	Failure factors
Trained staff	Low participation of the work team in decision-making processes
Usage of development methodologies	Inadequate change control
Client and user satisfaction	Inadequate schedule follow-up
Communication	No risk management
Management designation	Lack of training management
Quality	Few financial bonuses
Project completion within estimated time frame and costs, with functionality and quality agreed at the beginning of the project	Few rewards for good performance
Designation of responsibilities	Few rewards for completing the project on time
Designation of resources	Few rewards for surpassing expectations
Designation of commitments	Few projects create a new market penetration
Leadership	Few projects bring new infrastructures and technologies
Schedule flexibility	
Compliance with client requirements	
Long product life cycle	
Easy to use product	
The final system contributes to the improvement of the client's processes	

Table 4-1 Factors for success and failure in Parquesoft companies

The very personal responses, such as failure factors of few financial bonuses and few rewards for surpassing expectations look at some basic issues that probably have a lot more to do with the morale of team members than is always realised or acknowledged.

Software Technology Transfer Finland (STTF) has specialised for several years in gathering data which has led to developing improved process and project management tools and training. This work suggests key productivity factors that range from very low if the project manager has to develop standards during the project through very high if project member use new standards, which are not familiar in the industry, but must be followed (Maxwell and Forselius 2000).

A consultant and client on a successful SPI programme together have suggestions to improve the likelihood of success (Brodman and Hannigan 2003):

- Use an internal expert or external consultant—someone to lead the way
- Focus on configuration management early so process documentation is controlled, managed and accessible
- Set reasonable expectations for success and for level of resources needed to achieve it
- Try to keep going once you start so you keep momentum and commitment
- Do not underestimate preparation time for an assessment or audit
- Make sure policies, procedures and plans add value

Some of the lessons learned by the Ericsson groups implementing SPI were different (Börjesson and Mathiassen, 2004).

- Focus on implementation, not just planning
- Establish the culture of improvement with motivation and commitment
- Implement a recognition and reward system for those who do improve and follow the new ways
- Iterate over and over again; the new process has to be put into practice and become the way of life
- Expect chaos and be prepared to handle resistance and barriers to change
- Focus on action, not words
- Organise dedicated initiatives that solve specific problems

Börjesson and Mathiassen (2004) measured SPI success through implementation success—what SPI led to actual change in practice? They analysed eighteen SPI initiatives at Ericsson to see how they fared. Time-keeping data was used to determine number of weeks, person-hours and participants for each project. Projects covered various improvement areas. They grouped the projects as shown in Figure 4-1.

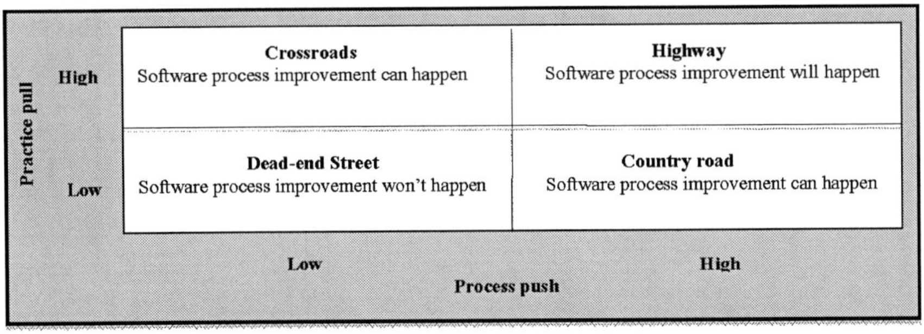

Figure 4-1 Four roads to process implementation

The seven Dead-end Street initiatives focused on the process itself—specifically on process definition and specification. They targeted several of the company's units but then were often hard to apply because too many compromises had to be made.

The Country Road initiative targeted a specific project's engineering practices. The process engineers worked in the project and understood that particular set of culture and practices. However, the practitioner commitment and motivation were weak. This combination of high process push and low practice pull can work but it is slow and likely to be less than totally satisfactory.

The three Crossroads initiatives targeted several company-level units with similar requirements. The practitioners understood the need for the new processes and were committed to using them, but the process engineers had not allocated sufficient time and resources to help them through the improvement process.

The seven Highway initiatives targeted practices in a single unit or project. The main focus was on solving problems identified by the software practitioners themselves. Both they and the process engineers were committed and time and resources were allocated. These initiatives were also the only ones to have more than one process improvement cycle. Every Highway initiative had at least three full cycles; most had four. This meant the improvements were analysed and followed long enough to become institutionalised. (Börjesson and Mathiassen 2004).

In adopting the CMM in a small IT organisation, factors for success were separated into two categories, environmental-dependent and environmental-independent (Guerrero and Eterovic 2004). Figure 4-2 shows this.

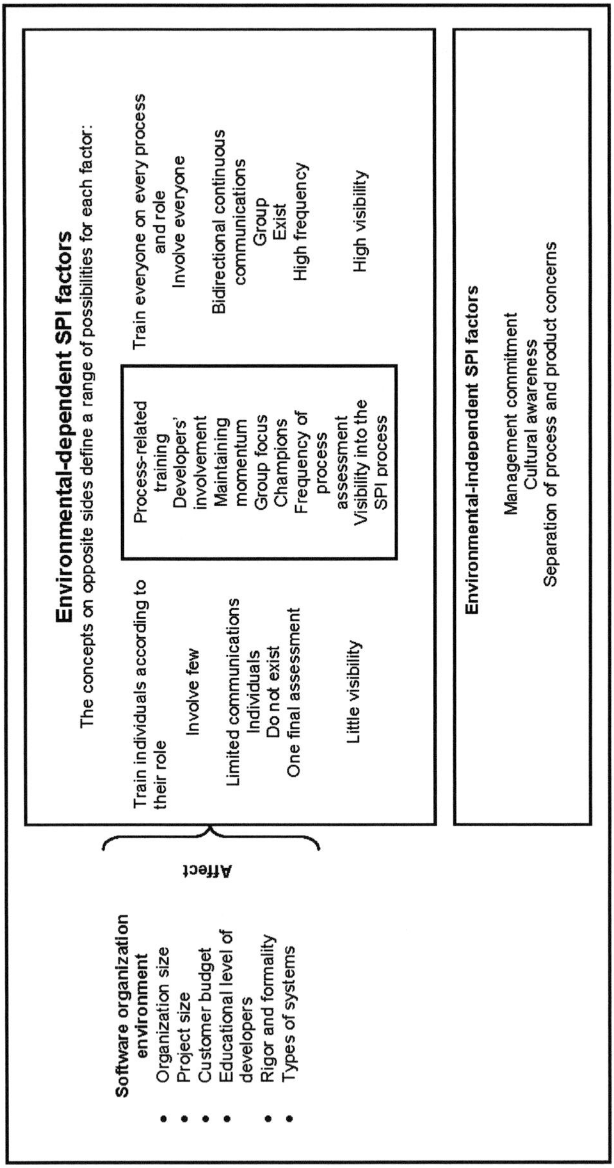

Figure 4-2 Organisational environment factors

Finally, one author compares our computer-driven lives to Eastern thinking, comparing the perfection of computers to our imperfect selves, pointing out that SPI in an uncertain context requires insight, understanding and a spirit of risk. In successful development projects, developers identify characteristics of projects and contexts, and vary their approach accordingly (Zhiying 2003). This would of course lend itself to the flexibility of a continuous model, like SPICE, rather than a staged model like the CMM.

CHAPTER FIVE

THE RESEARCH ENVIRONMENT

5.1 Introduction

Between 1994 and 1999 the European Commission (E.C.) sponsored the development of programmes to transfer knowledge on how best to implement SPI so as to help make European companies more competitive in a global marketplace. Two of the programmes were conducted in Ireland only, the others throughout different European countries. These programmes were diverse and used either different standards (CMM, ISO 9001, SPICE), or simple good practice, thereby leading to potentially very different types of software environments in the companies taking part. The author worked on the development of two of these programmes and the implementation of them all.

5.2 Development of the methodology

5.2.1 Introduction

The research methodology had to include various components: a process to find and find out about companies, development of a model to collect and compare data and an analysis process to turn those comparisons into useful information.

To ensure coverage of all the relevant issues and possibly a higher rate of return, interviews were chosen as the way to gather information, rather than just sending out questionnaires. In an article about requirements elicitation, Dieste *et al.* (2008) note that interviews were determined to be the best way to gather requirements although they were not always the most efficient. They further state that interviews remain the primary technique for requirements elicitation for good reason, expecting that some level of structure is provided. This was deemed to be true in this case, though the interview was for a different purpose.

To answer the research questions, this research is a based on interviews which use both questions to get qualitative information about the organisation and its temporal experiences with SPI and an assessment tool to get more specific details about current software processes. It is a descriptive study to produce information on groups and phenomena that already exist (Fink, 1995), as shown in Figure 5-1.

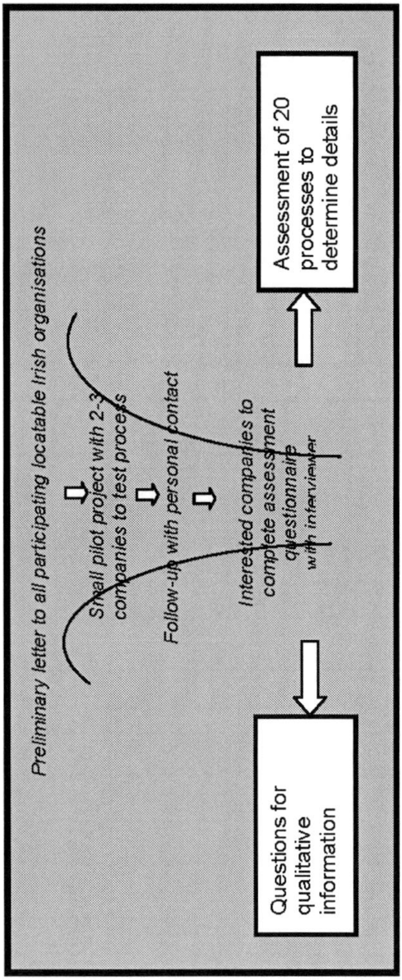

Figure 5-1 Planned research for gathering data on improvements

5.2.2 Define research tasks and select population

Following the suggestion of Oppenheim (1966), the research plan was developed by starting at the back and working forward:

Conclusions→
Results to give the conclusions→
Data needed to get the results→
Collection method to get the data

The tasks to accomplish this are described in the next parts of the chapter.

Phase I, preliminary research
1a. Non-client research tasks

- Develop criteria for and select SPICE-assessment tool

  Several SPICE-assessment tools were evaluated for the right combination of manageability, modifiability, usability, availability and price. However the decision was made that use of a PC-based tool would be too cumbersome and time consuming for this type of interview. Instead, paper tools to gain information about the company and details about use of specific practices were used in the interview, and the results transcribed to an electronic file as soon as possible after each interview.

- Develop SPICE profile including processes shared by CMM, ISO 9001 : 1994, SPICE standards

  One of the concerns had been how to compare companies that followed different standards or none. For example, what is a basic model of improved processes that could be applied to a company following ISO 9001 and another one that learned the CMM?

  The option chosen to answer this question was to create a basic SPICE profile using SPICE as it was designed—a framework for other standards. This covered all the Level 2 and some of the higher-level CMM processes, and most of the software-related ISO 9001 processes, making allowances for the different wording of the language. If the answers to the questions indicate that the organisation believes it has improved, an assessment can be used to enable quantification of the current environment. If the organisation believes it has not improved, the choice would be theirs on whether or not it is worthwhile to have an assessment of their software management processes. In the actual research ten organisations agreed to have assessments and one said they had rejected the idea of ISO 9001 so an assessment of improvements based on SPI assistance would not be reasonable.

1b. Client pre-research tasks

- Update database: earlier and current information
- Document early short-term benefits as printed in contemporary case studies or presentations by the organisation
- Finish with profile of client then and now

Organisations were chosen as candidates for assessment if they took part in one or more of the improvement programmes being reviewed and are located in the Republic of Ireland. Because it would be difficult to sort out benefits that can be assigned directly to a specific programme being studied vs. any other training or consulting the organisations had, the research looked at past improvements, the current environment for software and plans for the future. Since these E.C.-sponsored programmes were the first step on the improvement ladder for nearly all the organisations involved, a case can be made that the programmes at least helped to achieve the goal of encouraging a "culture of improvement" for those that participated. It is accurate to say that some interest had to exist for the companies to participate in the first place, but this does not mean any improvements are invalid and cannot be attributed at least partly to the improvement programmes.

Organisations were included if they were still in business and their current information was available. Much printed historical information exists for some companies; none at all exists for others. Some web sites open the door and introduce the viewer to everyone in the company; some do not share anything about the organisation or its people and some companies do not have web sites at all. Therefore, the available information about the companies being researched was variable.

The intent was to create for each organisation a profile of as much as is known about the past and as much as can be gathered about today. This serves as a background for the interviews and assessments.

1c. Client pre-interview tasks

- Develop cover letter

In an attempt to get more companies interested in participating in this research, the letter was designed to get the attention of the reader.

- Develop interview guide

A format was used which had the following characteristics:

Closed questions were used, but the interviewee was encouraged to add details for enrichment. Questions were asked about the general organisation, past improvements, the current environment for SPI and plans for future improvements to determine if a consistent culture for improvement exists. Questions about specific processes used in software management were used for the more detailed assessment. Capability levels were noted on the assessment instrument for discussion with the interviewees at the time of assessment. This format was verified by a number of experts.

5.3 Summary of interviews

The target population was 80 companies. After a variety of responses to phone calls and visits (number not in service or disconnected, no software development any more, etc.) this number was reduced to 23 possible companies worth further contact. Seven companies responded to a telephone invitation to interview. Three more were added after cold calling in person. This response rate was due to the low number of companies contactable, still in business or willing to participate in the research. The companies that had interviews and assessments are briefly described in Table 5-1.

Co.	Description
DTG	Financial products; 28 employees, 23 in software
FD	Database management system; ~60,000 employees world-wide, 40 software people in department assessed
FM	Business software; 24 employees, all in software
JC	Financial products and services; ~60 employees, 15 in software
MM	Business management software; 7 people, 2-1/2 in software
OS	Investment management; over 100 people in software alone

SI	Testing products; 15 employees, 1 software engineering, mostly maintenance
SM	Financial service provider; over 1000 employees, 20-30 software personnel at any given time
TM	Printing systems; 14 employees, 4 software engineers, mostly maintenance
TS	Middleware for tourism industry; ~250 employees, ~120 in software

Table 5-1 Companies which had interviews and assessments

CHAPTER SIX

DEVELOPMENT OF THE MMAI FOR SPI CULTURE ASSESSMENT

6.1 Introduction

Each of the participating companies received SPI assistance. Since participation in the SPI programmes was the first step on the SPI ladder for most companies, if a continuing environment for improvement exists, then the argument is that there were indeed long-term benefits from the programmes. These improvements are unlikely to be only because of the improvement programmes, but it is equally likely the SPI programmes had good effect.

The first part of the MMAI was designed to enable the author to understand the environment in which improvements took place. Massive changes in the organisation or personnel, continuity (or the lack of continuity) in improvement initiatives, evolution from what was done in the past to plans for the future, successes and failures in SPI and other issues all provide a context for understanding the assessment scores and how important they are to each organisation.

When the assessment instrument is used to add data about the performance of specific processes, a picture emerges about just how much has been accomplished in process definition, management and improvement. The information about the organisation enables a better analysis of what has been accomplished in SPI and why. Thus, both parts of the model are required, one to give data about the presence of specific processes, and the other to add depth and meaning to the scores.

6.2 Development of the MMAI, Part A

The rationale for the overall interview guide design is to determine the information about the organisation which might be pertinent to the improvement programme's success or failure. Added to this is information about improvements that were made in the past, the current culture for improvement and any plans for future improvements.

Questions about the organisation and its culture for SPI came from several sources, including questions used by different researchers, and training and assessment programmes developed and used by the author. Comparisons can be used to see what kind of differences might affect the SPI process. This could be useful if enough interviews are performed to see patterns. For example: does the type of organisation have any relationship to why improvements were made in the past? Does the role in the organisation of the interviewee shows different business needs for different roles? If so, that might explain at least partially why SPI fails to address a wide enough spectrum of concerns to present a universally accepted solution. Further comparisons are made with specific processes.

In ***Part I Organisation profile***, questions were asked about the organisation, partially to get answers to questions like:

- Is there a difference between type of organisation and the size and composition of teams?
- Are there differences in the size of the organisation and the sizes of teams and software departments?
- Did the numbers of people and type and length of projects have any effect on the improvements that were made?

In ***Part II Past culture for improvement***, improvements that were made in the past were discussed. Of particular interest are comparisons of what happened in the past to the culture of today and plans for tomorrow. All successes, failures and changes in both have to be put in the context of the evolution of the business environment.

Senior management support is the single factor that the literature universally identifies as required for SPI to succeed. Questions and comparisons about senior management support were asked to either support or contradict this finding.

In ***Part III Current culture for improvement*** questions that deal with the current environment and how it compares with other questions made about the current organisation were asked. These questions try to tease out how well employees throughout the organisation appreciate the goals of the organisation and how much of this is due to senior management support.

The next section, ***Part IV Plans for the future***, questioned the future to try to understand if plans are grounded in reality or just something to do when it is convenient.

6.3 Development of the MMAI, Part B

Development of this assessment instrument was rigorous. The process is illustrated through using the "Configuration management" process as an example.

1. A spreadsheet was developed with a column for each standard used in different SPI programmes—SPICE, CMM, ISO 9001: 1994, plus ISO 9001: 2000.
2. A keyword search of the spreadsheet was performed for common words, such as requirements, design, quality, testing and configuration management. Each of these key words had its own worksheet (See Table 6-1) and each paragraph or more on the subject in the standards was copied to the worksheet. Where SPICE, the CMM and ISO 9001 have a similar requirement, it is included in the model of good practice.

SPICE	**CMM**	**ISO 9001 : 1994**	**ISO 9001 : 2000**
SUP.2 Configuration management (establish and maintain the integrity of all the work products of a process or project)	Software subcontract management: activity11 (the prime contractor's software configuration management group monitors the subcontractor's activities for software configuration management according to documented procedure) Software configuration management (CM)/L2-repeatable (establish and maintain the integrity of the products of the software project throughout the project's software life cycle)		

Table 6-1 Initial Configuration Management processes

3. Because not all standards call the same action by the same words, it was necessary to look at those processes or practices that have a different name but should be treated as activities with the same intent. One example is ISO 9001: 1994 *4.8 Product identification and traceability*. This activity is called "Configuration Management" in other standards. Careful study of the wording to understand the intent was required to obtain consistency. This produced a file such as that in Table 6-2 for each of the processes defined in any one standard:

Configuration management processes
SPICE SUP.2 Configuration management (establish and maintain the integrity of all the work products of a process or project)
CMM ***Software subcontract management*** Activity 11 (the prime contractor's software configuration management group monitors the subcontractor's activities for software configuration management according to a documented procedure) Activity 12 (the prime contractor conducts acceptance testing as part of the delivery of the subcontractor's software products according to a documented procedure) ***Software configuration management*** Activity 1 (a SCM plan is prepared for each software project according to a documented procedure) Activity 2 (a documented and approved SCM plan is used as the basis for performing the SCM activities) Activity 3 (a configuration management library system is established as a repository for the software baselines) Activity 4 (the software work products to be placed under configuration management are identified) Activity 5 (change requests and problem reports for all configuration items/units are initiated, recorded, reviewed, approved, and tracked according to documented procedure) Activity 6 (changes to baselines are controlled according to a documented procedure)
ISO 9001 : 1994 ***4.8 Product identification and traceability*** Where appropriate, the supplier shall establish and maintain documented procedures for identifying the product by suitable means from receipt and during all stages of production, delivery and installation. Where and to the extent that traceability is a specified requirement, the supplier shall

establish and maintain documented procedures for unique identification of individual product or batches. This identification shall be recorded.
ISO 9001 : 2000 ***7.3.7 Control of changes*** Design and development changes are approved and documented. The effectiveness of various interactions are analysed and review of changes are documented.[9]

Table 6-2 Configuration management processes

This process created the start of the preferred model as the basis for all assessments to be performed. It is not intended to be used for procurement where certain critical capabilities may be required. However, the research goal was to see if the model could be used for such assessments and where improvements have been made, to look for differences and commonalities. The model was built up from processes in the five SPICE process categories to determine which processes are common to all three standards. The format for description of each SPICE process category is:

- A spreadsheet and figure for processes and which are in CMM, ISO 9001 : 1994 and ISO 9001 : 2000, as well as SPICE.
- A table which shows the content of each process in SPICE, CMM and ISO 9001 : 1994, the basic set of commonalities required.

Evaluation of the changes between ISO 9001 : 1994 and ISO 9001 : 2000 showed that while the standard has indeed changed as it has evolved, including processes from the newer version was rejected. Using ISO 9001 : 2000 would not change the model substantially and not using it allowed consistency in choosing only the versions of any standard that were used in SPI assistance programmes. ISO 9001 : 2000 is included in the high level figure and table for each process category to show this, but is not included in the detailed tables.

Customer-supplier process category

Figure 6-1 shows the overall dimension of what was selected from SPICE, CMM and ISO 9001 processes, in the Customer-Supplier process category.

[9] Current ISO standards must be purchased from your national standards body and are not directly quoted in this book.

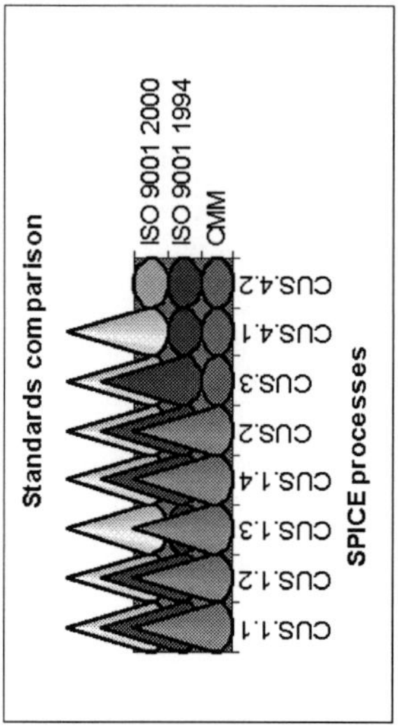

	SPICE Process	CMM	ISO 9001 1994	ISO 9001 2000
Review req.	CUS.1.1	1	1	1
Select supplier	CUS.1.2	1	1	1
	CUS.1.3	1	0	1
Customer A/T	CUS.1.4	1	1	1
Contract agreement	CUS.2	1	1	1
	CUS.3	0	1	1
	CUS.4.1	0	0	1
	CUS.4.2	0	0	0

Figure 6-1 Customer-supplier profile

Phrased simply:

- Make sure needs of the order, acquisition or software requirements are understood and any differences are resolved;
- Ensure qualified suppliers are selected and a contract is established;
- Ensure acceptance and verification of supplied products according to an established contract.

Table 6-3 lists those processes from the three standards (SPICE, CMM, ISO 9001 : 1994) that share intent, if not words. The SPICE Customer-Supplier process category can be used to assess capabilities as a supplier or as an acquirer. To bring a level of consistency to SPICE, the CMM and ISO 9001 : 1994, the first three processes were assessed for the organisations as acquirers.

SPICE	CMM	ISO 9001 : 1994
CUS.1.1 Acquisition preparation (establish the needs and goals of the acquisition); the concept or the need to acquire, develop, or enhance a system, software product or software process will be established; the customer's software and/or system requirements will be produced; an acquisition strategy will be developed; acceptance criteria will be defined./L2-managed	Requirements Management (RM)/ Activity 1 (the software engineering group reviews the allocated requirements before they are incorporated into the software project./L2	4.3.2 Review Before submission of a tender, or the acceptance of the contract or order (statement of requirement), the tender, contract or order shall be reviewed by the supplier to ensure that: b) any differences between the contract or order requirements and those in the tender are resolved;
CUS.1.2 Supplier selection (choose the organisation that will be responsible for the implementation of the project defined in CUS.1.1); the acquisition requirements will be produced; the supplier will be selected based upon the	Software subcontract management (SM)/repeatable (select qualified software subcontractors and manage them effectively)/L2	4.3.2 Review Before submission of a tender, or the acceptance of the contract or order (statement of requirement), the tender, contract or order shall be reviewed by the supplier to

evaluation of the supplier's proposals; a contract will be established and negotiated between the customer and the supplier./L2-managed		ensure that: c) the supplier has the capability to meet the contract or order requirements.
CUS.1.4 Customer acceptance (approve the supplier's deliverable when all acceptance conditions are satisfied); acceptance will be based on the acquisition strategy and conducted according to the agreed acceptance criteria; the delivered software product and/or service will be evaluated with regard to the agreed reuirements./L2-managed	SM, Activity 12 (the prime contractor conducts acceptance testing as part of the delivery of the subcontractor's software products according to a documented procedure)/L2	4.6.4.2 Customer verification of subcontracted product Where specified in the contract, the supplier's customer or the customer's representative shall be afforded the right to verify at the subcontractor's premises and the supplier's premises that subcontracted product conforms to specified requirements

Table 6-3 The organisation as an acquirer

"Supply" is assessed with the organisation as a supplier. The requirement is to make sure requirements are understood and documented, as well as managed during the development and installation process. This is shown in Table 6-4.

SPICE	CMM	ISO 9001 : 1994
CUS.2 Supply (provide software to the customer that meets the agreed requirements); a response to customer's request will be produced; a contract will be established between the customer and the supplier for	Requirements management (establish a common understanding between the customer and the software project of the customer's requirements that will be addressed by the software project/L2; Software project planning (PP)/repeatable (establish	4.3.2 Review Before submission of a tender, or the acceptance of a contract or order shall be reviewed by the supplier to ensure that: a) the requirements

developing, packaging, delivering, and installing the software product and/or service; a software product or/or service that meets the agreed requirements will be developed by the supplier; the software product and/or service will be delivered to the customer and installed in accordance with the agreed requirements./L3-established	reasonable plans for performing the software engineering and for managing the software project)/L2; Software project tracking & oversight (PT&O)/repeatable (provide adequate visibility into actual progress so that management can take effective actions when the software project's performance deviates significantly from the software plans)/L2; SQA, Activity 5 (the SQA group audit designated software work products to verify compliance)/L2	are adequately defined and documented; where no written statement of requirement is available for an order received by verbal means, the supplier shall ensure that the order requirements are agreed before their acceptance;

Table 6-4 The organisation as a supplier

The remaining SPICE Customer-Supplier processes (1.3, 3, 4.1, 4.2) appear in only one of the other standards or neither.

Engineering process category

Figure 6-2 shows the profile for engineering processes.

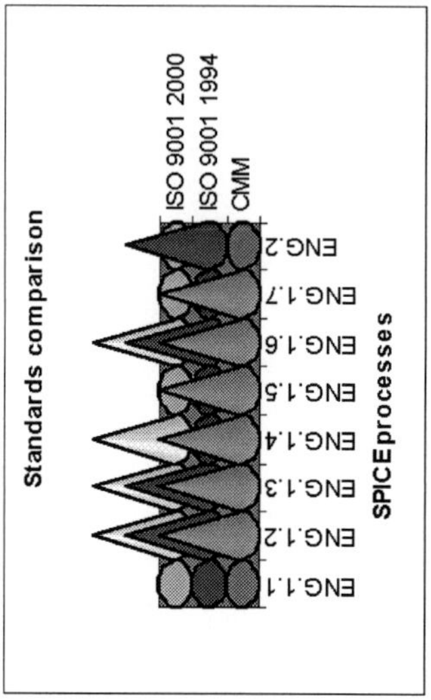

	SPICE Process	CMM	ISO 9001 1994	ISO 9001 2000
	ENG.1.1	0	0	0
Req. analysis	ENG.1.2	1	1	1
Design	ENG.1.3	1	1	1
	ENG.1.4	1	0	1
	ENG.1.5	1	0	0
S/W testing	ENG.1.6	1	1	1
	ENG.1.7	1	0	0
	ENG.2	0	1	0

Figure 6-2 Engineering profile

Some CMM processes listed in Table 6-5 are taken from Product Engineering, which is at Level 3, the software life cycle steps. Only CMM Level 2 was taught in SCATE, although the last meeting covered the Level 3 processes to introduce them. These processes were chosen from Level 3 because without doing so, there would be no assessment of any software life cycle steps and it was hard to see how a software assessment could legitimately ignore any parts of the life cycle.

SPICE	CMM	ISO 9001 : 1994
ENG.1.2 Software requirements analysis (establish the requirements of the software components of the system)	Requirements management (establish a common understanding between the customer and the software project of the customer's requirements that will be addressed by the software project/L2; PE, Activity 2 (the software requirements are developed, maintained, documented and verified by systematically analysing the allocated requirements according to the project's defined software process)/L3	4.4.4 Design input, Design input requirements relating to the product, including applicable statutory and regulatory requirements, shall be identified, documented and their selection reviewed by the supplier for adequacy. Incomplete, ambiguous or conflicting requirements shall be resolved with those responsible for imposing these requirements.
ENG.1.3 Software design (define a design for the software that implements the requirements and can be tested against them)	PE, Activity 3 (the software design is developed, maintained, documented and verified, according to the project's defined software process, to accommodate the software requirements and to form the framework for coding)/L3	4.4.2 Design and development planning, The supplier shall prepare plans for each design and development activity. The plans shall describe or reference these activities, and define responsibility for their implementation. The design and development activities shall be assigned to qualified personnel equipped with adequate resources. The plans shall be updated as the design evolves.

ENG.1.6 Software testing (test the integrated software producing a product that will satisfy the software requirements)	PE, Activity 5 (software testing is performed according to the project's defined software process)/L3	4.10.1 General, The supplier shall establish and maintain documented procedures for inspection and testing activities in order to verify that the specified requirements for the product are met. The required inspection and testing, and the records to be established, shall be detailed in the quality plan or documented procedures.

Table 6-5 Engineering processes

Support process category

Figure 6-3 shows the profile for support processes.

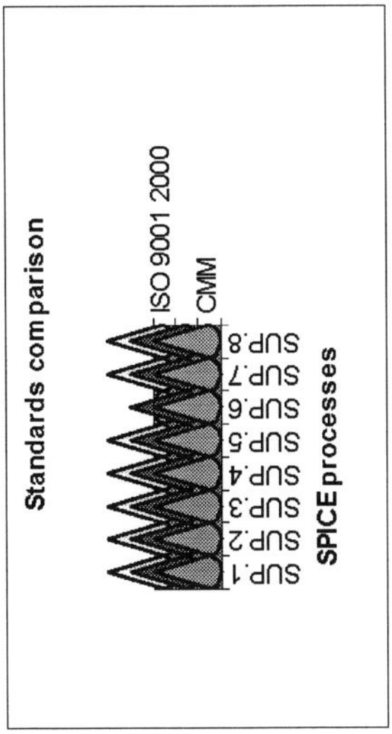

	SPICE Process	CMM	ISO 9001 1994	ISO 9001 2000
Documentation	SUP.1	1	1	1
Configuration Man.	SUP.2	1	1	1
Quality assurance	SUP.3	1	1	1
Verification	SUP.4	1	1	1
Validation	SUP.5	1	1	1
Customer review	SUP.6	1	1	0
Audit	SUP.7	1	1	1
Problem resolution	SUP.8	1	1	1

Figure 6-3 Support profile

Support functions are included in each of the standards followed in these SPI programmes. This is the only SPICE process category where all processes are in SPICE, the CMM Level 2 and ISO 9001 : 1994, as shown in Table 6-6.

SPICE	CMM	ISO 9001 : 1994
SUP.1 Documentation (develop and maintain documents that record information produced by a process or activity)	PE, Activity 8 the documentation that will be used to operate and maintain the software is developed and maintained according to the project's defined software process)	Records shall be maintained for qualified processes, equipment and personnel, as appropriate.
SUP.2 Configuration management (establish and maintain the integrity of all the work products of a process or project)	Configuration management (SCM)/(establish and maintain the integrity of the products of the software project throughout the project's software life cycle)/L2	Where appropriate, the supplier shall establish and maintain documented procedures for identifying the product by suitable means from receipt and during all stages of production, delivery and installation. Where and to the extent that traceability is a specified requirement, the supplier shall establish and maintain documented procedures for unique identification of individual product or batches. This identification shall be recorded.
SUP.3 Quality assurance (provide assurance that work products and processes of a process or project comply with their specified requirements and adhere to their established plans)	Software quality assurance (SQA)/provide management with appropriate visibility into the process being used by the software project and of the products being built/L2	The supplier shall identify and plan the production, installation and servicing processes which directly affect quality and shall ensure that these processes are carried out under controlled conditions.

SUP.4 Verification (confirm that each software work product and/or service of a process or project properly reflects the specified requirements)	SQA, Activity 4 (the SQA group reviews the software engineering activities to verify compliance.)	4.2.3 Quality planning/ f) the identification of suitable verification at appropriate stages in the realisation of product; 4.4.7 Design verification, At appropriate stages of design, design verification shall be performed to ensure that the design stage output meets the design stage input requirements. The design verification measures shall be recorded.
SUP.5 Validation (confirm that the requirements for a specific intended use of the software work product are fulfilled)	SQA, Activity 8 (the SQA group conducts periodic reviews of its activities and findings with the customer's SQA personnel, as appropriate)	4.2.3 Quality planning/g) the clarification of standards of acceptability for all features and requirements, including those which contain a subjective element; 4.4.8 Design validation, Design validation shall be performed to ensure that product conforms to defined user needs and/or requirements.
SUP.6 Joint review (maintain a common understanding with the customer of the progress against the objectives of the contract and what should be done to help ensure development of a product that satisfies the customer; joint reviews are at both project management and technical levels and are held throughout the life of the project)	PT&O, Activity 13 (formal reviews to address the accomplishments and results of the software project are conducted at selected project milestones according to a documented procedure)	4.4.6 Design review, At appropriate stages of design, formal documented reviews of the design results shall be planned and conducted. Participants at each design review shall include representatives of all functions concerned with the design stage being reviewed, as well as other specialist personnel, as required. Records of such reviews shall be maintained.

SUP.7 Audit (independently determine compliance of selected products and processes with the requirements, plans and contract as appropriate)	SQA, Activity 5 (the SQA group audit designated software work products to verify compliance)/L2	Internal quality audits shall be scheduled on the basis of the status and importance of the activity to be audited and shall be carried out by personnel independent of those having direct responsibility for the activity being audited.
SUP.8 Problem resolution (ensure that all discovered problems are analysed and resolved and that trends are recognised)	SQA, Activity 7 (deviations identified in the software activities and software work products are documented and handled according to a documented procedure)	4.1.2.1 Organisation responsibility and authority/b) identify and record any problems relating to the product, process and quality system; c) initiate, recommend or provide solutions through designated channels; d) verify the implementation of solutions; e) control further processing, delivery or installation of nonconforming product until the deficiency or unsatisfactory condition has been corrected.

Table 6-6 Support processes

Management process category

The project planning and management profile is shown in Figure 6-4.

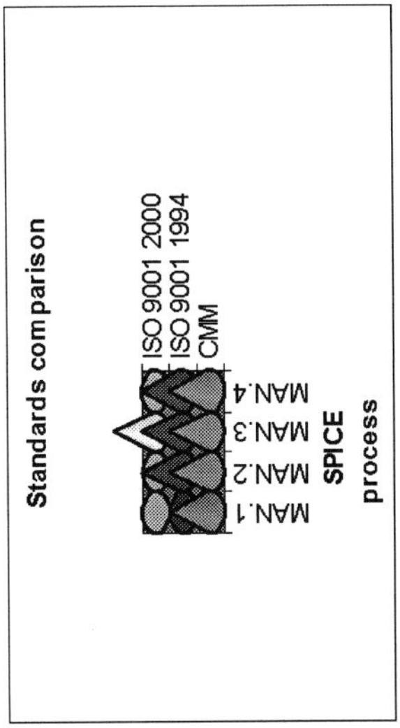

	SPICE Process	CMM	ISO 9001 1994	ISO 9001 2000
	MAN.1	1	0	0
Project management	MAN.2	1	1	0
Monitoring quality	MAN.3	1	1	1
Risk management	MAN.4	1	1	0

Figure 6-4 Project planning and management profile

Project planning and management activities are described in Table 6-7, including quality and risk management.

SPICE	CMM	ISO 9001 : 1994
MAN.2 Project management (identify, establish coordinate and monitor activities, tasks and resources necessary for a project to produce a product and/or service meeting the requirements)	Software project planning (PP)/L2-repeatable (establish reasonable plans for performing the software engineering and for managing the software project); Software project tracking & oversight (PT&O)/L2-repeatable (provide adequate visibility into actual progress so that management can take effective actions when the software project's performance deviates significantly from the software plans)	4.1.2.2 Resources, The supplier shall identify resource requirements and provide adequate resources, including the assignment of trained personnel, for management, performance of work and verification activities including internal quality audits.
MAN.3 Quality management (monitor the quality of the project's products and/or services and to ensure that they satisfy the customer)	SQA, Activity 5 (the SQA group audit designated software work products to verify compliance)	4.1.2.1 Organisation responsibility and authority, The responsibility authority and the interrelation of personnel who manage, perform and verify work affecting quality shall be defined and documented, particularly for personnel who need the organisational freedom and authority to: a) initiate action to prevent the occurrence of any nonconformities relating to the product, process and quality system; Inspection, measuring and test equipment shall be used in a manner which ensures that the measurement uncertainty is known and is consistent with the required measurement capability.

MAN.4 Risk management (identify and mitigate the project risks continuously throughout the life cycle of a project; the process involves establishing a focus on monitoring of risks at both the project and organisational levels)	PP, Activity 13 (the software risks associated with the cost, resource, schedule and technical aspects of the project are identified, assessed and documented)	Any corrective or preventive action taken to eliminate the causes of actual or potential nonconformities shall be to a degree appropriate to the magnitude of problems and commensurate with the risks encountered.

Table 6-7 Management processes

Organisation process category

The profile for organisation processes is shown in Figure 6-5.

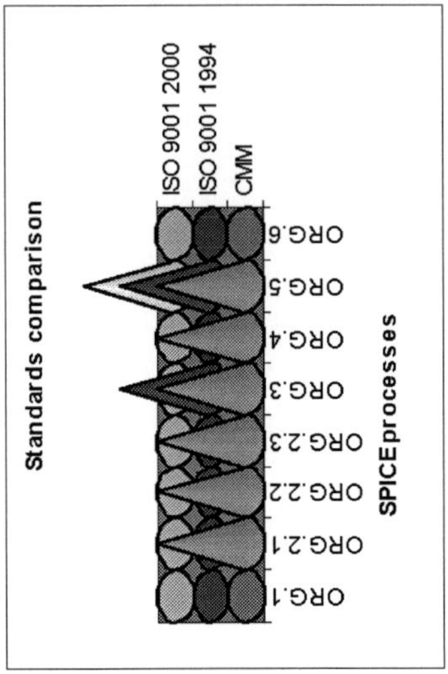

	SPICE Process	CMM	ISO 9001 1994	ISO 9001 2000
	ORG.1	0	0	0
	ORG.2.1	1	0	0
	ORG.2.2	1	0	0
	ORG.2.3	1	0	0
Training	ORG.3	1	1	0
	ORG.4	1	0	0
Measurement	ORG.5	1	1	1
	ORG.6	0	0	0

Figure 6-5 Organisation profile

Table 6-8 shows the last processes selected for the assessment model—training and measurement.

SPICE	CMM	ISO 9001 : 1994
ORG.3 Human resources management (provide the organisation and projects with individuals who possess skills and knowledge to perform their roles effectively and to work together as a cohesive group)	OPF, Activity 6 (training for the organisation's and projects' software processes is coordinated across the organisation)	4.18 Training The supplier shall establish and maintain documented procedures for identifying training needs and provide for the training of all personnel performing specific assigned tasks shall be qualified on the basis of appropriate education, training and/or experience, as required. Appropriate records of training shall be maintained.
ORG.5 Measurement (collect and analyse data relating to the products developed and processes implemented within the organisational unit, to support effective management of the processes and to objectively demonstrate the quality of the products)	Measurement and analysis, common feature/all levels (measurements are made and used to determine the status of the activities)/L2 process	4.11.1 Inspection, measuring and test equipment shall be used in a manner which ensures that the measurement uncertainty is known and is consistent with the required measurement capability.

Table 6-8 Organisation processes

In summary, the model for assessment was developed to include that set of good software practices that were common to all the standards used in training and consulting in the SPI programmes covered in this research. Because one of the SPICE functions is to act as a framework for assessment of organisations using other standards for SPI, selected SPICE processes were chosen to create the model for assessment.

The processes being assessed evaluate many aspects of the business. Processes covered at the organisation level are the organisation as supplier and acquirer, important parts of the development lifecycle which should be a good representation of the quality of the whole lifecycle, and support functions that enable proper control and management of the software development process. Relevant processes for management and control are assessed. Enabling functions to assist throughout the software development processes are also covered.

The processes from the standards discussed above were chosen because these were the standards used with the companies in earlier programmes. However, it is appropriate at this stage to mention ISO/IEC 29110, the new standard for very small entities. The entry and basic profiles are designed for an organisation of 25 people or fewer while an intermediate profile is planned for somewhat larger groups. The concept is that for smaller organisations the overhead required to implement ISO 9000 or one of the other extensive standards is simply not available. ISO/IEC 29110 contains only the basic processes that any organisation of any size should be confident about to ensure a quality product, managed projects and effective customer support. Initial components include:

- Requirements analysis (identification, refinement and analysis, verification and validation, change management);
- Architecture and detailed design;
- Construction and unit testing;
- Software testing (planning, design, verification of test cases and procedures, performance);
- Product delivery (define delivery instructions with customer, formalise completion);
- Version control (planning and setting up repository, version identification, change control);
- Project management (planning process, plan execution, assessment and control process, project closure);
- Verification and validation;
- Self-assessment (planning, data collection, data validation, process attribute rating, reporting).

Initial deployment of the standard started in 2010.

6.4 Summary

An interview guide was developed to gather information about:

- The organisation and its history of involvement with SPI processes, from participation in one or more of the SPI assistance programmes reviewed through the current environment and plans for future improvements,
- The existence of 20 software processes common to SPICE, the CMM and ISO 9001 : 1994 and the organisation's performance to achieve the desired outcomes.

Once this guide was developed, it was used in the interviews to determine how well each organisation incorporated their training in their software processes and management. Any organisation can use it in the same way to determine strengths and weaknesses in how it is managing software.

CHAPTER SEVEN

COMPANY PROFILES

7.1 Introduction

This chapter contains the case studies that were written to document the results of interviews. They are presented here to help the reader understand what real companies have done to improve their software development and maintenance environment. This may help readers to visualise what might be done in their own organisations.

7.2 DTG Profile, interview with Managing Director

Organisation profile

The company has grown from 8 to 28, with 23 of the employees in software. The average team size is three to four, two in software and the rest project management, testing and training. Projects are generally less than a month long. The existing system is being converted to a Windows-based system.

Past culture for improvement

The company took part in two improvement projects, TRI-SPIN and a PIE. The improvements were to solve several problems, most notably software versions and distribution of features were poorly controlled, and all knowledge of software was concentrated in one person, the senior programmer. These problems were solved and several processes put in place. These included: development of a software life cycle, documented control of requirements and the changes to meet them, development of a simple measurement system to track how time was being spent, implementation of management tools, development of a help desk to control access to the software staff and track common problem areas and development of a release system to balance special developments for individual customers and standard maintenance releases.

Senior management support for improvements has been very strong from the beginning. Staff understanding might have been weak on how improvements in software could be linked to business goals, but this did not keep the software staff from being most cooperative through the improvement programmes. Improvements included better quality and more reliable products, more predictable schedules and improved revenue. Most of the improvements made have persisted; measurement has fallen off, but increased use of tools has led to data being collected automatically. This hasn't so far been used in the business decision-making process, but customer complaints are down so the right changes seem to have been made.

No written documentation is available for the TRI-SPIN programme, but from the PIE final report, quoting the Managing Director of the company as it was organised then: "The project has generated the following major results for DTG:

- 57% increase in software installation sites
- Costing/estimating processes improved
- No longer dependent on key staff—this has been tackled by documenting the life cycle and software

Prior to the project, DTG felt that they were unable to grow their software business. As a result of implementing the project life cycle in the department, they have been able to increase the level of business significantly. This is reflected in the fact that at the start of the experiment their main software was installed at 35 sites, but this figure is now approaching 55 sites and is still growing."

Current culture for improvement

The current organisation includes a dedicated trainer and two project managers, one for installations and one to manage the programming. The vision is clearly presented and the organisation is supportive of whatever changes are needed to meet this vision. Business objectives and goals are well understood. No factors can be identified in the current culture that would interfere with making improvements. Better schedule and cost control were identified as important needs for the business as well as better infrastructure. Expenses, particularly wages, were highlighted as an area of concern. Good customer service and high quality software are considered to be the most important views of the customers; they have noted and approved of improvements.

Plans for the future

An IT strategy is being put together. DTG needs to have a more universal product which can be exported and hopefully the new product just rolled out is that. The goal is to triple customers in the next 5 years and this can only be done with exports. All the expansion plans are documented in a current business plan. The next need for hiring is to have a part-time HR person who can put some more structure into personnel issues.

Past	*Now*
II-4 Senior management support for SPI? *Very good*	*III-1 Senior management support for SPI?* *Very good*
II-5 SPI linked to business goals? *Poorly*	*III-2 Employees informed about business objectives, vision and goals?* *Very well* *III-5 Groups understand link between business objectives and goals and SPI* *A Senior management?: Very well* *B Middle management?: Very well* *C Technical management?: Very well* *D Software developers and maintainers?: Very well*
II-6 Vision lived by people?: 50% of the time	*III-3 Employees live vision?: Always*
II-7 Respected, senior SEs embrace SPI?: Always	*III-4 Respected, senior SEs embrace SPI?: Always*

Table 7-1 DTG changes over time detail

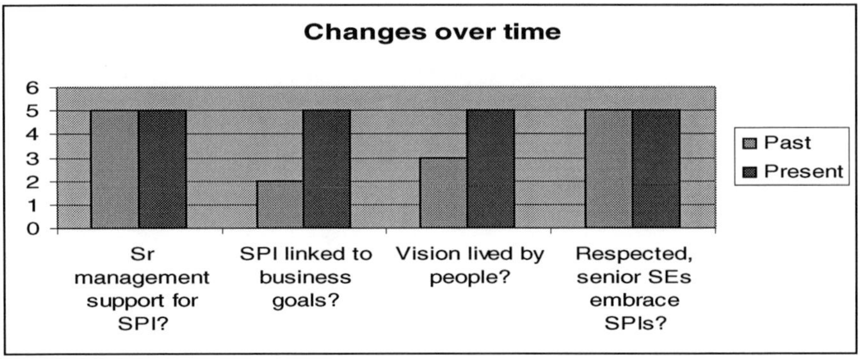

Figure 7-1 DTG changes over time

The link between business goals and SPI has changed dramatically. The author talked with several people who are happy to show what they are doing and how they are doing it.

The qualitative information from the questionnaire and evaluation of the overall organisational software management environment shows a strong management commitment and a workforce which is increasingly committed to improvements. The following more detailed assessment results can be put within this context.

Subject	Score	Any explanatory comments on rationale for scoring
Organisation as purchaser: Acquisition preparation Supplier selection Customer acceptance	 F F F	Whole systems are delivered to customers. DTG has long-term arrangements and periodic review meetings with companies for system components.
Organisation as supplier: Supply	 F	Contracts exist with all customers with requirements specified. An installation specialist does formal installations with release notes, lists of what is to be delivered and put in place. A training specialist works with customers on a daily basis to make sure the systems are operated correctly.

Steps of software life cycle: Software req. analysis Software design Software testing	 F L L	Written requirements are received and a specification written on how to transform the business requirements into software. A meeting is held with the supplier of the requirements to agree how they will be implemented. The design is documented informally as it is updated. More formality is not deemed to be necessary because of strong domain and customer knowledge. Unit, system, acceptance and regression testing are done in a controlled environment by the installation specialists using test scripts. It isn't clear how much documentation of test results exists and the process is dependent upon the "goodness" of one person, as much as anything.
Support processes: Documentation Configuration management Quality assurance Verification Validation Joint review Audit Problem resolution	 F F F P F F P L	 Release notes are created for deliveries. PVCS is used for configuration management and this produces documentation of status of the software components as the system is updated. Even in the beginning of the SPI process 12 years ago, the lead programmer was extremely careful about managing version control and organisation of software. Now the company uses PVCS rigorously and manages their libraries. A separate tester does the quality assurance, pulling in customer support for acceptance testing. No release goes out, no matter what the pressure, unless it is right. Verification does take place but informally, with perhaps not as much documentation as the standards would like. However, customers are brought in at every stage. This is monitored and as long as it is a small, concentrated group, this is probably OK. Validation is nearly always performed by customers as well as the tester acting for the customers. Regular reviews are held with the User Group and specific customers to make sure the software is correct and what is wanted

		and needed. The new product developed by the joint venture will be audited by a company that describes themselves as "forensic auditors". This will be used for all future releases. Two people staff the help desk at any given time to gather customer complaints and log them using "Gold Mine" and do the analysis of what needs to be done. The only reason this is designated "largely" instead of "fully" is because nobody uses this data to analyse trends or look for other information and this is required by all standards.
Management processes: Project management Quality management Risk management	 F N L	A specialist project manager handles all software projects and upgrades and a specialist project manager handles everything to do with the customers and installations. There is no formal quality strategy and goals. However, plenty of opportunity is given to customers to raise issues at meetings and through the help desk. No risk management plan exists that is called that but an extensive business plan covers many of the risky areas and shows forethought in planning for the future.
Organisation processes: Human resources management Measurement	 N N	The company is considered too small for any formal human resources management. However, the next hire planned is a part-time HR to handle the complexities of buying and absorbing new companies. Some data is collected but it is not really analysed or used to improve the decision process.

Table 7-2 DTG assessment results

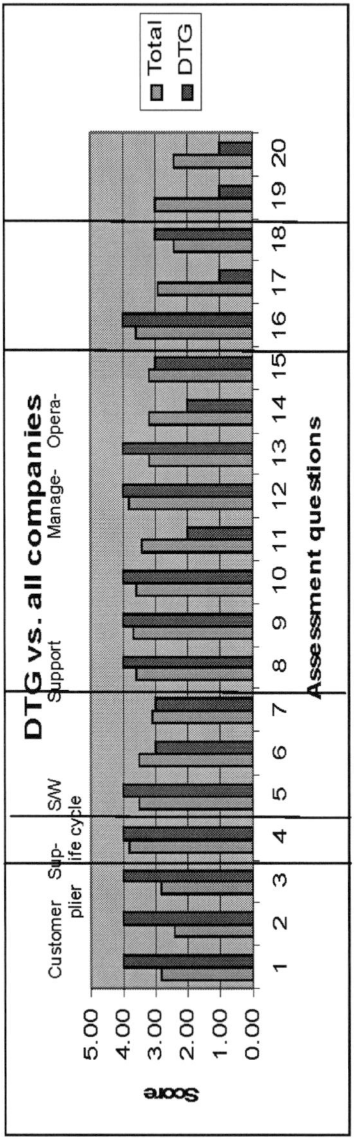

Figure 7-2 DTG scoring comparisons

Results of the assessment confirm the organisation as one with the majority of processes (11 fully, 4 largely, 2 partly and 3 N/A) compliant with the assessment instrument. Quality management, human resources management and measurement are the processes without formal implementation; there has been little or no presumption of the need for any of them as long as the company was so small. This is likely to change as the company grows.

The qualitative information obtained from the questionnaire shows an organisation which has consistently improved or sustained support and vision at all levels. The quantitative information obtained from the assessment show an organisation with strong software management processes which support the information gained through the initial questions.

Conclusion

The first objective of the research concerns individual organisations: to determine if a culture of improvement exists in the organisation. Both the interview and the assessment show that such a culture does exist and can be attributed at least in part to the improvement programmes since the improvements have been continual and most of the original improvements made are still are in place.

7.3 FD Profile, interview with Sr Manager in Engineering Group

Organisation profile

FD develops and supports a general software tool. The world-wide organisation is large, but the local engineering group the interviewee answered for is about 40 software engineering people. Average team size, sometimes all software people, is 1-10, although the preferred size when possible is 3-5. For most projects quarterly releases are normal but projects have been known to go as long as 3 years. Products are both web-based and distributed.

Past culture for improvement

FD sent one student to SCATE, the training programme based on the CMM. As the group involved "took on more and more development projects, the challenge was to establish processes in the new groups and to build on each project's success. Efficient Project Planning was seen as a common factor across the organisation."

The project chosen was a small team of three people. The project was new, there were no processes identified, there was nothing used previously to go on and there needed to be a way of recording the steps through the first project (each project lasts three months) to avoid duplication of work and delays in subsequent projects.

All three members of the group were keen to establish some processes and improve their project management skills, both for the sake of the project and for themselves.

The project began in October and the team wanted to have repeatable processes by Christmas and to ensure that they would release on time in subsequent projects.

The project achieved not only this goal, the team took on board many other valuable lessons including Requirements Management and Project Tracking.

The company goal (to retain our existing customer-base and attract new customers by providing products which meet and exceed their expectations and to deliver these products in a timely manner) was achieved through the hard work of the individuals to get the project right. Delivery was on time and the team members felt more confident in deciding their own time scales based on true experience.

The documentation of the processes proved to be of benefit as one of the team members left the company and although the other team members had a lot more to do, they were able to continue to use the new processes.

The project was seen to be success, running from Oct '97 to Mar '98. There were plans to repeat this success with some of the other development teams within the company.

The manager who sent the student to SCATE was very process-oriented. The interviewee knew of the SCATE attendee but not about SCATE; she doesn't believe that attendance at SCATE actually caused changes to happen because the student was from a different location and went on to do different things. However, one could surmise that the attitudes that caused her to be sent to SCATE in the first place meant that a process-oriented environment was being nurtured and supported at FD. This environment is evidenced by both the interview and the assessment.

ISO 9001 was adopted and is credited as being helpful with definition of the processes which have been built on over the years to become the present set. A few years ago FD decided the benefit of ISO 9001 had been exhausted and it was dropped. Management support for process improvement has been very strong for many years and is closely linked to understanding customer expectations and business goals. Technical personnel were supportive, although it tended to go in cycles sometimes.

Process improvement is credited with bringing better quality and more reliable products, improved revenue and more predictable schedules.

Current culture for improvement

Level of support for process improvement continues to be strong at all levels. Understanding of the link to business objectives can be variable among the technical staff but is generally high. Training continues—several personnel have just taken a project management course. FD products are sold on knowledge, quality and features rather than low cost so it is important to keep skills up. The current set of processes includes use of a code component library and code reusability to ensure continuity of product and wise use of resources. No factors exist to inhibit SPI, and many factors are in place to support it.

One area currently being examined is to make sure there are strong links between the business needs and the technical solutions.

Plans for the future

The interviewee described plans as being a fine-tuning process. Some of the areas being addressed are: code reviews, requirements gathering in a different way, and better design documentation. The strategy to make this happen is in place. FD, as a major multi-national corporation, has a continual issue with optimising low cost vs. high cost locations and regional vs. international development. They seem to be winning.

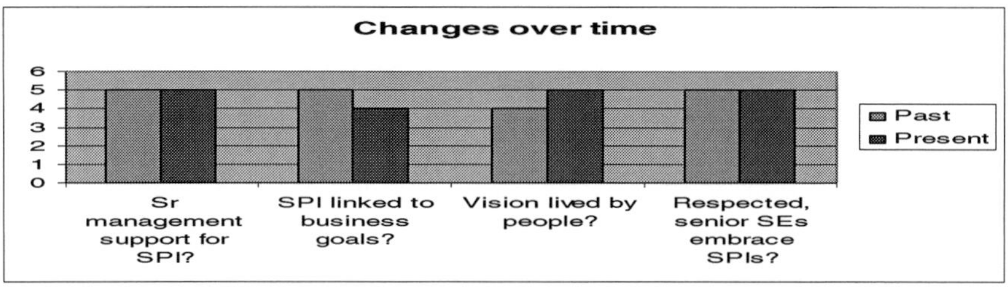

Figure 7-3 FD changes over time

Past	*Now*
II-4 Senior management support for SPI? *Very good*	*III-1 Senior management support for SPI?* *Very good*
II-5 SPI linked to business goals? *Very well*	*III-2 Employees informed about business objectives, vision and goals?* *Very well* *III-5 Groups understand link between business objectives and goals and SPI* *A Senior management?: Very well* *B Middle management?: Very well* *C Technical management?: Very well* *D Software developers and maintainers?: Very well usually, but can be variable, so scored as largely*
II-6 Vision lived by people?: Largely—sometimes it's a bit of trouble	*III-3 Employees live vision?: Very well*
II-7 Respected, senior SEs embrace SPI?: Always	*III-4 Respected, senior SEs embrace SPI?: Very well*

Table 7-3 FD changes over time detail

Subject	**Score**	**Any explanatory comments on rationale for scoring**
Organisation as purchaser: Acquisition preparation Supplier selection Customer acceptance	 N/A N/A N/A	Platforms are stable and any purchasing is done through formal corporate contracts and formal processes
Organisation as supplier: Supply	 F	Software is distributed on line after formal contracts have been established.
Steps of software life cycle: Software req. analysis Software design Software testing	 F F F	Requirements are gathered by working with the customers. There are nightly builds with formal, automated regression testing.

Support processes: Documentation Configuration management Quality assurance Verification Validation Joint review Audit Problem resolution	 F F F F F F F F	A technical writing group is responsible for documentation. All processes are acceptable within ISO 9001 even though formal certification has been dropped. Developers have quality assurance responsibilities themselves and there are independent QA resources across projects. Bugs are monitored throughout the life cycle, with all artefacts defined and all software meeting defined criteria before being released. User acceptance testing is part of the defined life cycle. Weekly meetings are held with customers. All bugs are tracked and issues resolved.
Management processes: Project management Quality management Risk management	 F F L	The project managers get extra resources as needed. Quality management is an integral part of the software process; bug reports are used as a measure of customer satisfaction by senior management. All projects are rated as green, yellow or red, with red as a high risk project. Open issues are tracked to closure with each open issue given an associated risk. An Executive Summary Report covers high level risks and their management for senior managers. This is scored as largely because the process can be variable over projects.
Organisation processes: Human resources management Measurement	 F L	 The measurement system for the entire company is very structured with data gathered about bugs, each one given a severity and criticality, and trends evaluated. However, for the smaller group being looked at here specifically, this level of trending doesn't always make sense because projects are frequently short term. Therefore the score given is a largely.

Table 7-4 FD assessment results

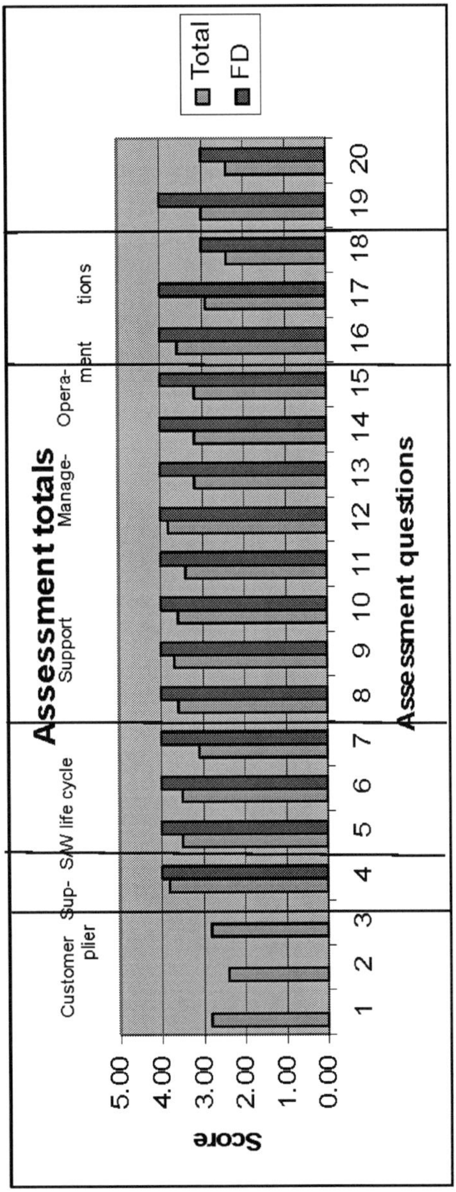

Figure 7-4 FD scoring comparisons

Results of the assessment confirm the organisation as one with the majority of processes (15 fully, 2 largely and 3 N/A) compliant with the assessment instrument.

This is a very organised, process-oriented company. As the interviewee stated, "They can't compete on costs so have to compete on quality and knowledge." The only thing listed as an important need for the business is to ensure the link between business and solutions—are their products really what the businesses need?

The qualitative information obtained from the questionnaire shows an organisation which has continuously sustained support for SPI at all levels. The quantitative information obtained from the assessment shows an organisation with strong software management processes which support the information gained through the initial questions. Not everything is perfect, but "holes" in the process are recognised and being addressed in both management and technical issues.

Conclusion

The first objective of the research concerns individual organisations: to determine if a culture of improvement exists in the organisation. Such a culture definitely exists at FD, but it is impossible to connect with the improvement programme in which it took part.

7.4 FM Profile, interview with the Commercial Director

Organisation profile

FM provides a range of business software applications and software related services. At the time of the early improvement project, FM had about 12-14 people. This has grown to 24, all in software; administration and other support services are handled centrally by the parent company.

The average total team size, all software people, is 2-3. Development is performed in phases—a six month project would be a big one. Products are web-based and for PCs.

Past culture for improvement

FM took part in ISCP and later in SPIRE, where the company aimed for ISO 9001 certification. The interviewee was a part of both improvement initiatives. Several improvements took place as a result, including adoption of ISO 9001. Also, new tools and processes were adopted, testing and quality improved, and better project management was put in place. In addition, the approach to work was improved, with better structure in the organisation and clearer focus on goals.

At the time of the initial improvement project, management support for improvement was very strong but there was a difficulty implementing new processes, partly because improvements were put in place before goals were clearly understood. In the second improvement project, a quality team from the working population, not the managers, was put in place to drive the improvements from the bottom up. Staff were generally supportive of the changes and understood why they were being made; one individual needed some encouragement to embrace the changes.

Some improvements included better quality products with less rework required, but delivery of products slowed at the same time. The changes forced individuals to evaluate what they were doing and the way work was being done. The only major attempt at improvement that tailed off was incorporating use cases, which proved to be difficult to adapt throughout the organisation and failed to show value for the time and effort required.

Current culture for improvement

The entire organisation now embraces the need for quality in the processes followed. There could still be some improvement at all but the highest level in understanding the link between business goals and the improvement regime.

Their ISO 9001 certification is a few months old now so the environment which led the company to take part in improvement projects still seems to be in existence. The only factor identified as possibly inhibiting more improvements is that some people have resisted an attempt to understand and improve the productivity of the individual.

The most important needs for the business were identified as better schedule control and faster time to market. The greatest area of concern is rising expenses. Customers appreciate FM as supplying the best products and the best people to service them. This is confirmed by positive comments from customers on better testing and the improvement in quality. Some of these comments have been received through an active help desk.

The interesting response to what a good organisation looks like was: innovative, efficient, reactive and a "joy to deal with". The response to what the company looks like today was, "hard work to get something done, but get good services". The interviewee believes more communication of the mission/vision/goals would help to align the hoped for and the actual views.

Plans for the future

Over the next three years, FM has goals to be the largest reseller of their third-party software in Ireland. The interviewee is developing a set of KPIs to tell them how well this goal is being met. The strategy is in place to make this happen. The one change the interviewee would like to see is a stronger customer sales focus.

Past	*Now*
II-4 Senior management support for SPI? *Very good*	*III-1 Senior management support for SPI?* *Very good*
II-5 SPI linked to business goals? *First time: poorly* *Second time: Very well*	*III-2 Employees informed about business objectives, vision and goals?* *Very well* *III-5 Groups understand link between business objectives and goals and SPI* *A Senior management?: Very well* *B Middle management?: Well* *C Technical management?: Well* *D Software developers and maintainers?: Well*
II-6 Vision lived by people?: Always	*III-3 Employees live vision?: Always*
II-7 Respected, senior SEs embrace SPI?: Always	*III-4 Respected, senior SEs embrace SPI?: Always*

Table 7-5 FM changes over time detail

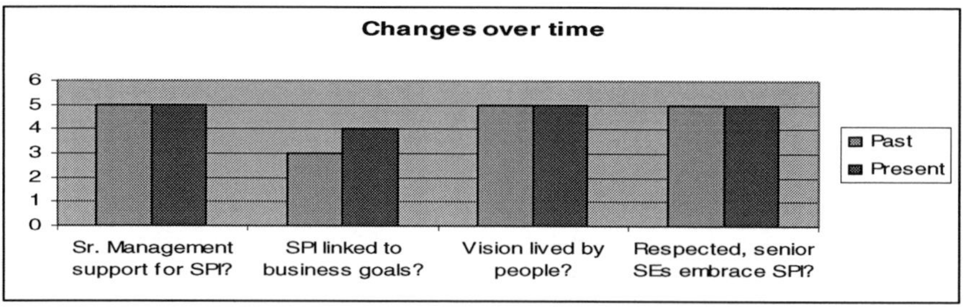

Figure 7-5 FM changes over time

The link between business goals and SPI is variable and depends on when improvements were implemented and who is the subject so it is only given a 3 (average) in the past and 4 (well) in the present. As explained earlier, because the company took part in two SPI programmes, one of which did not lead to ISO 9001 certification and one that did, scores are given for both, where appropriate.

The qualitative information from the questionnaire and evaluation of the overall organisational software management environment shows a strong management commitment and a workforce which is increasingly committed to improvements. The following more detailed assessment results can be put within this context.

Subject	**Score**	**Any explanatory comments on rationale for scoring**
Organisation as purchaser:		
Acquisition preparation	F	The organisation is opportunity-driven with a strategy on how to buy product, how it fits in, how to make it successful.
Supplier selection	N/A	The platform is stable; any purchases are from known suppliers.
Customer acceptance	L	An evaluation process exists but often depends on the knowledge of senior people.
Organisation as supplier:		FM has just introduced selling to the retail sector, using a project plan with formalised requirements
Supply	F	and contract.
Steps of software life cycle:		
Software req. analysis	P	Some areas have full set of requirements and analysis, some are ad hoc. FM is struggling with this area.
Software design	F	Design is solid; most work uses existing products.
Software testing	P	Tests are performed on customer data and customers do formal acceptance tests, but no formal regression testing.
Support processes:		
Documentation	F	FM has standard documents and templates; some are mandatory.
Configuration management	F	Configuration management is quite strong.
Quality assurance	F	
Verification	F	
Validation	F	
Joint review	F	
Audit	F	
Problem resolution	F	

Management processes: Project management Quality management Risk management	 F F L	 Only bigger projects have a risk register.
Organisation processes: Human resources management Measurement	 F P	 One concern identified by ISO 9001 auditor is not enough measurement; this is improving.

Table 7-6 FM assessment results

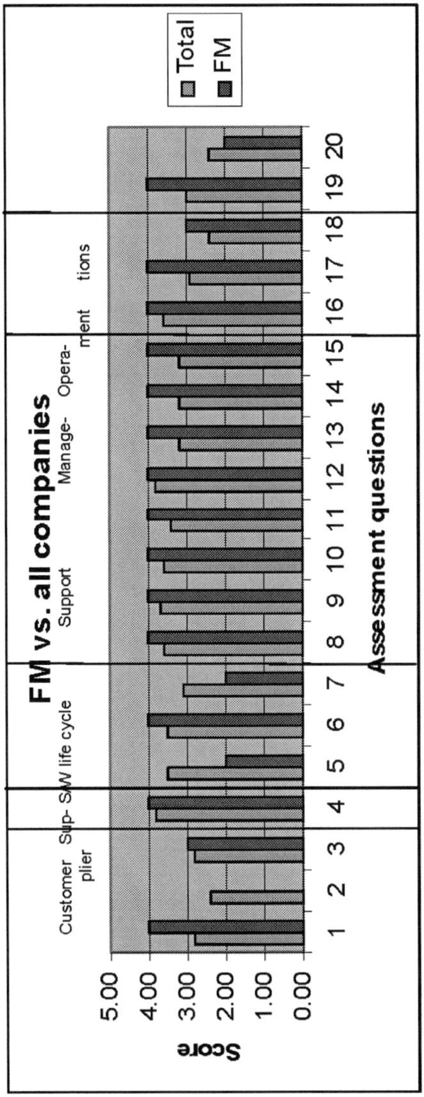

Figure 7-6 ***FM scoring comparisons***

Results of the assessment confirm the organisation as one with the majority of processes (14 fully, 2 largely, 3 partly and one N/A) compliant with the assessment instrument.

Conclusion

The first objective of the research concerns individual organisations: to determine if a culture of improvement exists in the organisation. The results of both the questionnaire and the assessment indicate the answer is yes. In particular, the interview showed that while implementation of process improvement has had to grow gradually, management has always been strong. In light of this, a case can be made for the benefits of the improvement programmes in making this happen.

7.5 JC Profile, interview with the COO/Software Manager[10]

Organisation profile

JC is a niche-supplier of products and services. The organisation has expanded and contracted but is now, at around 60 employees, about the size it was when it took part in ISCP. Fifteen of these employees are in software, with an average team size of three people, two of them software. Development projects are typically six months or less and are described as web-based.

Past culture for improvement

The interviewee didn't know about the ISCP programme but did know about the quality manager who was there during the programme and remembers the quality manager who followed. JC did go on to adopt ISO 9001 after the improvement programme. Senior management support for improvement has fluctuated drastically from "very good" to "poor" support as people have come and gone. Employees—including senior software engineers—have shown "about average" understanding of business goals and their support of these goals in daily work has also fluctuated, with room for improvement cited.

One result of the adoption of the Standard was more predictable schedules. This affected senior people the most because they had to do a better job of setting things up, using a more structured framework. Some improvements were tried and not sustained, such as transferring functional

[10] After the interview, the interviewee indicated that he was under a great deal of pressure and the answers may have come across as more negative than is actually warranted. Presumably the opportunity to make any changes he wanted to make provided the opportunity to bring any discrepancies into alignment. No further comments were received by the author.

requirements to technical requirements and using a tool for performance measurement of software, test and code coverage.

Current culture for improvement

Senior management support for change/improvement in software management was cited as "good" recently, a slight improvement. Equally, the employees' understanding of business objectives, vision and goals was described as "fluctuated" in the past but improving today. The incorporation of these business objectives in daily work is improving from "50% of the time" to "often". The software engineers understand the process of improvement "50% of the time" and this understanding needs improvement.

The use of business goals and objectives to drive improvements is cited as very well understood by senior business managers, but "well" by other management groups and software developers. Lack of senior management support, loss of face, resistance to change and the pressure of getting through daily work were cited as factors which might inhibit a culture of improvement.

The most important needs for the business today are high quality services and moving into more service contracts. Areas of greatest concern are getting the right experienced developers to create a culture of peer pressure-led improvements. The answer to the question about how customers view the organisation, led to a discussion of confusion on the part of the customer sometimes. Business intelligence and quality are sometimes undervalued because the customers think low cost is more important. This view has been expressed as both positive and negative on occasion.

The description of a "good" organisation was one where all levels have the same understanding of the customer and the same priorities. The current organisation is described as busy and inefficient, but surviving well. The only comment on why there is a difference between the two was that improving efficiency of the management team leads to improved efficiency of the operations team.

Plans for the future

Most important changes being made are to ramp up profitability by improving efficiency. The strategy to accomplish this is in place. The change most wished for is for the operational staff to improve business knowledge of the industry and company.

Past	*Now*
II-4 Senior management support for SPI? *Fluctuated as people came and went; scored as average*	*III-1 Senior management support for SPI?* *Average, at least recently*
II-5 SPI linked to business goals? *Average*	*III-2 Employees informed about business objectives, vision and goals?* *Average, poor in the past* *III-5 Groups understand link between business objectives and goals and SPI* *A Senior management?: Well* *B Middle management?: Average* *C Technical management?: Average* *D Software developers and maintainers?: Average*
II-6 Vision lived by people?: Fluctuated with room for improvement; scored as 50% of the time	*III-3 Employees live vision?: 50% of the time has improved to often*
II-7 Respected, senior SEs embrace SPI?: 50% of the time	*III-4 Respected, senior SEs embrace SPI?: 50% of the time, still needs work*

Table 7-7 JC changes over time detail

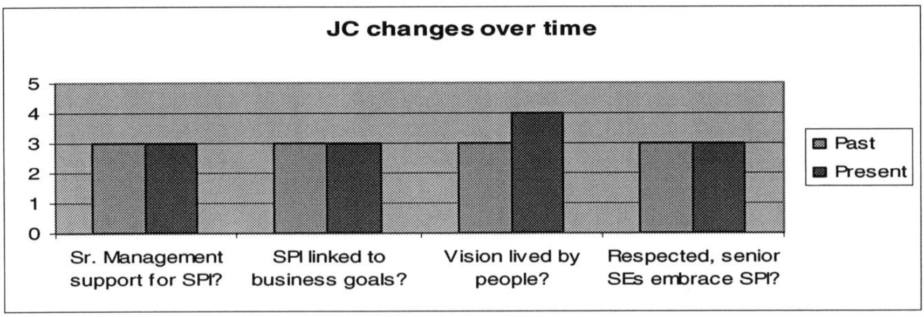

Figure 7-7 JC changes over time

Subject	Score	Any explanatory comments on rationale for scoring
Organisation as purchaser: Acquisition preparation Supplier selection Customer acceptance	 F F F	The first three questions have to do with acquisition as a customer. The service agreement and other arrangements with one supplier are covered by this, with an acquisition strategy and agreed requirements in place.
Organisation as supplier: Supply	 L	This question applies to the company as supplier and includes steps from formal response to a customer's request through delivery and installation according to agreed requirements. While a process is in place, better detail is needed to bring it up to fully. For example, customer requirements are in place but not in detail.
Steps of software life cycle: Software req. analysis Software design Software testing	 P P L	These are steps of the software life cycle. As part of the description of JC's processes the statement was made that the company is largely driven by schedule.
Support processes: Documentation Configuration management Quality assurance Verification Validation Joint review Audit Problem resolution	 P L L P L L F F	These processes are defined as support to the software life cycle. In response to the questions about testing, in particular, the interviewee noted that Quality Assurance is sometimes cut short by schedule constraints. Since only the audit and problem resolution processes—required by ISO 9001 compliance—are defined as fully performed, this might indicate that schedule constraints are a problem in many areas. When asked about joint review, indications were that all projects are different in level of review.
Management processes: Project management Quality management Risk management	 L F P	Risk management is described as part of project planning and management, and not a separate function.
Organisation processes: Human resources management Measurement	 L F	

Table 7-8 JC assessment results

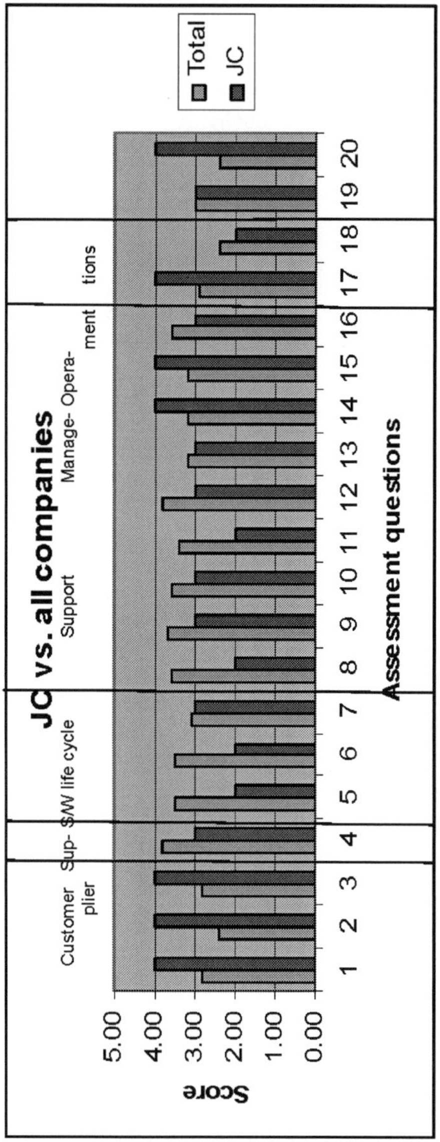

Figure 7-8 ***JC scoring comparisons***

Results of the assessment confirm the organisation as one with the majority of processes (7 fully, 8 largely and 5 partly) compliant with the assessment instrument.

There is a certain discrepancy between the answers to the questionnaire, which indicate a lack of support and understanding at all levels for SPI, and the fact the organisation has had ISO 9001 consistently since taking part in ISO 9001 training and has relatively good assessment results.

This may indicate that the interviewee's comments about his answers being more negative than warranted are true.

Conclusion

However, the first objective of the research concerns individual organisations: to determine if a culture of improvement exists in the organisation. The results of the ISO 9001 certification and the assessment at least indicate the answer is yes. The results of the questionnaire do not. Therefore, that culture of improvement is questionable with this company.

7.6 MM Profile, interview with Senior Sales Consultant

Organisation profile

MM has been through many changes since participating in SCATE. The company has expanded to as many as 35 people in two different countries but is now back to 7, about the same number as when involved in SCATE. The company makes niche software for business management. Two and one-half people are responsible for software development and maintenance, with three people on most development teams. Development projects are short, with a new software release every quarter.

Past culture for improvement

The interviewee himself took part in SCATE. Improvements were made, particularly with the larger, distributed team. Strong support for process improvement was shown across the management and employee spectrum. According to the interviewee, the changes made included better quality products and more predictable schedules. Testing and quality assurance became stricter, although reviews and measurement didn't continue as part of the software process.

From the overview of a case study written by the interviewee after SCATE: "At the beginning of SCATE there was a high level commitment to software process improvement. However, the effort required for SCATE was underestimated. During the course of SCATE improvements have taken place. The need for improvements in the software process is recognised by both the management and the developers. The areas for improvement have been identified and plans are being developed to implement these improvements. The improvement areas cover better design analysis of requirements, improving time estimates and better project tracking. One of the key lessons learned is that time must be invested by the champion in planning software process improvement."

The following detailed benefits were noted in the case study, although no specific improvement project was undertaken within the SCATE timescale for various reasons.

- Better time management and time tracking. A simple time tracking tool, recommended during one of the SCATE sessions, was invested in at an extremely low cost. The time tracking tool helped developers to focus on time spent on tasks and how they are progressing.
- Better guidelines on estimating time and effort were developed. The real benefit of the time tracking tool is to track time on individual project tasks. This information will then be used to review original estimates and redefine existing guideline on estimates.
- More review meetings to track project progress.
- Requirements gathering has improved and all staff have received further training in recording change requests from customers. Requirements gathering has always been a strong feature of MM meeting customer satisfaction and requirements gathering has improved.
- All staff have been given further training in using internal suggestions and discussion topics systems.
- All staff have been trained on using personal Calendar system in Lotus Notes.
- Internal IT infrastructure upgraded, network improved, e-mail system made more efficient.
- Improvements in technical support procedure. Technical Support is provided by the development team. Initial results from time tracking showed that technical support was taking up more resources and time than originally suspected. As a result, the technical support procedure was improved. The changes have resulted in more discipline by individuals in dealing with calls and more efficient handling of calls.

Lessons learned included:

- Significant time needs to be invested by the champions to make software process improvement a real success.
- Process improvement has to be planned, it will not just happen. Both management and development team at MM see the need for improvement, but the improvements require planning.
- Small changes can make a difference.

The results documented at the end of SCATE improvements are consistent with what the interviewee remembers today: better quality products and more predictable schedules. Testing and quality assurance became stricter, although reviews and measurement didn't continue as part of the software process.

Statements made in the case study and at the time of the interview contained the theme of not enough time. In the case study, one plan for the future that was never implemented was ISO 9001 certification.

Current culture for improvement

MM has been refocusing its business after cutting back. Some of the improved processes, such as testing, have somewhat reduced in formality, although they are still practiced. The slimmed down organisation is concentrating on the business objectives and how to best satisfy the customers. Predictably for a small company, primary inhibitions to a culture of improvement are getting swamped in the day-to-day business and simply not having the time or resources to concentrate on improvements. Efforts are spent on ensuring a high quality product and providing friendly, reliable support. Keeping up with changes in technology is a special area of concern. Customers provide feedback and have regularly noted improvements in the products and services. The company is stretched for resources and needs more people, once that becomes feasible in the current business climate.

Plans for the future

MM wants to stabilise its new product and expand into additional product areas, possibly something completely different like products that support alternative energies. One strong desire is to hire more people.

Past	*Now*
II-4 Senior management support for SPI? *Very good*	*III-1 Senior management support for SPI?* *Very good*
II-5 SPI linked to business goals? *Very well*	*III-2 Employees informed about business objectives, vision and goals?* *Very well* *III-5 Groups understand link between business objectives and goals and SPI* *A Senior management?: Very well* *B Middle management?: Very well* *C Technical management?: Very well* *D Software developers and maintainers?: Very well*
II-6 Vision lived by people?: Always	*III-3 Employees live vision?: Always*
II-7 Respected, senior SEs embrace SPI?: Always	*III-4 Respected, senior SEs embrace SPI?: Always*

Table 7-9 MM changes over time detail

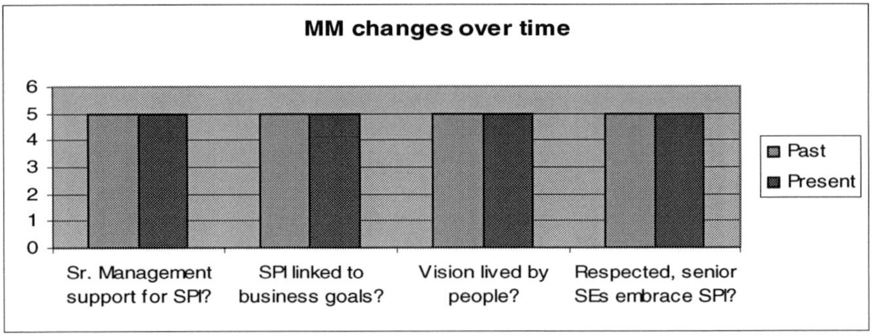

Figure 7-9 MM changes over time

Assessment results

After discussion of the different levels of the SPICE assessment the interviewee agreed that with few exceptions MM would be at the performed level rather than anything higher (managed, established, predictable, optimising)

Subject	Score	Any explanatory comments on rationale for scoring
Organisation as purchaser: Acquisition preparation Supplier selection Customer acceptance	 N/A N/A N/A	MM develops software which runs on other people's computers. They have no hardware purchase to do with distributing their product.
Organisation as supplier: Supply	 F	Contracts exist with all customers with requirements specified. MM responds to the customer tender process and frequently has a Statement of Work to follow.
Steps of software life cycle: Software req. analysis Software design Software testing	 F F P	MM uses management software which tracks documentation, action items, etc. through the software process. Requirements→design→development→ testing is all tracked throughout the quarterly release and other development processes. Software testing is only partly because there is no regression testing and some of the other testing is treated somewhat informally in the smaller organisation.
Support processes: Documentation Configuration management Quality assurance Verification Validation Joint review Audit Problem resolution	 F F P L F F N P	Documentation includes requirements and design specifications as well as release notes, upgraded user instructions and review reports Tools are used for formal code control and the release process. A quality assurance process is followed, but independence is sometimes difficult, so quality assurance is only given a partly. The verification process is followed but not always thoroughly documented so it is given a largely. Validation is always performed by customers. On larger projects weekly telephone conversations are held with the customer to discuss status, issues are tracked and people are assigned to deal with problems. All action items are tracked with customers. There are two full versions of each product so it is mostly a maintenance environment. A new product is being developed and new products are being discussed. MM has no formal ISO 9001 or other standard to audit against but one recommendation was they could and possibly

		should audit against how well they follow their own software process. Problems and their resolution are tracked but no attempt is made to then use the data for trend analysis, determining weakness in various components of the software, etc.
Management processes:		
Project management	L	The work is planned and tracked, actions taken to correct deviations, etc. however some tasks are handled informally.
Quality management	N	There is no formal quality strategy.
Risk management	N	No risk management is performed or has ever been considered.
Organisation processes:		
Human resources management	P	The company is considered too small for any formal human resources management. MM knows they would like to have more people but it isn't always clear exactly who to hire and why.
Measurement	P	Some data is collected but it is variable and data is seldom turned into knowledge. More measurement was in place when the company was distributed and larger.

Table 7-10 MM assessment results

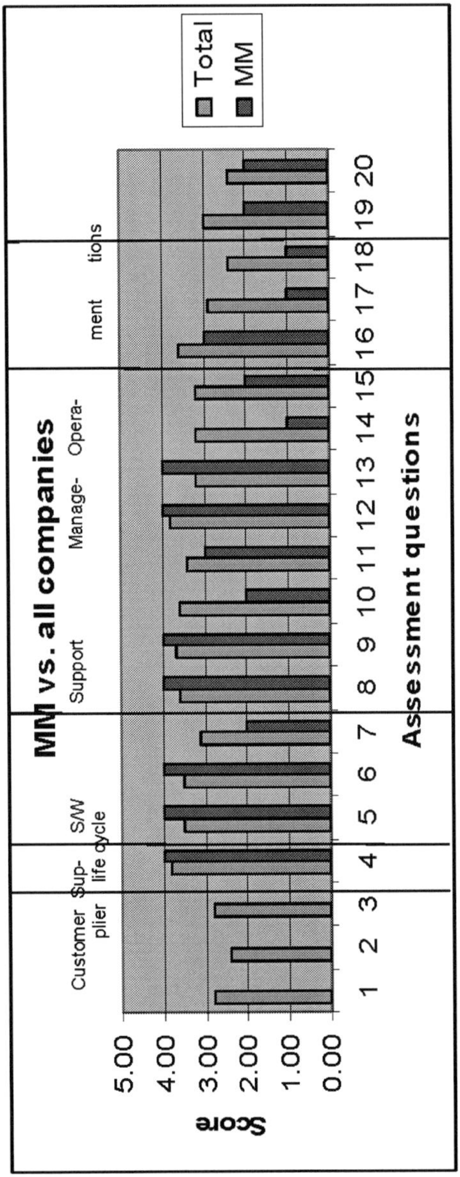

Figure 7-10 MM scoring comparisons

Results of the assessment show the organisation as one with the majority of processes (7 fully, 2 largely, 5 partly, 3 no and 3 N/A) compliant with the assessment instrument, at least to some extent. This is a company which has gone through a great many changes and it is to their credit that so many processes are still in place, although many have been modified.

Conclusion

The first objective of the research concerns individual organisations: to determine if a culture of improvement exists in the organisation. Both the interview and the assessment show that such a culture does exist, although some is very limited, and can be attributed at least in part to the improvement programmes since the improvements continued through great changes and some of the original improvements made are still in place.

7.7 OS Profile, interview with Project Manager

Organisation profile

The current organisation isn't the same as the one which took part in the PIE, however the interviewee was the manager of the PIE. The original organisation was spun off and merged with another to form this company. Responses about an initiative which took place so many years ago may be understandably a bit fragmented at times. This is a large organisation compared to many software organisations in Ireland, with over 100 employees in software alone. The average team size may be about 12 or so, with 5-8 software personnel on each team for short projects of a few months. Products are internal bespoke developments for the front office. Three-tier applications are sometimes web-based or distributed.

Past culture for improvement

At the time of the PIE, several initiatives were adopted to strengthen and improve the organisation. The PIE in particular was focused on better project management methods and measurement. As a result, a cut-down version of PRINCE[11] was implemented, along with function point counting. Both were considered very powerful and successful. Senior management and others strongly supported the improvements, which were driven from IT to develop better quality software in a timelier manner. Benchmark exercises with a consultant were valuable to show where

[11] PRojects IN Controlled Environments

improvements were needed. All levels grasped the business objectives and were willing to make changes to meet them.

New software processes were put in place to create a reasonably agile environment, but with quality assurance walkthroughs, review of code developed by beginners, with level of review required being determined by senior personnel. In addition, better products, clearer specifications and better estimates ensued.

From the PIE final report, written by the research interviewee: "The primary benefits expected from the Application Experiment were improved estimates on projects leading to better delivery, increased client participation on software engineering projects by adopting PRINCE methodology and improved Project Management, specifically in the areas of project planning and control.

Overall the project achieved its objectives."

Current culture for improvement

Support for changes has been sustained, and frequently improved at all levels, although sometimes it does get over-ridden by the need to be both agile and productive in the daily work. A constant focus on business concerns drives a need to be more efficient. Customer approval of improvement initiatives has been expressed in regular customer satisfaction surveys.

Many of the improvements made are still in place but most of them have been modified. For example, function point counting had an important role to play in helping reach better understanding of what was needed, but over time seemed too labour-intensive and of limited value. If tools existed to automate a lot of the functions it might have been different. The response to the questions about adjectives to describe the current organisation vs. a "good" organisation, led to a discussion of the need for straight, efficient processes to link the decision, investing and funding management functions of the business. Improved technology would help smooth out these processes in the current organisation.

Plans for the future

The general manager has developed a five-prong approach to improvements:

- IT governance (prioritisation and approval process)
- IT strategy, including the architectural role in the organisation
- Service management (change control, problem resolution, issues management)

- Time recording and measurement
- Testing, including user acceptance and regression testing

Some activities are finished, some ongoing and some planned. All are in aid of smoothing out the processes and improving linkages. Consultants were brought in to review best practices across the organisation and recommend where they can be implemented in new ways. Particularly since the organisation is a merger of components of different companies, many of the same activities were performed in different ways and great efficiencies can be recognised by adopting best practice across the entire organisation.

Past	*Now*
II-4 Senior management support for SPI? Very good	*III-1 Senior management support for SPI? Very good*
II-5 SPI linked to business goals? Very well	*III-2 Employees informed about business objectives, vision and goals? Very well III-5 Groups understand link between business objectives and goals and SPI A Senior management?: Very well B Middle management?: Very well C Technical management?: Well D Software developers and maintainers?: Well Because not all levels were at "Very well" this was scored as "Well"*
II-6 Vision lived by people?: Largely—sometimes it's a bit of trouble	*III-3 Employees live vision?: Often—focus is on daily jobs.*
II-7 Respected, senior SEs embrace SPI?: Always	*III-4 Respected, senior SEs embrace SPI?: Always*

Table 7-11 OS changes over time detail

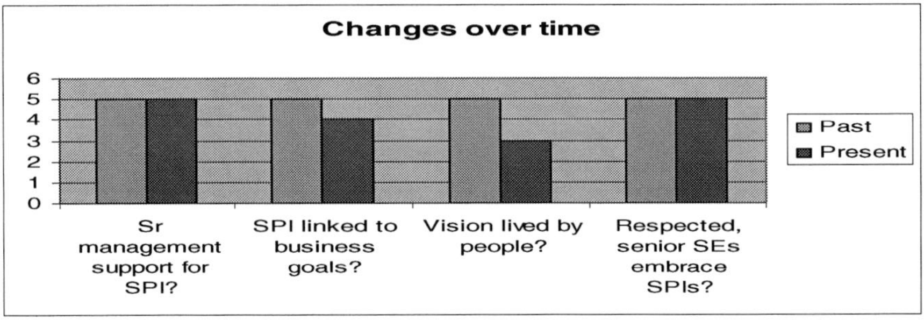

Figure 7-11 OS changes over time

It might be difficult to actually compare past and present in one sense because the organisation itself is different today.

Subject	Score	Any explanatory comments on rationale for scoring
Organisation as purchaser: Acquisition preparation Supplier selection Customer acceptance	 F F F	
Organisation as supplier: Supply	 F	
Steps of software life cycle: Software req. analysis Software design Software testing	 F F L	Software testing is given a "Largely" because regression testing is only done when deemed necessary.
Support processes: Documentation Configuration management Quality assurance Verification Validation Joint review Audit Problem resolution	 F F F F F F F L	Quality assurance is performed on all deliverables as part of the life cycle. User acceptance testing is part of the life cycle. The process is practiced but fragmented until recently; a new Help Desk is coming in.

Management processes: Project management Quality management Risk management	 F F F	 This is part of the process and a feature of the initial documentation; critical success factors are identified and internal audits held to ensure accuracy.
Organisation processes: Human resources management Measurement	 F P	 Data is collected but not always used although there is a quarterly review of all statistics.

Table 7-12 OS assessment results

Results of the assessment confirm the organisation as one with the majority of processes (17 fully, 2 largely and 1 partly) compliant with the assessment instrument.

The interviewee described the company as "one that has good people that operate well when given the space to do it." The biggest difficulty is pressure—so much to do, so little time.

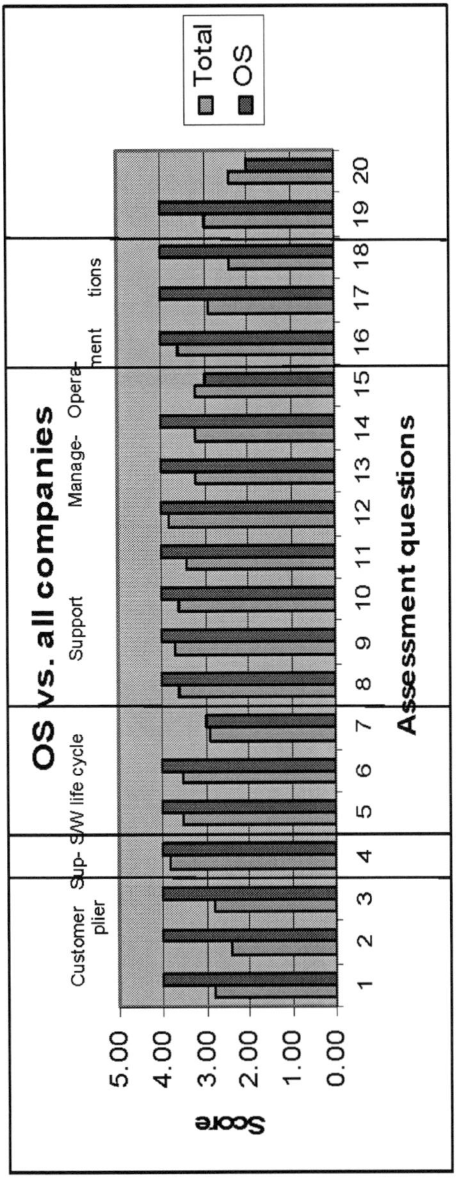

Figure 7-12 OS scoring comparisons

Conclusion

The first objective of the research concerns individual organisations: to determine if a culture of improvement exists in the organisation. This has been demonstrated; a consultant was brought in to review best practice across the organisation, displaying a continuing commitment to improvement. The interviewee definitely gave credit to the improvement programme even though specific processes implemented then have been overtaken by decisions affected by mergers and reorganisation.

7.8 SI Profile, interview with Engineering Manager

Organisation profile

SI has gone through massive changes since taking part in the process improvement programmes of the past, having been bought several months ago from the parent company and now returned to being called its original name. The local company now has 15 employees, including one software engineer, who make bespoke products for nearly 100 customers. Currently, most projects are short maintenance upgrades, sometimes to embedded systems and sometimes to PC-based management tools. Some new product development is being discussed.

Past culture for improvement

Under the former parent company, process improvement programmes were allowed in a hands-off environment where the local company could make such decisions independently. In such an environment, local SI took part in TRI-SPIN, SCATE and SPIRE. Improvements made include more structure in using a formal life cycle, using peer and technical reviews and better project management, including processes and procedures consistent with ISO 9001:1994.

From the TRI-SPIN case study, written by the then Quality Manager: "SI, although still at an early point in the introduction of Peer Reviews, believe it to have been successful. By calculating the estimated time saved through early detection and setting that against the overhead of holding Peer Reviews, SI estimated they have saved around 27 hours of developers time for around 1 month's worth of reviews. They currently save 2 hours development time for every hour spent reviewing."

From the SCATE case study, written by the same Quality Manager: "The SCATE Project goal was to implement project management and controls consistent with the CMM level 2 KPAs of Project Planning, and Project Tracking and Oversight on the development project. However, the attempts to implement changes on a baseline project failed. Both the

Managing Director and the Software Manager left during this time and management commitment to the baseline project faltered. So the Quality Manager decided to focus on education and hold several workshops to train people in the KPAs and current barriers they see to product design quality and the improvement which need to be put in place."

Lessons learned included:

- "No matter how many times you are told 'Process Improvement and organisational changes' are much more difficult than you expect. Appreciataion and expertise in this area can only be mastered through knowledge and experience in much the same way as people become expert in medicine. Knowledge alone is not sufficient and you only gain more expertise through experience combined with learning.
- Goals need to be very well understood. This is not only the commitment by the individual(s) involved but from the point of view of the commitment required by the organisation if the goal(s) are to be realised. Although the SCATE programme was very well structured in relation to goal setting I now feel we did not have a sufficient understanding of the commitment which would be required to meet our SCATE goals. Also our goals were aligned with the baseline project which effectively was put 'On-Hold'.
- Because of our relatively 'process immaturity' we would have benefited from more support in the selection of goals. Less ambitious goals with milestones aligned with the SCATE activities and defined deliverables at each of these milestones would help the goals be more realistic.
- Success in implementing new processes is a multistage process itself; firstly it requires the knowledge as to how the process should be, then it requires continuous and sustained effort to convince the people that this is the way and it will be worth all the effort. To make the change requires more than being aware that the change will be good for you, you also need constant gentle persuasion. We all know that smoking, driving too fast, drinking too much alcohol and lots more are bad for us but we continue to do it."

SI was already approved for SPIRE while they were still trying to finish SCATE. The same subjects were basically being being addressed under an equally changing environment.

From the SPIRE case study, written by the same Quality Manager: "So many changes were taking place simultaneously that it was difficult to gather measurements against original goals for SPIRE. However, we are very pleased with what we accomplished in such a relatively short timeframe. Our second assessment against the SPICE model showed an improvement in the capability of ten of the nineteen areas including project management (which increased from 0.25 to 0.75) and software requirements analysis (which increased from 0.25 to 0.5). Staff attitudes have improved dramatically with staff who were previously unhappy with the existing processes now making a conscious effort to improve them. A customer representative visited SI towards the end of the project, to follow-up on a previous project audit. He remarked on the improvement in the development process, stating that he had a lot more confidence in SI's ability to meet his needs."

This was particularly difficult because the Quality Manager knew his job was being terminated at the same time SPIRE was to end at the end of August 1998. It is to his credit that he worked so hard on this programme and documented the results so thoroughly.

Current culture for improvement

SI is currently certified to ISO 9001 : 2000, undertaken while it was still part of the former parent company. Project management and other activities integrated in process improvement initiatives are still followed, although the adherence is variable depending on the size and criticality of the project. Code reviews instigated as part of TRI-SPIN did not continue to be useful. Software is generally considered a strength in the products since there are few service calls or complaints on software/firmware. The Engineering Manager describes the entire staff as consistently being very customer-oriented.

Plans for the future

SI plans to keep its ISO certification, even though it means upgrading the quality system at a time it is trying to simply stay in business. As part of better cost control a basic measurement system is planned, as well as updating some of the current processes to adapt them to the smaller company.

Past	*Now*
II-4 Senior management support for SPI? *Average; the support of local management is defined as very well and the support of the Swiss parent company is not at all.*	*III-1 Senior management support for SPI?* *Good; the new owners of the company have been supportive but their main concern today is simply staying in business.*
II-5 SPI linked to business goals? *Well*	*III-2 Employees informed about business objectives, vision and goals?* *Very well* *III-5 Groups understand link between business objectives and goals and SPI* *A Senior management?: Very well* *B Middle management?: Very well* *C Technical management?: Very well* *D Software developers and maintainers?: Very well*
II-6 Vision lived by people?: Always	*III-3 Employees live vision?: Always*
II-7 Respected, senior SEs embrace SPI?: Always	*III-4 Respected, senior SEs embrace SPI?: Always*

Table 7-13 SI changes over time detail

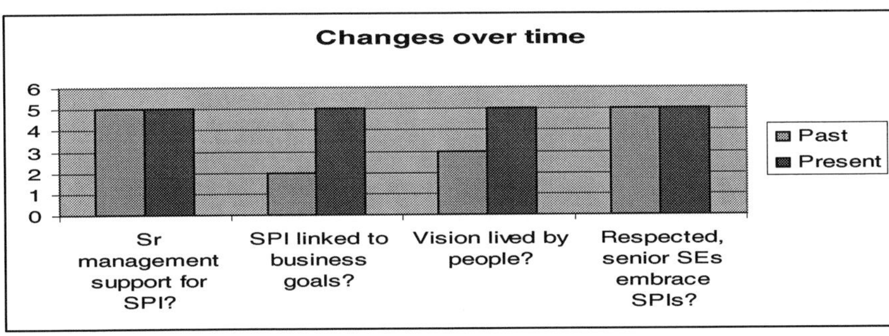

Figure 7-13 SI changes over time

Subject	Score	Any explanatory comments on rationale for scoring
Organisation as purchaser: Acquisition preparation Supplier selection Customer acceptance	 N/A N/A Partly	Very little new equipment is purchased, but when things are, most of the processes in customer acceptance are followed informally. This may change when they actually start to go to new interfaces for their equipment. No work is contracted out to subcontractors and when work is done as a supplier they have contracts or a PO before any work is done. When they are suppliers, the customers nearly always have acceptance criteria.
Organisation as supplier: Supply	 L	Usually, contracts exist with all customers with requirements specified.
Steps of software life cycle: Software req. analysis Software design Software testing	 F P P	As a result of the improvement programmes and ISO 9001, the link between requirements and design is strong and well documented. At the moment, work is mostly just improvements to the existing systems but the company has ideas for the future and more new design is likely to take place. Testing is performed, but they had never considered the importance of regression testing.
Support processes: Documentation Configuration management Quality assurance Verification Validation Joint review Audit Problem resolution	 P F L L L L P N	The level of documentation depends on the size of the project. Sourcesafe is used for controlled access and structured configuration management. Both quality assurance and verification are performed but are being reassessed for the new company structure. They could be better at field failure analysis and fault finding. Validation is nearly always performed by customers. The point was made that for a large capital expenditure customers will not spend that money without making sure of the product. On larger projects weekly conversations are held with the customer to discuss status, issues are tracked and people are assigned to

		deal with problems. This may fall down a bit on smaller activities. This is covered by their ISO 9001 certification, but internal audits may be slim. Under the former parent company the quality goals and system worked, but has to be revised for the new organisation. The point was made that software has never been the problem. Very few service calls are required over software problems.
Management processes: Project management Quality management Risk management	 P P N	 As with other things, this has to be revised for the new circumstances. As with other things, this has to be revised for the new circumstances. The current system is partial, but nebulous, and based on on-time delivery. No risk management is performed or has ever been considered.
Organisation processes: Human resources management Measurement	 P P	 The company is considered too small for any formal human resources management. Some data is collected but it is variable and data is seldom turned into knowledge.

Table 7-14 SI assessment results

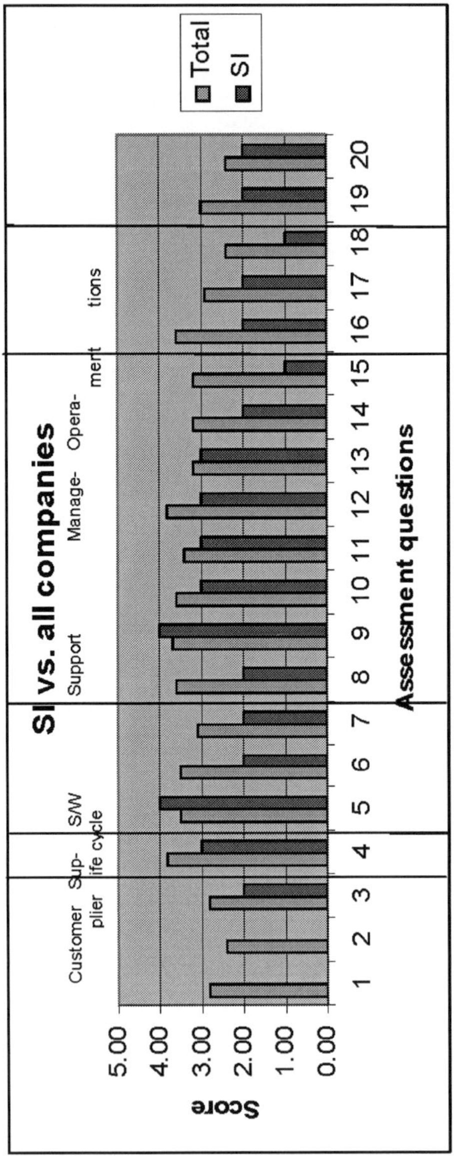

Figure 7-14 SI scoring comparisons

Results of the assessment show the organisation as one with the majority of processes (2 fully, 5 largely, 9 partly, 2 no and 2 N/A) compliant with the assessment instrument, at least to some extent. The whole thing is a bit confused because the assessment was done so soon after the company was sold off as an independent company. It was actually quite surprising to find so many of the documented process improvement initiatives still in place and actively being used even though current staff had nothing to do with these improvement programmes and didn't know they took place.

External concerns include: lack of control over the ups and downs of the electronics industry in general; holding on to a niche market when so much manufacturing is moving elsewhere; exchange rates outside of the Euro zone.

Internal concerns include: need for reorganisation to reflect the current reality of the new business; improvement needed in selling the products properly; the small size of the business which makes each employee unique and imposes a potential vulnerability in getting out the work or employee turnover; the fact that all employees except the new owners have been there so long there is a lack of exposure to other ways of doing things and a certain amount of inertia may have set in.

Conclusion

The first objective of the research concerns individual organisations: to determine if a culture of improvement exists in the organisation. Both the interview and the assessment show that such a culture does exist, although some is very limited, and can be attributed at least in part to the improvement programmes since the improvements continued through great changes and some of the original improvements made are still are in place.

7.9 SM Profile, interview with Middle Manager

Organisation profile

SM is an organisation of over 1000 employees which can be most accurately described as a service provider, but it also develops the niche software necessary to support the services. Software employees (21-30 in number) are used in small teams of 1-6 people, 1-4 of which are software personnel. Although the company has had a couple of big projects lasting up to 2 years, most projects are short-term iterations of 1-6 months. Developments are described as transaction based since most applications involve money transfer.

Past culture for improvement

The current IT Manager took part in a 1996 TRI-SPIN Focused Process Improvement in test methods for client server application development. Additionally, the interviewee took part in ISCP 10 years ago. Although the organisation did not choose complete installation of ISO 9001 procedures, many changes were made including improved testing and other quality tasks, configuration management, the creation of documented procedures which allowed standardisation of various activities and the introduction of an internet-based formal quality system which is still in use.

The level of senior management support for change was described as "good" although the link to business goals was non-existent as far as employees were concerned. The organisation vision and mission was described as being lived by the people "50% of the time". Most senior and respected software engineers had trouble supporting the process of making improvement.

There was some change in the day-to-day workings of the organisation but not the level of change required for ISO 9001 certification. The standardisation changes that *were* made resulted in:

- Cheaper costs and improved revenue
- Improved customer confidence
- Improved ability to get tenders from the government
- Improved recruitment by providing a standardised process and mentoring of new employees.

From a presentation on the TRI-SPIN improvement initiative, given by the person who is currently the IT Manager: "Process improvement goal: to develop and implement methods and processes which are appropriate for client server application development using our selected tools and platforms. The tool was Microsoft Solutions Framework, a knowledge base of concepts, guides and assistants (including tools, templates and case studies). The TRI-SPIN project was developing an appropriate test method for client-server application development." This presentation was made during the project so no results are included in the presentation.

Several improvement initiatives tailed off, including code reviews and internal auditing once standards and procedures were in place. NOTE: since an auditor performs regular audits which include IT processes, web site performance and problems and other issues to do with software, the internal auditing was perceived to be not needed. That attitude may be changing today with the realisation that the auditor continues to find similar problems that maybe could have been identified and addressed before the next audit.

Current culture for improvement

Senior management support for improvement still is classed as "good". Today's employees are "very well" informed about the business goals and objectives, although employees are described as living this vision only "50% of the time". Senior software engineers have moved up to "often" in support of change.

Business objectives now described as driving improvement and change are at a level of "well" for all levels of management and "average" for software developers and maintainers.

Several factors were described as possible inhibitors for a culture of improvement:

- Lack of sufficient senior management support
  - Senior management decisions don't always reflect what people on the ground see needs to be done
  - Sometimes managers are obsessed with a certain way of doing things which might not always be universally the best way to do things
- Resistance to change for fear of loss of face or seniority

However, even with these possible barriers the company has adopted an agile software process with determination. Pair programming, customer involvement, stand-up meetings, changes recorded on cards on the wall and other concepts have been embraced to the extent of completely revamping the room to create a bullpen supporting the new open process. This has been in place for two years now and seems to be working well generally although improvements are still being made.

In response to the question about the most important need for the business there were several choices offered on the questionnaire that were accepted as important (higher quality products, better schedule control, better cost control, faster time to market and tighter security) but the one especially mentioned was cutting cost to better compete in the market.

The greatest area of concern for IT noted was depending on internal businesses within the company for support and revenue. Parallel to this was a sense that customer expectations aren't always clearly understood coupled with a mixed response from customers about changes and improvements made. Customer feedback has been good about the new openness and communication that has accompanied the agile environment.

A "good" organisation was described as one which has clear objectives and vision openly communicated so everyone can know what they are doing and close customer involvement is made possible. The current environment is about 50% there. Any differences between the two are put down to management "to-ing and fro-ing", as well as a sometimes difficult organisation with several remote customers.

Plans for the future

The agile process is still being refined and improved, with individual processes being adapted and modified as appropriate. As part of this, improvements are being made to the measurement and tracking systems.

The new general manager comes from a manufacturing background and is looking at putting Six Sigma in place as a broader strategy for improvement.

One of the identified problems is a lack of understanding about some customer views and requirements. Service Level Agreements were being implemented to help solve this problem. In general, an overall strategy for improvements is in existence and being updated regularly.

When asked what one thing should be changed, the interviewee said more motivation and proactivity was needed because there is still a middle management culture of resistance.

Past	*Now*
II-4 Senior management support for SPI? *Good*	*III-1 Senior management support for SPI?* *Good*
II-5 SPI linked to business goals? *Not at all*	*III-2 Employees informed about business objectives, vision and goals?* *Very well* *III-5 Groups understand link between business objectives and goals and SPI* *A Senior management?: Well* *B Middle management?: Well* *C Technical management?: Well* *D Software developers and maintainers?: Average* *Even though the answer for software developers to III-5 was only "average", the answer to III-2 was "very well" and*

	all others were "well"; so overall scoring was "well"
II-6 Vision lived by people?: 50% of the time	*III-3 Employees live vision?: 50% of the time*
II-7 Respected, senior SEs embrace SPI?: Never	*III-4 Respected, senior SEs embrace SPI?: Often*

Table 7-15 SM changes over time detail

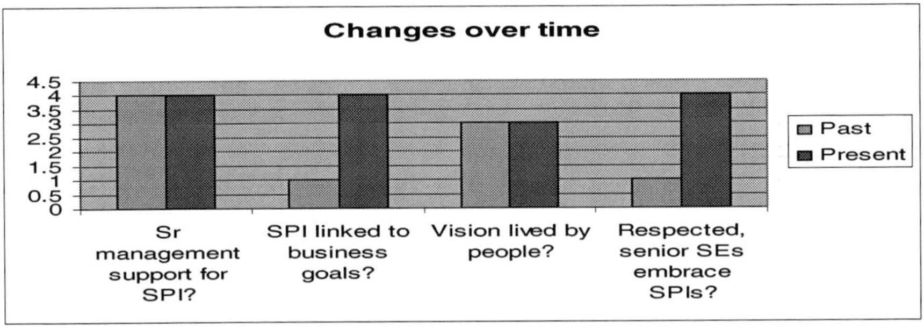

Figure 7-15 SM changes over time

A history of the company shows a series improvements over time. This makes a rating of only "good" for senior management support somewhat surprising.

Subject	Score	Any explanatory comments on rationale for scoring
Organisation as purchaser: Acquisition preparation Supplier selection Customer acceptance	 F F F	A corporate contract with the manufacturer provides all the computer equipment needed. The rest of the business has formal product selection process.
Organisation as supplier: Supply	 F	Customers are involved in product development, directly as part of the development team whenever possible. All work packages are signed off by the customer before development.
Steps of software life cycle: Software req. analysis Software design	 F F	Pair programming and the attendant communications protocols are used to ensure thorough and shared understanding of requirements, design changes and testing

Software testing		sign-offs. Tests are written from specifications early in the development process.
Support processes: Documentation Configuration management Quality assurance Verification Validation Joint review Audit Problem resolution	F F F F F F F F	The development process is light on documentation by some standards but follows strictly the agile process requirements of notes on the wall to document current status and changes. The specific words of the assessment instrument say: • A strategy identifying the documents to be produced during the life cycle of the software product will be developed • The standards to be applied for the development of documents will be identified • All documents to be produced by the process or project will be identified • The content and purpose of all documents will be specified, reviewed and approved • All documents will be developed and published in accordance with identified standards • All documents will be maintained in accordance with specified criteria By these criteria, even though the documentation is very focused and lighter in quantity than might be expected, all requirements are met to give it a fully. Tools are incorporated in the development process and system. Again, quality assurance, verification and validation are built in to the agile process. Customers are involved in development whenever possible. Joint reviews are held where this is not. However, one might question the results of these are as effective as they might be since there are still some issues about what the customers actually want.

		Auditors perform regular audits which include IT as well as the rest of the company. Included as part of the agile process, all problem reports are prepared and followed through to correction. Trends are noted and acted on.
Management processes:		
Project management	F	The project management process isn't document heavy but is robust within the agile environment.
Quality management	L	The audits and follow-on activities cover most of the components of quality management. In addition, the coming implementation of a Six Sigma ethos addresses others. However, the comment was made that sometimes the same problems surfaced from one audit to another, indicating that "appropriate action" is not always taken "when quality goals are not achieved".
Risk management	P	No risk management plan exists and is called that but planning for new applications and business ventures must include some risk management.
Organisation processes:		
Human resources management	F	Included in the human resources of a large company is a mentoring program for new IT employees. In addition, the use of pair programming is a training process in itself.
Measurement	L	A measurement programme is in place and being expanded. How much the measurements are being used to support the decision process isn't clear.

Table 7-16 SM assessment results

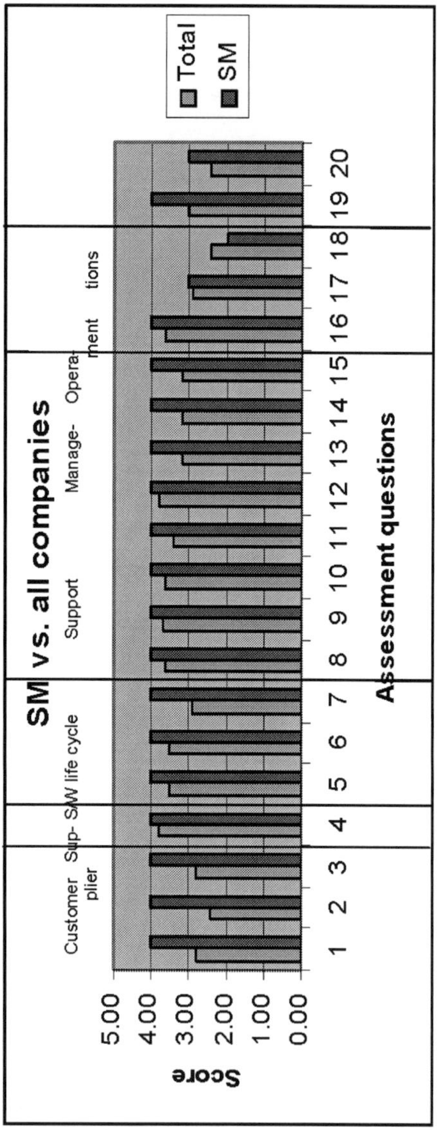

Figure 7-16 SM scoring comparisons

Results of the assessment confirm the organisation as one with the majority of processes (17 fully, 2 largely and 1 partly) compliant with the assessment instrument.

Conclusion

The first objective of the research concerns individual organisations: to determine if a culture of improvement exists in the organisation. This has been demonstrated by a continuing review of processes and updating as the business has changed and grown.

7.10 TM Profile, interview with the Engineering/Quality Manager

Organisation profile

TM develops IT software, but it is not in a traditional sense. The company buys hardware components and integrates them into a system which is controlled by a PC with software and one board of firmware. The software can be updated remotely; plans are in train to do remote updates of the firmware. As a small company, it is driven by revenue and will develop or modify systems as required.

The interviewee was both engineering manager and quality manager. The company has 14 employees, with 4 to support ~50 customers for at least 60 projects. Teams are usually small (1-6) people with 1-4 software engineers on each team. Development projects are usually 1-6 months, understanding this is a maintenance environment supporting a few related products. Within this environment, new feature implementation or system enhancements can take a few days to a few months. The interviewee said the company couldn't be described as one doing development.

Past culture for improvement

NOTE: The author worked with TM in a TRI-SPIN improvement programme to implement ISO 9001 and filled in answers about the changes in the past from a presentation made by the Director of Engineering after the programme was finished. Nobody currently in the company was there at this time. At the time of the interview, TM had just sold off the part of the business which took part in the earlier TRI-SPIN programme and were now in a completely different type of business which developed over the last several years.

From a presentation on the TRI-SPIN improvement initiative, given by the Engineering Manager: achievements under the TRI-SPIN programme were training needs addressed, customer interface improved, documentation for better specs defined, needs of individuals addressed, configuration management improved, useful reusable modules identified, software libraries started, awareness of software management and quality issues raised, procedures put in place leading to ISO 9001 certification. The company was more organised with better control and more structure. There is no existing knowledge about any improvement initiatives that may have tailed off.

Current culture for improvement

The level of senior management support for SPI is described as "good" with most employees having an "average" understanding about overall business goals and an ability to live them 50% of the time. The most experienced and respected software engineers often embrace the process of change. Understanding of the link between business objectives and SPI activities is given an "average" for all levels of management and "poor" for developers and maintainers. However, since most employees were given an "average" understanding about overall business goals in an earlier question, the overall scoring was given an "average" for question III-5.

Since the author worked with TM on the earlier improvement project, she happens to know about the strong management support at the time and the co-operative environment of the employees.

Factors which might inhibit a culture of improvement today were given as pressure of simply getting through the business day, with no time to worry about how things are done and it is difficult to get people to change when they perceive what they have works. The most important need for the business today was defined as better schedule control and faster time to market. The greatest area of concern was rising expenses. TM customers appreciate high quality, innovation and customer service. Customers have been very favourable to changes which have improved customer service. The interviewee had no experience in different companies so had no idea what difference might between the existing company and a "good" company.

Plans for the future

The company has gone through many changes in size and product since the Quality Manual was developed. It is being updated to reflect these changes using a contractor who was hired for this specific task. Changes are recommended to the Engineering/Quality and Service Managers for their review before suggested changes are actually made. If the interviewee could change one thing he would hire more software developers to write "clean code" for the systems to replace the systems which have grown with enhancements by different people over the years.

Past	*Now*
II-4 Senior management support for SPI? *Was excellent with the original company owners and managers*	*III-1 Senior management support for SPI?* *Good*
II-5 SPI linked to business goals? *As a small company, all employees understood what was needed.*	*III-2 Employees informed about business objectives, vision and goals?* *Average* *III-5 Groups understand link between business objectives and goals and SPI* *A Senior management?: Average* *B Middle management?: Average* *C Technical management?: Average* *D Software developers and maintainers?: Poorly, but see answer to above question.*
II-6 Vision lived by people?: Employees clearly understood that quality was the principal need	*III-3 Employees live vision?: 50% of the time*
II-7 Respected, senior SEs embrace SPI?: Always	*III-4 Respected, senior SEs embrace SPI?: Often*

Table 7-17 TM changes over time detail

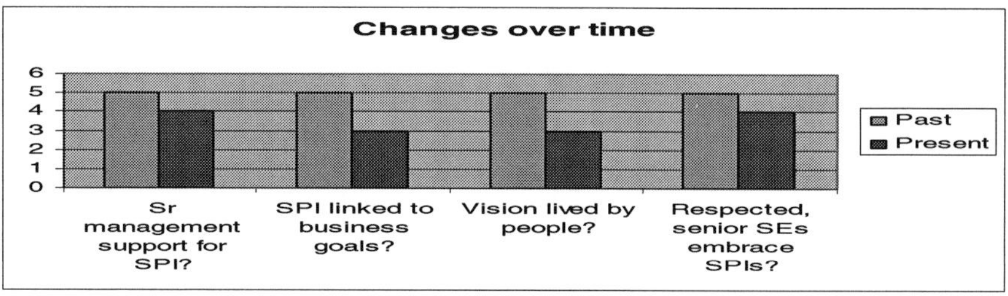

Figure 7-17 TM changes over time

To put the apparent negative answers to questions in context, the original owners and managers and employees are all gone, although the former Engineering Manager and joint owner occasionally comes back as a consultant. This is virtually a new company in contrast to all others interviewed.

NOTE: After discussion of the different levels of the SPICE assessment the interviewee agreed that with few exceptions the company would be at the performed level rather than anything higher (managed, established, predictable, optimising)

Subject	Score	Any explanatory comments on rationale for scoring
Organisation as purchaser: Acquisition preparation Supplier selection Customer acceptance	 F F L	The process of getting suppliers is usually to look on the web for a desired product and get in one for evaluation. Only after it has been decided that the product is a good candidate does the company enter into negotiation with the potential supplier. Contracts are drawn up with provisos such as "50 will be bought within the next year" and only after both sides have negotiated and agreed is a deal struck. Because nearly all these components are replacement parts, the formal acceptance criteria are doing a known function better. In the rare event of needing a new function, more formal documentation can be produced. Some processes are somewhat more informal than the standard requires but the process has worked well in this environment.
Organisation as supplier: Supply	 F	Contracts exist with all customers with requirements specified.
Steps of software life cycle: Software req. analysis Software design Software testing	 L F L	TM is not a development company but focus is on enhancements and new features for new customers. The process generally consists of a salesperson taking a potential new customer to an existing site to see a system which nearly resembles what the customer wants. If the customer decides to purchase the TM product, it is generally defined as the system they saw with additional features. The standard model is delivered with a mutual agreement on the time needed to deliver the additions.

		Development is done at the TM office, with as much testing as can be done there. If testing needs to be done on site, several customers have agreed to allow their sites to be used for this. No site which is dependent on an integrated TM product (which might bring the whole operation down if problems surface in testing) or which has a few short runs on an erratic schedule is used for testing. Release notes are created for major changes. Minor enhancements are documented with e-mails which go to all persons who are involved with the system, including an on-site field engineer who is doing the acceptance testing. The software is not released until the field engineer says the system has passed all the tests, including regression testing. The only problem identified by the interviewee is a tendency for developers to change the code but not necessarily the comments to go with it. This can lead to problems when a developer leaves and the person who takes over has to sort out what is correct and what is not. The "largely" given for both requirements analysis and testing is because although these functions are performed, formality may be less than desired sometimes when the changes are more than a simple maintenance change but less than addition of a large feature. The distinction of when formality is needed seems to be mostly a "seat of the pants" decision.
Support processes: Documentation Configuration management Quality assurance Verification Validation	 F F F F F	 These are all covered by their ISO 9001 certification. Customers go to sites to see their new systems working and to make sure it is what they want. All customers have a 30-day period to test and use their system in their

		own environment before accepting the equipment.
Joint review	N/A	TM is not a project company.
Audit	F	This is covered by their ISO 9001 certification.
Problem resolution	F	All problems are described and tracked. No problem can be closed until it is solved or the Engineering/Quality and Service managers agree it is no longer an open issue. For example, a problem may be overcome by events, such as a complete module replacement. All problems are tracked using a software tool, SalesForce. The two managers have a review of all open issues on a regular basis.
Management processes:		
Project management	F	TM is not a project-oriented company but major feature additions are treated as small projects with schedules, resource allocation, test plans, etc.
Quality management	F	This is covered by their ISO 9001 certification.
Risk management	N	No risk management is performed except for the health and safety of the building. There are no moving parts in the product requiring this kind of analysis. We discussed various risks—currency exchange rates, employee turnover, etc.—but identified no apparent risks. Some more thought might identify risks that should be addressed.
Organisation processes:		
Human resources management	F	Since the company has been slimmed down to support one product, the best, most highly trained and skilled employees were retained for that purpose. Neither people nor training are issues.
Measurement	F	Problems, bugs/defects, and other things are tracked, including length of time to closure. Trends can be analysed and some data collected is available to the customer.

Table 7-18 TM assessment results

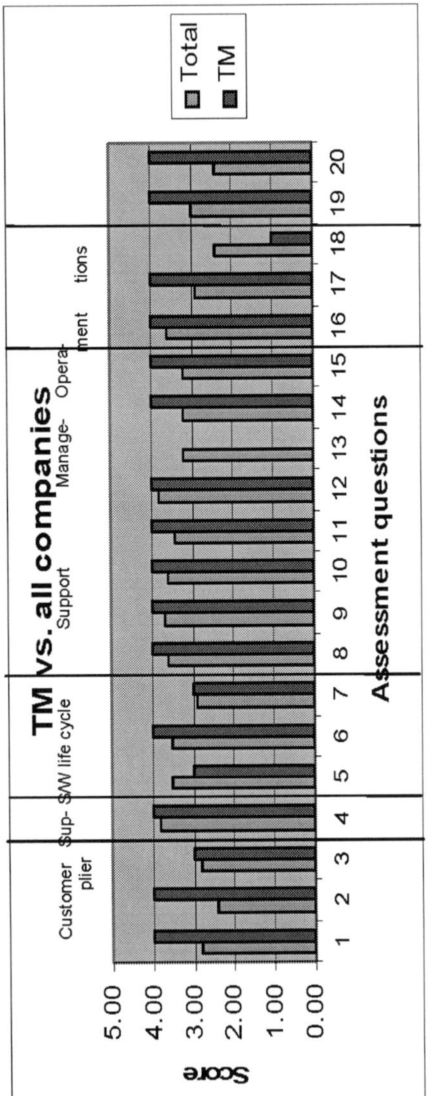

Figure 7-18 TM scoring comparisons

Results of the assessment confirm the organisation as one with the majority of processes (15 fully, 3 largely and 1 no and 1 N/A) compliant with the assessment instrument.

Conclusion

The first objective of the research concerns individual organisations: to determine if a culture of improvement exists in the organisation. The results of the ISO 9001 certification and the assessment indicate the answer is yes. This may at least in part be due to a continuing certification to ISO 9001 even through all the changes in business and personnel.

7.11 TS Profile, interview with the Development Process Manager

Organisation profile

TS is a producer and service provider of specialised middleware software. TS has about 250 employees, with about 120 software employees. Average project team size is usually around 12 people, with 6 of them in software. One development project last year lasted for around a year and another for 3 years but most are about 2 months. Development projects are both web-based and distributed.

Past culture for improvement

The interviewee has been with the company for 2-1/2 years. However, the former Quality Manager met with the reviewer informally to discuss the improvement programme in which he took place (SCATE). He indicated that as a result of participation in SCATE small changes did take place, but not the major improvements he had hoped to see due to lack of support—from senior management down to the software engineers. If anything, not only were improvements not made, the situation may have become marginally worse. When the same question was put to the interviewee, she agreed that small changes, not much, took place in the past due to lack of support. In response to the question about improvement initiatives that failed, various standards were documented but not used and there were no common testing tools or source control.

From the SCATE case study written by the former Quality Manager: "The engineering staff at TS agreed that since we were already working within the Capability Maturity Model (CMM) software process improvement framework on an ad hoc basis, it would do us no harm to join a group of like-minded companies to aid us in formalising our approach. TS employs 45 people, more than half of which are software developers. We have recently opened an office in the US.

Though we would consider ourselves to be a fairly conscientious bunch, a self-assessment quickly determined that we suffered most of the maladies of a process-immature organisation.

Specifically, the assessment showed that we needed to concentrate on improvement in the following areas immediately:

- Formulation and tracking of requirements
- Approach to planning projects
- Tracking of planned vs. actual
- Post-mortems after project completion
- Reporting and tracking to closure of problems
- Working together with common goals in mind

We decided to tackle entire CMM Key Process Areas (KPAs) individually, and the first area chosen was Requirements Management, as it was felt this would give us the most ‘bang for the buck’.

This first stab at implementing a KPA across the whole company failed quite miserably. We had entirely underestimated the ability of the sales team to be able to formulate customer requirements. Our products are quite complex, and we finally realised that it was unrealistic to expect Sales to generate ideas for new products without significant input from the engineering team. Our initial process design was flawed. However, all was not lost. Through this effort, we determined that we needed another group in our organisation to bridge the gap between sales and engineering, and are at this point in time (May 1998) forming a product development and strategy group which should help us to address this issue.

We learned quite a lot from this initial attempt to implement a KPA:

- Don’t try to bite off a big chunk of the problem all at once. Small improvements with *measurable* results are more important.
- Without management commitment, you will fail.
- Get all the staff involved and keep them informed. I felt that this was the main item I failed to deliver on as Quality Manager.

Since that nasty experience a few months ago, the situation has improved somewhat. We now have:

- Projects with well-defined requirements that are agreed to between sales and engineering before development commences. These projects are running on time!
- A comprehensive Problem Report and Tracking form
- Each project manager holds a weekly status meeting, and a report is generated.
- An understanding by management that Quality Assurance ≠ Testing. It's a start!

In order of priority, we still need to:

- Raise the awareness level about what we are doing
- Start producing metrics as a measure of progress
- Firm up on our project planning
- Figure out a way to give management more visibility into the development process
- Do project post-mortems
- Implement a Change Request form

All too often the 'We'll just write procedures that *will* be followed and everything else will fall into place' approach to process improvement is attempted…and inevitably fails.

In this respect, SCATE has been a small success for us. If anything, it repeatedly demonstrated that the emphasis of any software process improvement (SPI) programme needs to be directed at engendering a feeling of 'We can do this!' within the organisation.

I have this feeling that the 'iceberg' analogy applies very much to the SCATE experience: less than 10% of our SPI work has been accomplished during this 9-month programme. The rest will happen afterwards, but only if we're committed to making it happen!"

Current culture for improvement

Today support for improvements is better. The level of support from senior management was described as being "good", but this is better than in the past. Most employees have been informed about the business objectives and goals, although their willingness or ability to live them in daily behaviour is stated to be "often". However, the most senior and respected software engineers are leading the way by often being willing to make improvements, so continual improvements are expected. All levels of management are described as understanding the links between business objectives and changes/improvements in daily activities. Software developers and maintainers were described as "well" in their understanding of these links.

Several factors which might inhibit a culture of improvement were identified, including: cost of tools, time it takes to roll out a new process, and formerly, lack of senior management support. In one facility in England, a fear of openness because jobs might be sent elsewhere was identified. The important needs for the business were identified as faster time to market, and to a lesser extent, higher quality products. Staff turnover was described as an additional area of concern.

Several things contribute to the success of TS, including: low cost, a flexible system which allows clients to use any vendor and make changes at will, as well as a better price for some specific functions. Customers have responded positively to higher quality products. The interviewer described a "good" organisation as one having teamwork and the organisation today as one where each department works well as a team, and is starting to work better as a company. She describes the difference today as a result of time pressures, although in the past it may have had more to do with fear of jobs being lost.

Plans for the future

TS is testing the use of agile/Xtreme programming, calling it an agile strategy which will be rolled out across the company if it is successful. A measurement programme is being planned for the future. The one thing the interviewer would change is people's attitude to change itself.

Past	*Now*
II-4 Senior management support for SPI? *Poorly*	*III-1 Senior management support for SPI?* *Good*
II-5 SPI linked to business goals? *Poorly*	*III-2 Employees informed about business objectives, vision and goals?* *Average* *III-5 Groups understand link between business objectives and goals and SPI* *A Senior management?: Average* *B Middle management?: Average* *C Technical management?: Average* *D Software developers and maintainers?: Poorly, but see answer to above question.*

II-6 Vision lived by people?: Seldom	*III-3 Employees live vision?: 50% of the time*
II-7 Respected, senior SEs embrace SPI?: Seldom	*III-4 Respected, senior SEs embrace SPI?: Often*

Table 7-19 TS changes over time detail

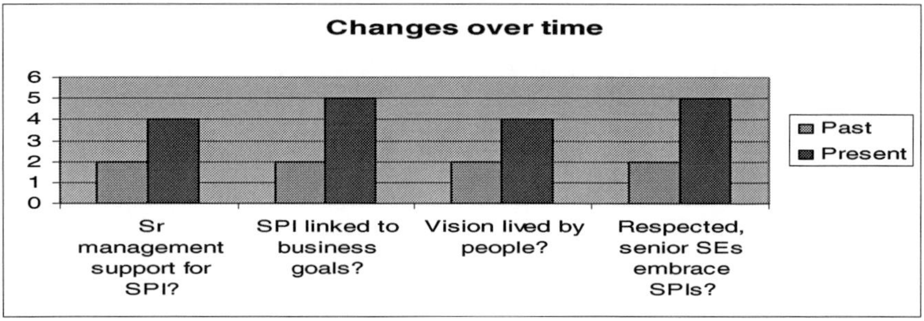

Figure 7-19 TS changes over time

Subject	Score	Any explanatory comments on rationale for scoring
Organisation as purchaser: Acquisition preparation Supplier selection Customer acceptance	 F F F	The platform is currently stable; tools are purchased according to formal criteria all the way through buying the license. In the future, more acquisitions to do with the platform and software products themselves may occur and the same processes should be followed formally.
Organisation as supplier: Supply	 F	
Steps of software life cycle: Software req. analysis Software design Software testing	 F F F	Part of the description of TS's processes includes use cases being updated and signed off by the customer, improved design of interfaces and a Quality Assurance department that runs separate User Acceptance Tests.
Support processes: Documentation	 F	With about 16 documents defining the software process, which is reviewed at the process level with any non-compliance

Configuration management Quality assurance Verification Validation Joint review Audit Problem resolution	P F F F P L L	reviewed and corrected, documentation can be defined as fully performed. Configuration management is given only a partially performed because no unique identifiers are assigned to software products and although source code is controlled and updated, no reporting is performed. Quality assurance, verification and validation are all described as fully performed. However, joint review is only partially performed. Although weekly or bi-weekly reviews with customers are held, the components of making results of the reviews known to all parties and tracking of all action items to closure appear to be missing. Audit is given a largely performed after discussion about the results and processes of code and end of phase reviews. Problem resolution is also given a largely performed because there is no attempt to recognise or act on trends in problems identified.
Management processes: Project management Quality management Risk management	 F P F	 Project management is given a fully performed even though each project manager does the job differently. A more cohesive strategy is being put together but not adopted yet. Quality management is given a partially performed because it was described as variable in performance among projects. Risk management gets full marks, particularly for keeping a risk register with a review every two weeks and the top five risks discussed and managed.
Organisation processes: Human resources management Measurement	 P N	 Human resources is given a partially performed because it is described as inadequate, with perhaps not enough training, although everyone gets at least one week. A measurement programme is being planned for the future.

Table 7-20 TS assessment results

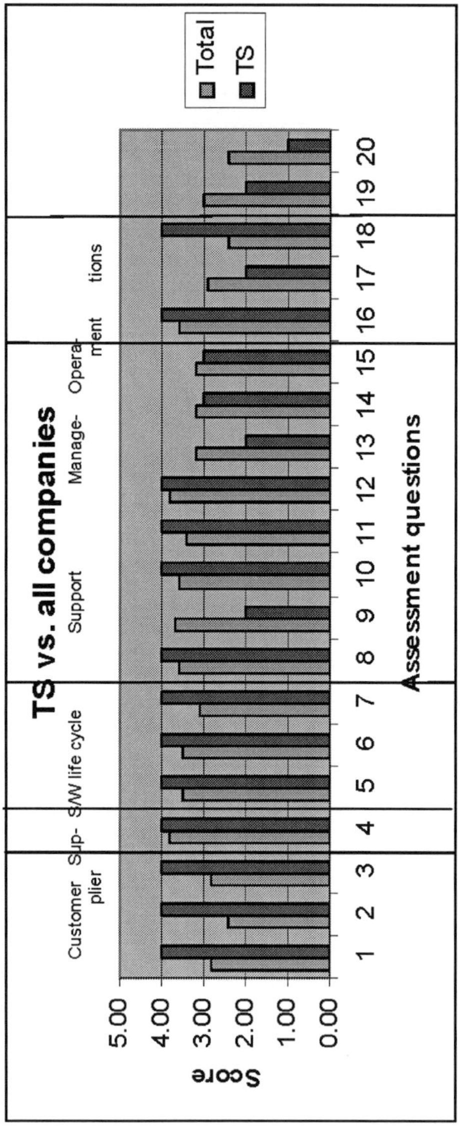

Figure 7-20 TS scoring comparisons

Results of the assessment confirm the organisation as one with the majority of processes (13 fully, 2 largely, 4 partly and one no) compliant with the assessment instrument. Support for process improvement has vacillated over time for all types of employees—management, software engineers and support staff.

Conclusion

The first objective of the research concerns individual organisations: to determine if a culture of improvement exists in the organisation. The results of both the questionnaire and the assessment indicate the answer is yes. But there is nothing to show that it is the result of the process improvement programme undertaken.

7.12 Summary

One of the more interesting aspects of this project was to see how companies with differing sizes and commercial needs implemented and used the information they gathered from these improvement initiatives. Mistakes were made but opportunities were seized to increase profitability through smarter work practices.

CHAPTER EIGHT

DATA COLLECTION AND EVALUATION

8.1 Introduction

This chapter describes the data collection and evaluation process using the MMAI in the ten companies that participated in the research project. The initial validation of the model is described in two initial interviews, followed by a discussion of each section of the interview guide, Part A, individual questions asked and a profile of the answers given. Any useful correlations or comparisons are described as part of the dialogue.

8.2 Interview results

Initial interviews were with two companies, both of which had current ISO 9001 : 2000 certification. The assessment scores derived are shown in Table 8-1.

		Company	
	Process	**SI**	**TM**
1	Acquisition preparation	0	4
2	Supplier selection	0	4
3	Customer acceptance	2	3
4	Supply	3	4
5	Software requirements analysis	4	3
6	Software design	2	4
7	Software testing	2	3
8	Documentation	2	4
9	Configuration management	4	4
10	Quality assurance	3	4
11	Verification	3	4
12	Validation	3	4
13	Joint review	3	0
14	Audit	2	4

15	Problem resolution	1	4
16	Project management	2	4
17	Quality management	2	4
18	Risk management	1	1
19	Human resources management	2	4
20	Measurement	2	4

Table 8-1 Test site scores for validation

SI had just been sold off a few months before the interview so the scores are somewhat lower than an ISO 9001 : 2000 might indicate. Yet, the scores that are lowest are in the areas being modified to suit the smaller, independent company so the scores do accurately reflect reality. The interviewee said the company is determined to keep their ISO 9001 : 2000 certification and is working to make adjustments to the quality system as needed to reflect its new status. All but one of the improvements made in the TRI-SPIN, SCATE and SPIRE improvement programmes are in place as part of the software management process.

TM has embraced a software process tightly integrated with a centralised management tool that allows customers using the web to track the status of their system while it is being created, see what problems have developed and how they are being treated. The ISO 9001 : 2000 certification is highly valued as both a way to help with tighter control on the development process and a marketing tool in a global marketplace. The high assessment scores reflect this dedication to quality and innovation.

8.3 Collecting and evaluating data

8.3.1 Introduction

Answers are listed in the order of questions on the interview guide, except where past and present comparisons are useful, such as looking at any changes in senior management support over time. Some of the initial questions are simply to provide a framework for answers to other questions and for possible correlations of answers showing differences, such as size of organisation vs. improvements made. After individual questions have been discussed, any significant comparisons that were made between them are discussed and the results noted. Then, the data gathered on specific processes in the MMAI are discussed and any particularly interesting findings noted.

8.3.2 Questions asked

Part I Organisation profile

Part I was designed to provide a rounded picture of the organisation, its changes over time, its people, the interviewee and the software employees and their role in the organisation. Having this knowledge enabled the author to put software processes in the context of what was happening with the rest of the business.

All but one organisation produces a software product and/or services; the other integrates hardware as well as software. Of those interviewed for this research, 5 of the 10 interviewees are niche producers. There are 11 answers for 10 interviewees because JC wanted to be considered both a producer and service provider.

The interviewees were middle manager (FD, OS, SM, TS), managing director (DTG), technical manager (JC, SI, TM), senior executive (FM, MM). The limited positions of interviewees for this research is not too surprising. In contacting companies, the author was naturally referred by receptionists to the manager or technical person in charge of software.

Numbers of employees varied from 6-10 (MM), 11-20 (SI, TM), 21-30 (DTG, FM), 31-50 (FD), 51-100 (JC), >100 (OS, SM, TS). The author believed that since all but one of the SPI programmes (PIEs) were geared to small companies, few respondents would fit into categories of 50 or more. However, that is not the case as nearly half are in this category of bigger companies. One reason for this may be as simple as more small companies believed they did not have the time to participate in the survey. Indeed, six people contacted by telephone either said they did not have the time or interest to participate or were clearly so busy they did not want to respond.

One large company (OS) is the result of the merger of three IT departments. Another's representative (FD) took SCATE as part of a small department in a very large company (3 in group that took SCATE, 40 in department assessed, ~60,000 worldwide) with no corporate processes; today that situation is reversed with company-wide software processes required for all. The remaining three larger companies (JC, SM, TS) have grown dramatically since participating in the SPI programmes but there is no reason to believe it has anything to do with the programmes themselves or better software process management.

Some information exists about how the sizes of companies have changed. As Figures 8-1 and 8-2 show, some of the changes have been dramatic. This information came from a combination of what is written in case studies, statements by the interviewees and memories of the author and is only presented to show one level of change companies had to manage.

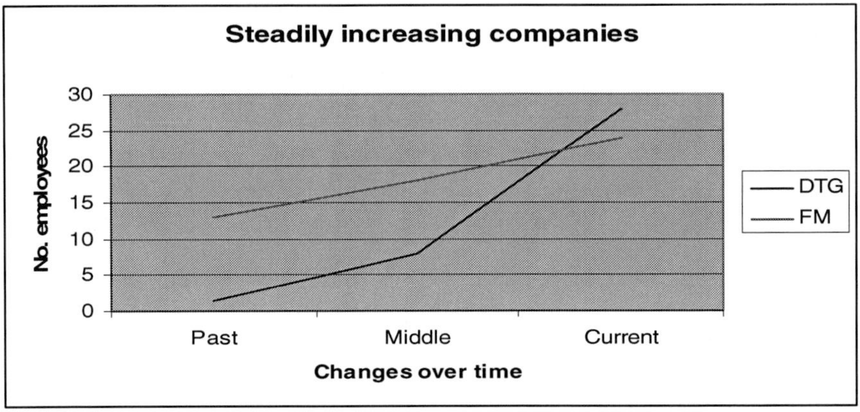

Figure 8-1 Steadily increasing companies

Two companies have steadily increased with DTG breaking off from the parent company to form a separate software company which supports a niche business market. FM has changed from software developing to providing software services, adapting third-party packages to individual customer needs. Each appears to have had a smooth transition to more formal processes as they expanded, with DTG looking ahead to extra support staff and processes that will be needed as they grow with new partnerships, divisions and products, and FM gaining a brand new ISO 9001 certification of which they are very proud.

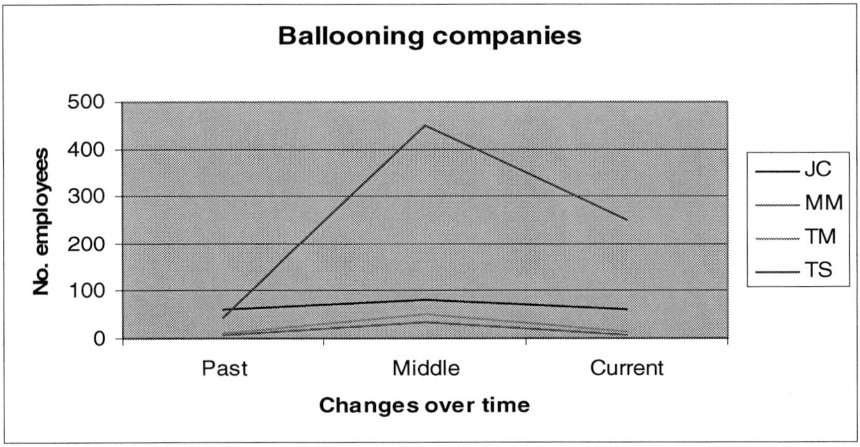

Figure 8-2 Ballooning companies

Perhaps the most difficult situation of all was for companies that ballooned in size and shrank again, most because they got caught in the "dot.com bubble bursting", according to the interviewees. TS went through the most dramatic changes from being a small Irish company that had just opened another office in the US to becoming a world leader in their middleware which is primarily for the tourist industry. It is still a world leader but according to the former quality manager is "a more manageable size". MM was in a major expansion programme with an office opened in the United States when the bubble burst. According to the interviewee, only the determination of the managing director kept them in business. TM grew while a subsidiary of a foreign company but it was not always an easy union. JC, being in the financial services industry, has expanded and contracted as the market has in a more commonly understood way. SI sold off most of the company, keeping a continuous ISO 9001 certification in the company interviewed.

Numbers of software employees ranged from 1-5 (MM, SI, TM), 11-20 (JC), 21-30 (DTG, FM, SM), 31-50 (FD), >100 (OS, TS) There seems to be very little correlation between number of employees and number of software employees. FD, FM and OS interviewees spoke for departments or divisions of only software people—all other work, administrative and support, is performed by parent companies or otherwise separate groups[12].

---

[12] In some cases specific numbers of employees were not given, but the answers were given within the stated ranges. In this case, an average number in the range

Average size of project team was 1-6 (DTG, FD, FM, JC, MM, SI, SM, TM), 7-12 (FD, OS, TS). One respondent, FD, said that teams have been as large as 10 people in the past but the current preferred size was a smaller team of six or less. The preference for smaller team sizes transcends size of the organisation or type of work being performed.

Average number of software employees on projects is 1-4 (DTG, FM, JC, MM, SI, SM, TM), 1-12 (FD), 5-8 (OS, TS). Even the large companies have small teams with small groups of software people although no specific comments about this were made. The percentage of software people per total team size is the same; the slightly larger teams have correspondingly more software people.

Typical length of development projects in months extended from 1-6 (DTG, FM, JC, MM, OS, SI, TM), 7-12 (TS) through 1-24 or more (FD, SM). One company, FD noted that at least one project had gone 3 years in the past, but now short projects of small teams are preferred. SM had a "couple of big projects" lasting between 7-12 months and one that lasted for 24 months, but the adoption of an agile environment has led to short delivery schedules.

Several companies have well-established platforms and databases; others are in the process of transferring to new types and supporting new and old. "Transaction" is used by any organisation involved in financial dealings. "Distributed" refers to distributed databases and other components and systems with on-line updates; most of these have been or are being converted to web-based systems.

Part II Past culture for improvement

Information on the past includes case studies, final reports or presentations provided by some of the companies. "MS" on the Table 8-2 means the author worked as a consultant with the company on that programme. Only JC had no written record of past participation in SPI programmes.

---

was used for this table with the exception of SM which was described as '1000+' and OS which was described as '>100'.

Co.	TRI-SPIN	Case study	ISCP	Presenta-tion	SCATE	Case study	SPIRE	Case study	PIE	Final report
DTG	MS								MS	**x**
FD					MS	**x**				
FM			MS				x	**x**		
JC			MS							
MM					MS	**x**				
OS									x	**x**
SI	x	**x**			MS	**x**	MS	**x**		
SM	x		x	**x**						
TM	MS			**x**						
TS					MS	**x**				

Table 8-2 Published material available for companies

Six of the interviewees remembered the SPI programmes (DTG, FM, MM, OS, SM) one knew the person involved (TS) and four knew nothing about it (FD, JC, SI, TM).

The interviewee (TS) who did not know about the SPI programmes but did know the person involved affirmed the company was following several of the processes which were established. JC knew nothing about the programme but had heard the name of the person involved and knew the company had been ISO 9001 certified continuously since that person was there. One interviewee who knew nothing about the SPI programmes (SI) read the case studies from TRI-SPIN and SPIRE improvement projects and noted that all improvements but reviews (started during TRI-SPIN) were a part of the company's normal software development process.

Nine of the ten companies that agreed to an interview were known to the author, who might not know a current employee but could "drop names" that were known to one or more of the current employees. The company response pattern was predictable since it was normal for companies who did not know about the SPI project or the author to refuse to take part in the research or simply not respond to phone calls or a letter, except for the gentleman at OS.

Seven interviewees (DTG, FM, JC, OS, SI, SM, TM) could point to specific improvements that took place, most to several improvements. As much as one can tell with ten interviews, there is a definite difference in success rates with methodology of technology transfer and standards used. The three (FD, MM, SM) who could not point to any specific major changes during the interview (although improvements might have been noted in case studies published just after the programmes) all referred to SCATE, a training-only programme based on the CMM. The other companies had consultants coming in on a regular basis to help solve small day-to-day problems and make sure the improvements were on-stream. All reported success, regardless of the standard they might have been using or if they had not been using any particular standard. Written documentation of past improvements exists for all but JC among the interviewed companies. No correlation seems to exist between size of company and the changes that were made.

FD said that no improvement took place as a result of one individual's attendance at SCATE, but stated that the manager who promoted it was known for his support of SPI in general so improvements may have taken place but not have been specifically known to the interviewee.

MM, who is the "sometimes" in the previous chart, is an unusual company because it has been responsible for consulting and tool development since its foundation. It is possible that one of the reasons the interviewee had difficulty remembering specific improvements is because improved processes are quickly absorbed into the company processes. In addition, the tools MM produces (and uses itself) are management-based and so improvements are incorporated within enhancements to their own products.

TS had a lack of support through all layers of its management and developers, although that has changed now and many improvements have taken place in the last few years.

Different types of changes took place in management of each organisation's software development and maintenance environment, as shown in Table 8-3.

Improvements	Organisations
Adopt standards or standardise process	DTG, FD, FM, JC, SI, SM, TM
Better project management	FM, JC, OS, SI
New tools	STG, FM, JC
Improved testing/quality	FM, JC, SM
Improved structure, approach	DTG, FM, SI
Added measurement	DTG, OS
Various small changes	MM

Table 8-3 Improvements in different organisations

Each of the changes listed in Table 8-3 were adopted by individual organisations. It is not surprising that companies reported multiple improvements, particularly when standards were involved, since all the standards emphasise multiple processes for improvement. Some companies have had continuous ISO 9001 certification since the improvement programme which helped them institute it. FM, JC, SI, TM are still certified and plan to continue ISO 9001 certification; all had had recent audits prior to the research interviews. FD was certified to ISO 9001 for several years but decided that the company had gained what it could and stopped certification after internal processes were instituted which were beyond ISO 9001: 2000 requirements.

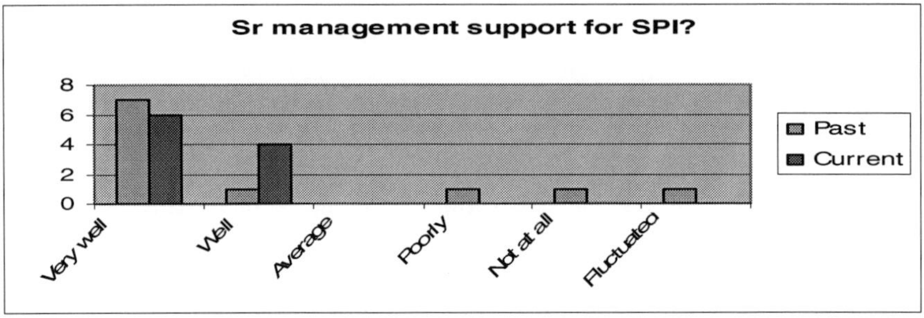

Figure 8-3 Change in senior management support for SPI

It would be expected that senior management support would be strong for the organisation to be involved with the SPI programme in the first place. The CEO of TS at the time of SCATE was very problematic according to the former Quality Manager, who was informally interviewed before the current Process Manager. The Software Manager at JC indicated that support for SPI "fluctuated" and it depended on what else was happening in the organisation[13].

Only SI showed that senior management support had decreased slightly from before and that they were one of the companies which had gone through massive changes in the intervening years. This change is slightly misleading since two scores in "past support of senior management" are "very strong" in relation to local management but "not at all" with respect to the parent company.

[13] This company has had continual ISO 9001 certification since the original ISCP programme, so the lows of 'fluctuated' might not have been so low.

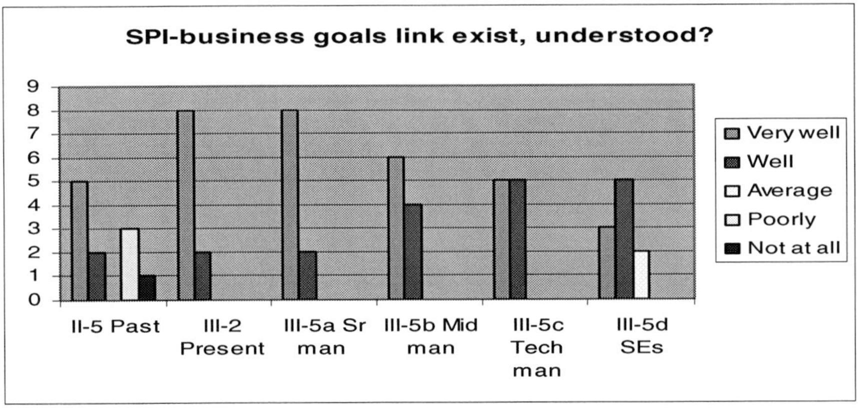

Figure 8-4 Changes in understanding of links between business and SPI

Two answers are given by FM to the questions about the past; "poorly" for the first attempt at implementing ISO 9001 and "very well" for the second time, which was led by employees, not managers.

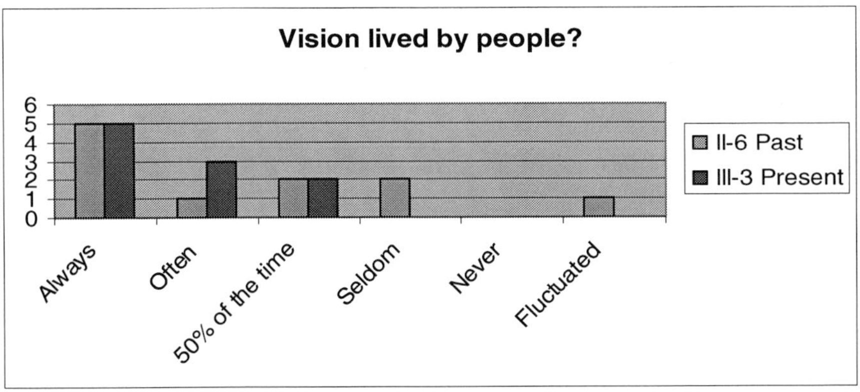

Figure 8-5 Changes in adoption of vision

Two companies, OS and TM are described as decreasing in people understanding with regard to the goals and vision of the company and the living out of same in their daily work. OS went through the merger of three IT departments and TM sold off a large portion of the company and is now working with a secondary product. SM showed no improvement in understanding but this may be due to any or all of several factors, amongst them the: expansion of the business into new areas and locations, the conversion to a completely agile environment and/or the coming of a new general manager who wishes to implement Six Sigma in this agile environment. Two responses are given for FM in relation to the past: "seldom" for the first attempt at ISO 9001 and "always" for the second successful time.

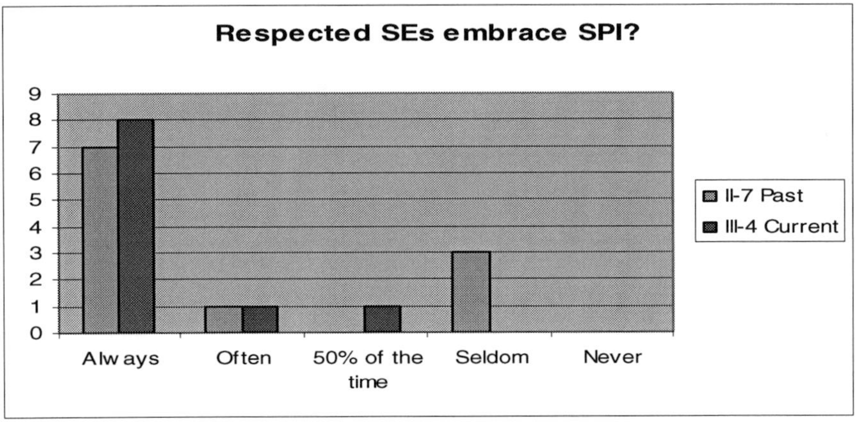

Figure 8-6 Changes in adoption of SPI by respected SEs

All interviewees except DTG, MM and TM commented on having at least one individual who resisted change for a bit. However, none noted this as instrumental in preventing new processes from being adopted. Again, two scores were given for FM in the past: "seldom" for the first time, and "always" for the second.

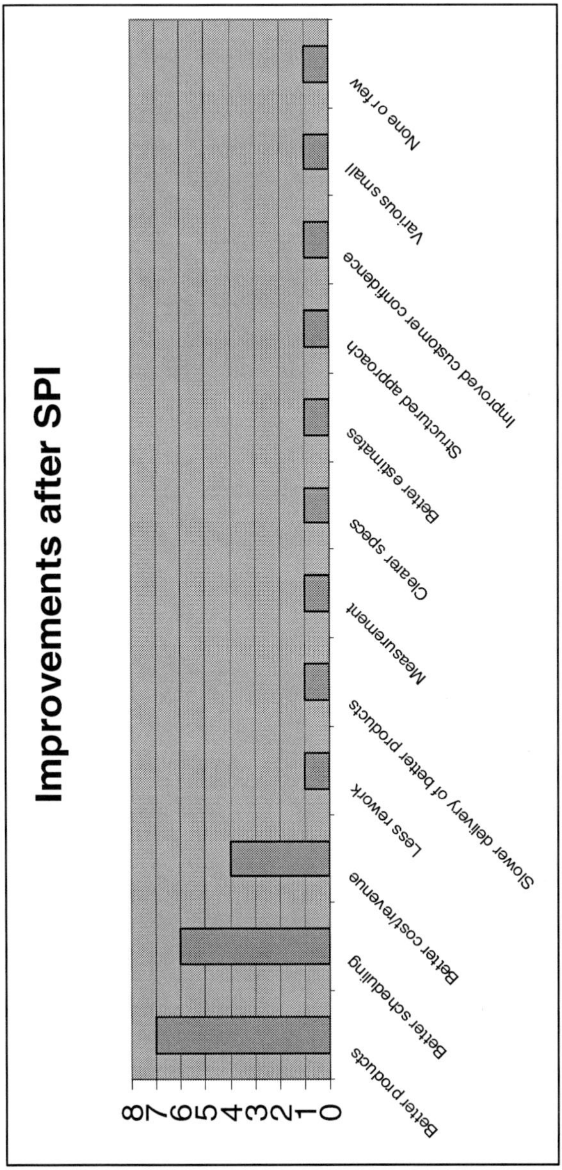

Figure 8-7 Improvements made after SPI assistance

Each of the improvements shown in Figure 8-7 was recorded by at least one interviewee. All but the first three (better products, better scheduling, better cost/revenue) were stated by the interviewees. SM stated that although ISO 9001 was not adopted after training, the processes used were standardised and this led to greater customer confidence, cheaper costs, and improved revenue. Clearly, improvements are not all at the same level, and they are closely related to what changes were actually made. This is shown in Table 8-4.

Past What happened?	vs.	Past What were the improvements after SPI?
New tools, transform processes/lifecycle, improved structure/approach to work, measurement	DTG	Better products, better scheduling, better cost/revenue
Transform processes/ lifecycle	FD	Better products, better scheduling, better cost/revenue
Adopt standards or processes, new tools, transform processes /lifecycle, improved testing /quality, better project management	FM	Better products, less rework, slower delivery of better products
Adopt standards or processes, new tools, transform processes /lifecycle, improved testing /quality, better project management	JC	Better scheduling
Various small changes	MM	Better products, better scheduling
Better project management, measurement	OS	Better products, measurement, clearer specs, better estimates
Adopt standards or standard process, transform processes/ lifecycle, better project management	SI	Better products, better scheduling, better cost/revenue, various small improvements
Adopt standards or processes, transform processes /lifecycle, improved testing /quality	SM	Better cost/revenue, improved customer confidence
Adopt standards or standard process	TM	Better products, better scheduling
Nothing	TS	None or few

Table 8-4 Past improvement activities vs. results

Table 8-5 shows what was in presentations, reports and case studies that were published during or shortly after the SPI programmes, as opposed to what the interviewee had stated about the improvements made. Where there are discrepancies they may be for a number of reasons, including a long-term view of results vs. short-term, responses from different people with different perceptions, either this interview or the reporting after the SPI programmes was influenced in order to present a biased picture for whatever reason or simply, they formed different ways to express similar results.

Co.	Improvements interviewees remembered	Improvements reported earlier[14]
DTG	Better products, better scheduling, better cost/revenue	Better quality and more reliable products, more predictable schedules and improved revenue, customer complaints down
FD	Better products, better scheduling, better cost/revenue	Retained existing customer-base and attracted new customers; on-time delivery; documentation of processes, useful when staff left.
FM	Better products, less rework, slower delivery of better products	Adoption of ISO 9001; new tools and processes; testing and quality improved, and better project management; approach to work improved; better structure in the organisation and clearer focus on goals.
JC	Better scheduling	No reports
MM	Better products, better scheduling	Better time management and time tracking. Better guidelines on estimating time and effort were developed. Requirements gathering improved; recording change requests from customers improved; improvements in technical support.
OS	Better products, measurement, clearer specs, better estimates	Improved estimates on projects leading to better delivery; increased client participation on SE projects by adopting PRINCE methodology; improved Project Management, specifically in the areas of project planning and control.

[14] In no case did the interviewee know about or remember case studies or other reports written after the SPI programme. These were not shown to the interviewees until they had contributed what they could.

SI	Better products, better scheduling, better cost/revenue, various small improvements	Peer Reviews (Not sustained); implement project management and controls, although not to the level expected; training of staff.
SM	Better cost/revenue, improved customer confidence	Process improvement goal: to develop and implement methods and processes; develop an appropriate test method for client server application development. This presentation was made during the project so no results are included in the presentation.
TM	Better products, better scheduling	Training needs addressed, customer interface improved, documentation for better specs defined, needs of individuals addressed, configuration management improved, useful reusable modules identified, software libraries started, awareness of software management and quality issues raised, procedures put in place leading to ISO 9001 certification; more organised with better control and more structure.
TS	None or few	Small changes took place.

Table 8-5 Past improvements from interviewees vs. documentation

In answer to the question, "How much did this improvement affect the everyday workings of the overall organisation?" eight of the ten organisations said "Well" or "Very well". This is closely related to the next question on *how* the organisation might have been affected. The answers are shown in Figure 8-8.

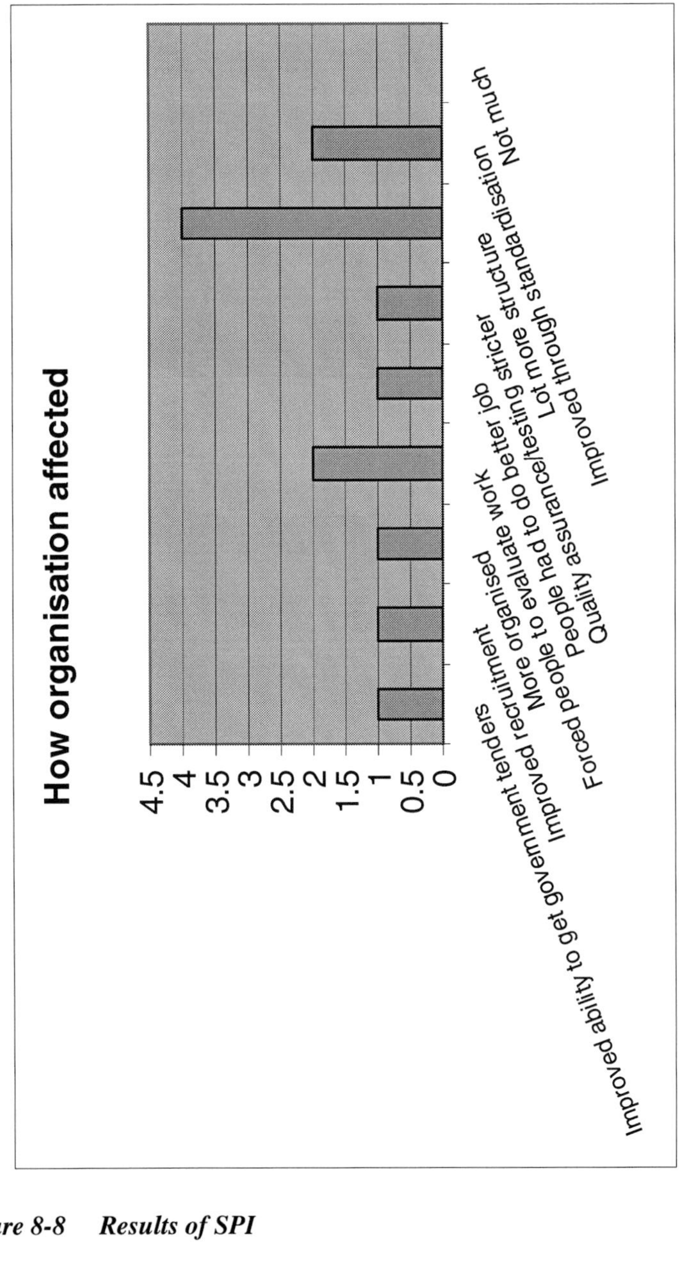

Figure 8-8 Results of SPI

Questions were asked to address "soft issues" such as the willingness of people to adopt change. However, as Figure 8-8 shows, most of the responses dealt with specifics. It was very difficult for both author and interviewees to remember exactly what had happened during this time and it may have been too much to expect this kind of information.

The following question was included to look at problem areas, "Were any improvement initiatives started that tailed off or were not widely implemented?" Particularly with tools, companies often see them fall into disuse once the "tool-master" leaves. Sometimes a methodology or standard is supported until the expert leaves, taking the real expertise away. This question was designed to determine if this had happened.

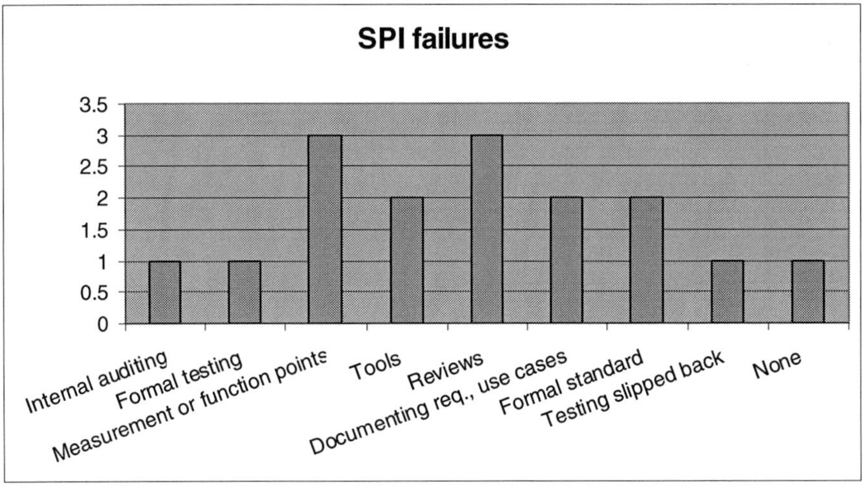

Figure 8-9 Past SPI failures

The interviewee noted that even though function points were abandoned at OS because the cost/benefit ratio was not acceptable, the act of performing the analysis was invaluable in determining the processes which were actually needed. "Reviews" included both code and design reviews.

Part III Current culture for improvement

Questions in this section were reviewed with comparable questions in Part II, the past culture for improvement. In addition, various factors about today's organisation were discussed, including: why improvements in software management might not have taken place, business needs and concerns, customer views, and interviewee views regarding the nature of the company and what it might look like in terms of structure.

An understandable response was that the daily pressure of work could interfere with SPI. There was no correlation between the reasons given for lack of improvement in the past by MM (massive changes in organisation) and TS (lack of support), and those factors which might inhibit SPI today (MM-daily pressure of work, TS-cost of tools and adequate time to roll out change).

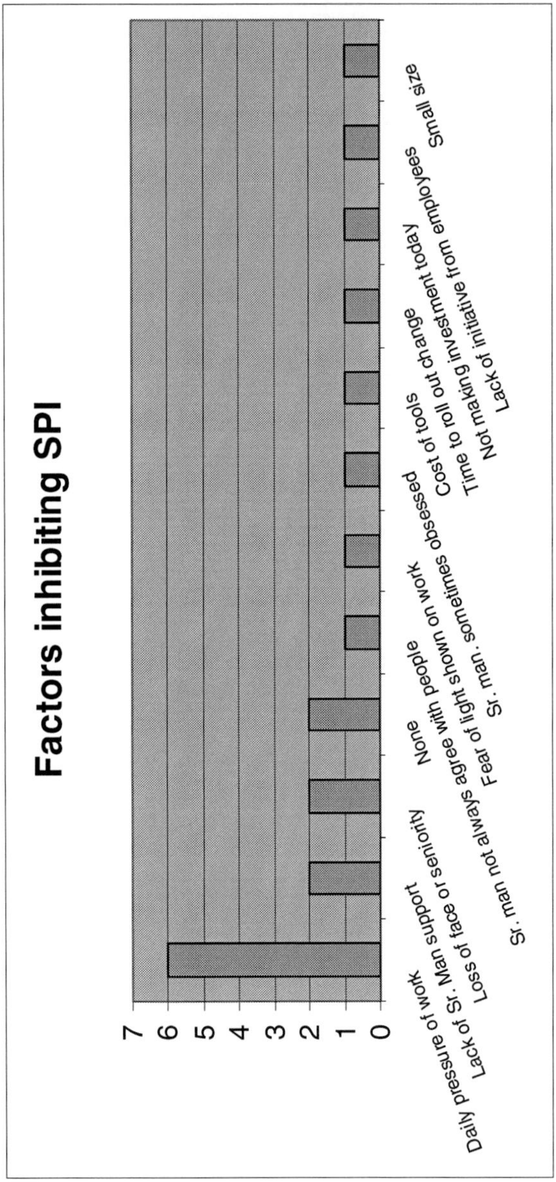

Figure 8-10 Current factors inhibiting SPI

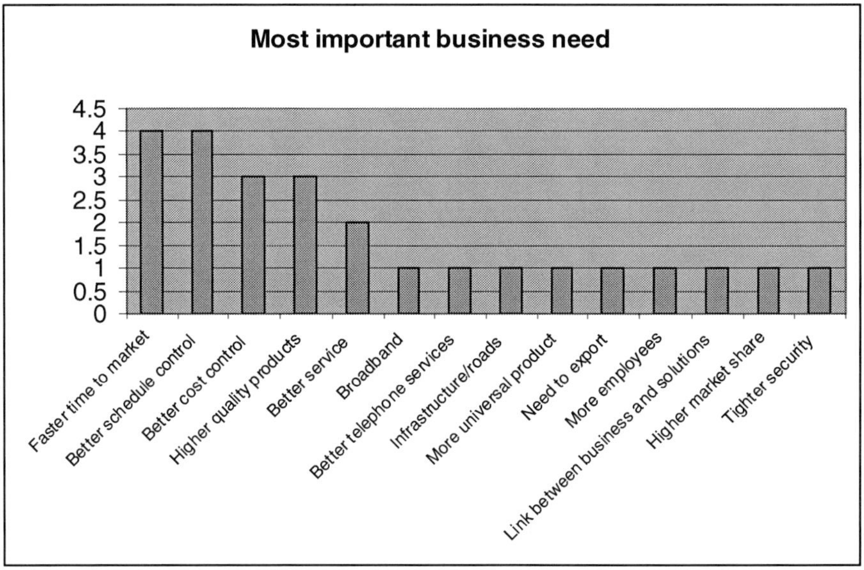

Figure 8-11 Current business needs

A general survey of business needs and concerns was used to assist with the results of the process assessment and guide the author in providing advice for improvements. This was discussed for each individual company in the company profiles in Chapter Seven.

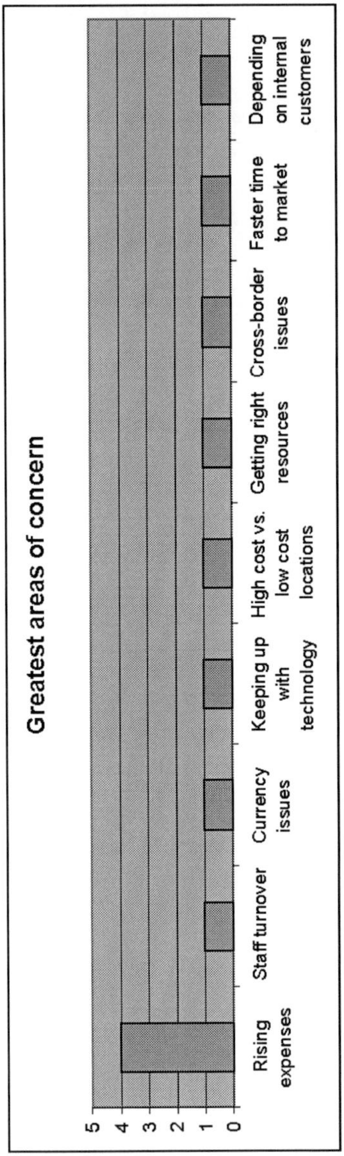

Figure 8-12 Current areas of concern

No assumptions were made about what interviewees in different roles would view as their most important business needs or their greatest areas of concern. It would not have been surprising if technical managers and business managers had shown different types of concerns but this did not prove to be the case. A larger survey might possibly have demonstrated more variations, however. Table 8-6 shows what responses there were. If no title is listed for role in organisation the interviewee has multiple roles

		Present	
	Co.	**Most important business need**	**Greatest concern**
Role in organisation			
Managing director/CEO	DTG	Better schedule control, better cost control, broadband, better telephone services, infrastructure/roads	Rising expenses, currency issues
Senior executive	FM	Better schedule control, faster time to market	Rising expenses
	MM	Higher quality products, better service	Keep up with technology
CTO/CIO/COO/EM	JC	Better service	Right resources
	SI	Better cost control	Currency issues
	TM	Better schedule control, faster time to market	Rising expenses
Middle manager	FD	Link between business and solutions	High cost vs. low cost locations
	OS	Higher market share	Rising expenses
	SM	Higher quality products, better schedule control, better cost control, faster time to market, tighter security	Depend on internal customers
	TS	Higher quality products, faster time to market	Staff turnover

Table 8-6 Role in organisation vs. business need and concerns

Customer views often influence how an organisation manages its improvement process. Figure 8-13 shows how well the interviewees believe they understand the customer's views.

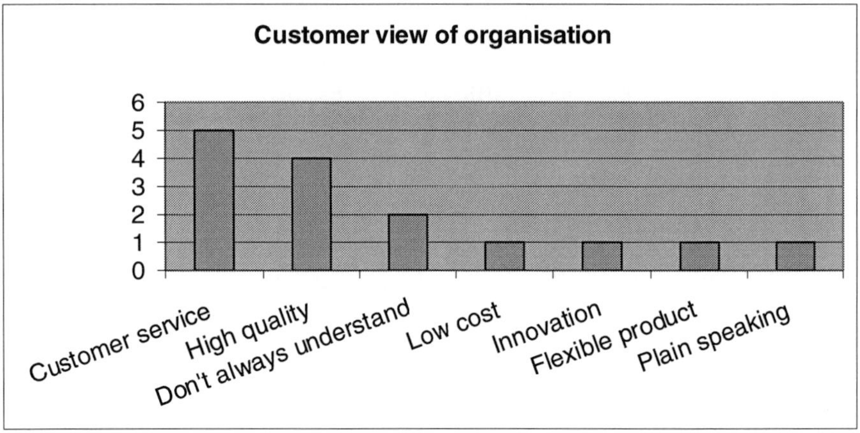

Figure 8-13 Current customer views

The interviewee at JC stated that customers do not always understand the knowledge and skill needed to provide the products and services required. This can lead to a conflict between high quality vs. low cost for clients. The SM interviewee describes a difficult organisation with often remote customers; however hopefully the planned Service Level Agreements will help solve the problem. Table 8-7 shows the correlation between the customer view vs. the most closely related process score which focuses on the necessity to provide software to the customer which meets the agreed requirements.

Present-How do customers view org?	Co.	Supply process
High quality, customer service	DTG	4
High quality	FD	4
High quality, customer service	FM	4
Do not always understand	JC	3
Customer service	MM	4
Plain speaking	OS	4
Customer service	SI	3
Do not always understand	SM	4
High quality, innovation	TM	4
Low cost, flexible product	TS	4

Table 8-7 Customer view vs. related process scores

Despite not always understanding what customers want or need, both JC and SM tested well in answer to assessment questions about customer issues.

Six of the interviewees said the customer view had improved. The others were not so positive or were both positive and negative. The interviewer at FM made a point of saying that the customer relationship had to be managed when improvements are made so that the customer understands the benefits they will gain in exchange for (possibly) some disadvantages. In their case, improvements necessitated longer schedules but a better product was delivered in the end.

Asking three questions about whether or not the organisation was a good one, and differences between the ideal and actual did not appear to be as effective as hoped but some answers were given as shown in Table 8-8.

		Current	
Is it a good organisation?	**Co.**	**Describe organisation**	**Why different from ideal?**
Do not know	TM	Do not know	Do not know
Independent	DTG	Need more people/specific person	No difference
Organised	FD	Organised	No difference
Common understanding of customers	JC	Busy, inefficient, surviving well	Lack of efficiency
Organised	MM	Hard to get work done, need more people/specific person	Do not know
Organised	SI	Need reorganisation	Do not know
Innovative and efficient	FM	Hard to get work done	Need better communication of goals
Innovative and efficient	OS	It's a good organisation	No difference
Objectives and visions openly communicated	SM	50% there	Senior management to-ing and fro-ing
Good teamwork	TS	Need more team work	Time pressures

Table 8-8 Views about organisations

The interviewee at TM had never worked anywhere else and could make no contribution about how things might be different. SM is a real enigma in some ways. It is very successful by any standards in software and in business but there is also definitely an undercurrent of unease with it as evidenced in these answers.

Part IV Plans for the future

Questions in the final section designed to show whether the company is looking at continuing improvements, indicating a "culture of quality".

In discussing planned changes (illustrated in Figure 8-14), measurements and reviews were the most frequently discarded SPI initiatives (3 each) while measurement was also the most frequently mentioned planned improvement. DTG, MM and OS all reported measurement programmes that were discarded. FM, SI, SM and TS are planning to implement measurement. In no case is any one company re-launching a failed initiative. Three companies (MM, SI and SM) got rid of design and/or code reviews and FD plans to implement them. These were the only subjects repeated in what SPI initiatives failed and what new SPI activities are planned for the future.

The last question was a part of CMM assessments at the last company where the author was employed as an internal quality consultant and process engineer. The answers can be insignificant or can unleash a torrent of words on what is wrong. Both happened during these interviews.

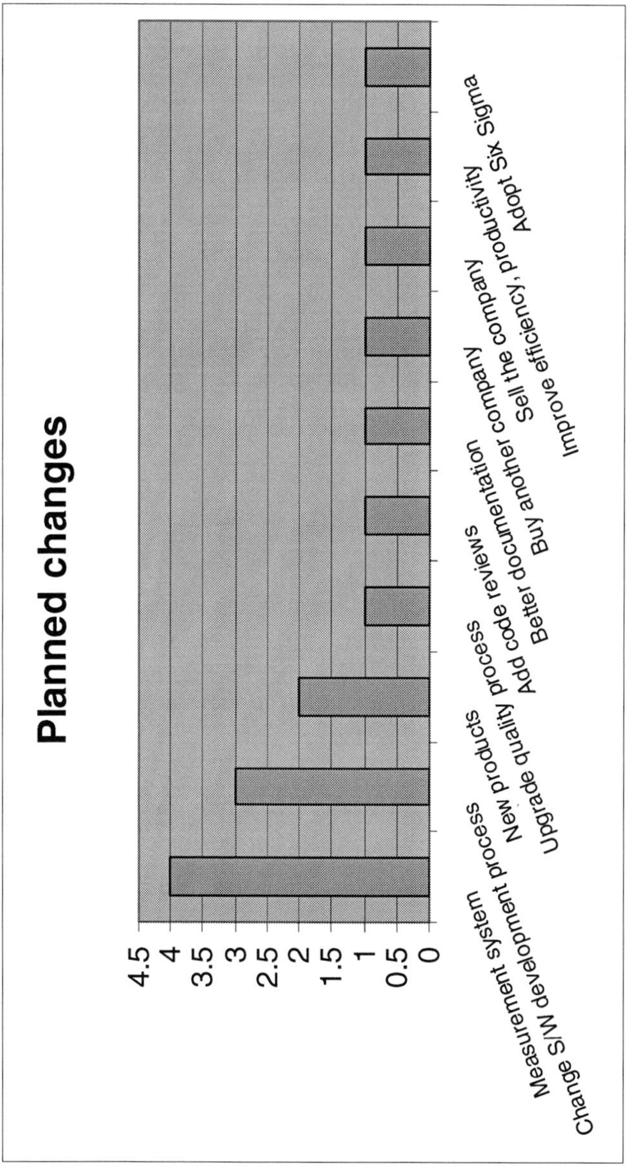

Figure 8-14 Changes planned for the future

"If you could change one thing—not your boss or your pay check—what would it be?"

MM wants to hire more people, although the interviewee said one of their problems was deciding just what skills are most needed. The interviewee at TM is the Engineering and Quality Manager and wants to hire people specifically to write "clean" code to replace code which has been modified and enhanced over several years. All other wishes were unique to one individual interviewee. The OS interviewee first said "nothing" then said that we "have good people; they operate well when given the space to do it." Both responses are recorded although they seem to indicate issues way beyond the scope of this research.

The two companies who do not yet have their strategic plan for improvement in place are MM and SI, two companies who have gone through massive change, including both expansion and contraction within the recent past. Table 8-9 compares plans to the existence of an overall strategy and what each interview suggested as a good change to make.

		Future	
Future-changes planned	**Co.**	**Overall strategy?**	**What would *you* change?**
Upgrade quality system	TM	Yes	Hire people to write clean code
New products, buy another company	DTG	Yes	Better traffic management
Change software development process, code reviews, better documentation	FD	Yes	Optimise processes
Improve productivity, sell the company	JC	Yes	Improve staff business knowledge
New products	MM	Working on it	More people
Measurement system	SI	Working on it	Get engineering budget
Measurement system	FM	Yes	Strong customer sales focus
Change software development process	OS	Yes	Nothing
Measurement system, adopt/adapt six sigma	SM	Yes	More motivation, proactivity
Change software development process, measurement system	TS	Yes	People's attitude to change

Table 8-9 Future wishes and plans

8.3.3 Process assessment

The tables and figures in this section show the responses to each of the 20 processes included in the MMAI. All scores are recorded as 4-fully, 3-largely, 2-partly, 1-not done, 0-not applicable. The last was used particularly when acquisition and supplier selection were not issues for the company since they had stable suppliers on long-term contracts or had fixed platforms and tools, requiring no purchases. Each case is described in more detail in the company profiles. No attempt was made to go above the SPICE "performed" level for the purposes of this research. Where organisations were well-managed and would clearly be at a higher level in a capability assessment, it is noted in the relevant company profile. Each assessment question is shown as SPICE process, purpose, and the expected outcomes that can be used as indicators of capability.

The organisation as acquirer (Acquisition preparation, Supplier selection, Customer acceptance)

SPICE process	Purpose	Expected results
CUS.1.1 Acquisition preparation	Establish the needs and goals of the acquisition	• The concept or the need to **acquire, develop, or enhance** a system, software product, or software process will be **established**. • The customer's software and/or **system requirements** will be produced, • An **acquisition strategy** will be developed. • **Acceptance criteria** will be **defined**.
CUS.1.2 Supplier selection	Choose the organisation that will be responsible for the implementation of the project identified in CUS.1.1	• The **acquisition requirements** (eg. request for proposal) will be **produced** • The **supplier** will be **selected** based upon the evaluation of the supplier's proposals • A **contract** will be **established and negotiated** between the customer and the supplier

CUS.1.4 Customer acceptance	Approve the supplier's deliverable when all acceptance conditions are satisfied	• **Acceptance** will be **based on** the **acquisition strategy** and **conducted according** to the **agreed acceptance criteria** • The **delivered software** product and/or service will be **evaluated** with regard to the **agreed requirements**

Table 8-10 Processes assessed for organisation as acquirer

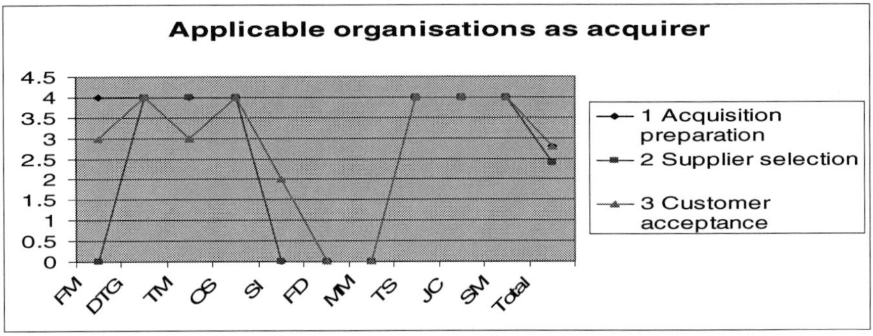

Figure 8-15 Scoring of processes assessed for organisation as acquirer

FM is included, even though Supplier selection is not applicable (stable platform) because they do have a process for when it is required. If this is taken into account, the set of processes covering the company as acquirer shows a high level of competence.

The organisation as supplier (Supply)

SPICE process	Purpose	Expected results
CUS.2 Supply	Provide software to the customer that meets the agreed requirements	• A **response to customer's request** will be **produced** • A **contract** will be **established** between the customer and the supplier for developing, packaging, delivering, and installing the software product and/or service

		• A **software product** and/or service that **meets the agreed requirements** will be **developed** by the **supplier** • The **software** product and/or service will be **delivered** to the customer **and installed** in accordance with the **agreed requirements**

Table 8-11 Processes assessed for organisation as supplier

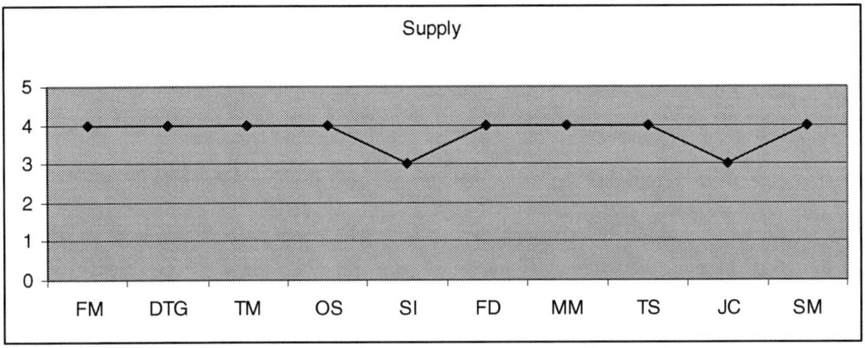

Figure 8-16 Scoring of processes assessed for organisation as supplier

Interviewees were generally proud to talk about their relationships with their customers. JC is the one who said that the customers did not understand about quality vs. cost. SI had just been sold off and was restructuring many things but yet the interviewee talked about close customer relationships, some of which were informal enough to score a "largely" instead of a "fully" on the assessment.

Engineering (Software life cycle steps—Software requirements analysis, Software design, Software testing)

SPICE process	Purpose	Expected results
ENG.1.2 Software requirements analysis	Establish the requirements of the software components of the system	• The **requirements** allocated to software **components** of the system and their **interfaces** will be defined to **match the** customer's **stated needs** • **Analysed, correct and testable** software **requirements** will be

		developed • The **impact** of software requirements **on the operating environment** will be **understood** • A **software release strategy** will be developed that **defines** the **priority** for implementing **software requirements** • The **software requirements** will be **approved** and **updated** as needed • **Consistency** will be established **between software requirements** and **software designs** • The **software requirements** will be **communicated to all** affected parties
ENG.1.3 Software design	Define a design for the software that implements the requirements and can be tested against them	• An **architectural design** will be developed that describes the major software components that will **implement the software requirements** • Internal and external **interfaces** of each software component will be **defined** • A **detailed design** will be developed that **describes software units** that can be built and tested • **Consistency** will be established **between software requirements** and **software designs**
ENG.1.6 Software testing	Test the integrated software producing a product that will satisfy the software requirements	• **Acceptance criteria** for integrated software will be developed that **verify compliance** with the **software requirements** • **Integrated software** will be **verified** using the defined **acceptance criteria** • **Test results** will be **recorded** • A **regression strategy** will be developed for **retesting the integrated software** should a change in software items be made • **Regression testing** will be **carried out** as necessary

Table 8-12 Processes assessed in engineering

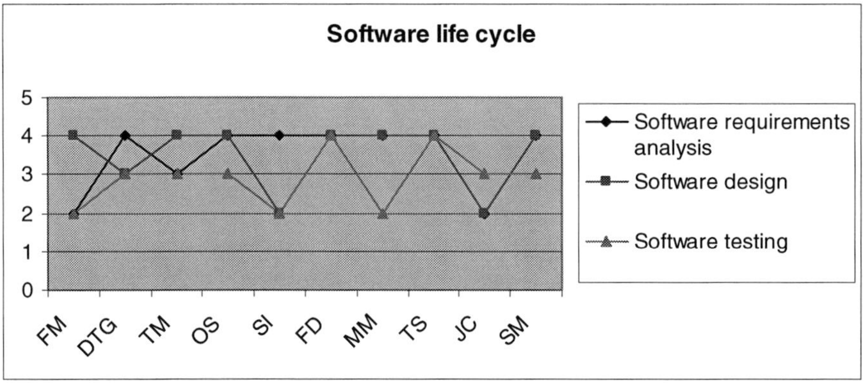

Figure 8-17 Scoring of processes assessed in engineering

This is where large differences between organisations begin to show themselves, with "testing" the issue needing the most attention. The lack of regression testing, the use of "informal" testing and the recording of test data, as well as a dependence on good people rather than detailed and documented processes were all factors in determining scores.

Support (Documentation, Configuration management, Quality assurance, Verification, Validation, Joint review, Audit, Problem resolution)

SPICE process	Purpose	Expected results
SUP.1 Documentation	Develop and maintain documents that record information produced by a process or activity	• A **strategy identifying** the **documents** to be **produced** during the life cycle of the software product will be developed • The **standards** to be **applied for** the development of **documents** will be **identified** • All **documents** to be **produced** by the process or project will be **identified** • The **content and purpose** of all documents will be **specified, reviewed and approved** • All **documents** will be developed and published **in accordance** with **identified standards**

		• All **documents** will be **maintained in accordance** with **specified criteria**
SUP.2 Configuration management	Define a design for the software that implements the requirements and can be tested against them	• A **configuration management strategy** will be **developed** • **All items** generated by the process or project will be **identified, defined and baselined** • **Modifications and releases** of the items will be **controlled** • The **status of** the **items and modification requests** will be **recorded and reported** • The **completeness and consistency** of the items will be **ensured** • **Storage, handling, and delivery** of the items will be **controlled**
SUP.3 Quality assurance	Provide assurance that work products and processes of a process or project comply with their specified requirements and adhere to their established plans	• A **strategy** for conducting the **quality assurance process activities and tasks** will be **developed, implemented and maintained** • **Evidence of** quality assurance **activities and tasks** will be **produced and maintained** • **Problems or non-conformances** with contract **requirements** will be **identified** • **Adherence** of software products, processes and activities **to the applicable standards, procedures and requirements** will be **verified objectively**
SUP.4 Verification	Confirm that each software work product and/or service of a process or project properly reflects the specified requirements	• A **verification strategy** will be **developed** and **implemented** • **Criteria for verification** of all required software work products will be **identified** • Required **verfication activities** will be **performed** • Identified **defects** will be **found and removed** from software work products

		• **Results of the verification activities** will be **made available to** the **customer and other** involved **organisations**
SUP.5 Validation	Confirm that the requirements for a specific intended use of the software work product are fulfilled	• A **validation strategy** will be **developed and implemented** • **Criteria for validation** of all required work products will be **identified** • Required **validation activities** will be **performed** • All **identified problems** will be **resolved** • **Evidence** will be **provided** that the software work **products as developed are suitable** for their intended use • **Results of the validation activities** will be **made available to** the **customer and other** involved **organisations**
SUP.6 Joint review	Maintain a common understanding with the customer of the progress against the objectives of the contract and what should be done to help ensure development of a product that satisfies the customer	• **Periodic reviews** will be held at **predetermined milestones** • The **status and products of an activity** of a process will be **evaluated** through **joint review** activities between the customers, suppliers, and other stakeholders (or interested parties) • **Review results** will be **made known** to all affected parties • **Action items** resulting from reviews will be **tracked to closure**
SUP.7 Audit	Independently determine compliance of selected products and processes with the requirements, plans, and contract, as	• An **audit strategy** will be **developed and implemented** • **Audits** will be **held** at **predetermined milestones** • **Compliance** of selected software work products and/or services or processes with requirements, plans, and contract will be **determined according to the audit strategy**

	appropriate	• The **conduct of audits** by an appropriate **independent party** will be **arranged** • **Problems** detected during an audit will be **identified, communicated** to those responsible for corrective action, and **resolved**
SUP.8 Problem resolution	Ensure that all discovered problems are analysed and resolved and that trends are recognised	• The **problem resolution activities** will be **identified** to ensure that all discovered problems are analysed and resolved • **Problem reports** will be **prepared** upon detection of problems (including non-conformances) • A **mechanism** will be **provide**d for **recognising and acting on trends** in problems identified

Table 8-13 Processes assessed in support

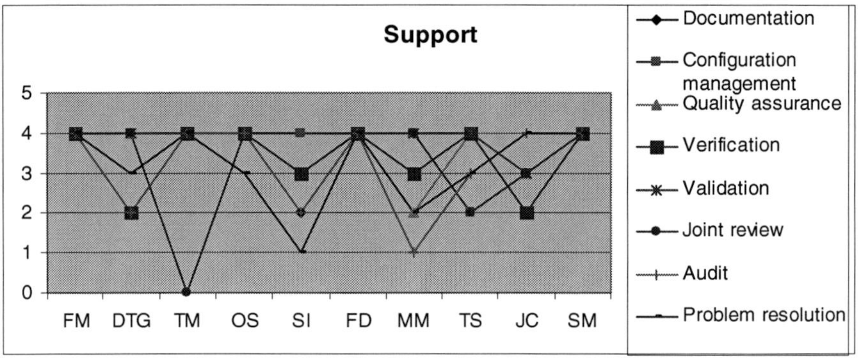

Figure 8-18 Scoring of processes assessed in support

Support functions have been adapted and adopted to each organisation's software processes. In many cases, there is probably nothing untoward with the processes being followed provided that nothing goes wrong, no experienced people leave, no computers go down unexpectedly, or no other unplanned events occur. As can be seen from Figure 8-18, configuration management is widely followed and various tools are used to support it. Indeed, interviewees were astonished that software had ever been managed any other way, in previous (earlier) years. Unfortunately, no documentation exists to show how uncommon configuration management was in the early days of these programmes.

Management (Project management, Quality management, Risk management)

SPICE process	Purpose	Expected results
MAN.2 Project management	Identify, establish, coordinate, and monitor--activities, tasks, and resources necessary for a project to produce a product and/or service meeting the requirements	• The **scope of the work** for the project will be **defined** • The **feasibility of achieving the goals** of the project with available resources and constraints will be **evaluated** • The **tasks and resources** necessary to complete the work will be **sized and estimated** • **Interfaces** between elements in the project, and with other projects and organisational units, will be **identified and monitored** • **Plans** for execution of the project will be **developed and implemented** • **Progress** of the project will be **monitored and reported** • **Actions to correct deviations** from the plan and to prevent recurrence of problems identified in the project, will be **taken when project targets are not achieved**
MAN.3 Quality management	Monitor the quality of the project's products and/or services and to ensure that they satisfy the customer. The process involves establishing a focus on monitoring the quality of product and process at both the project and	• **Quality goals**, based on the customer's stated and implicit quality requirements, will be **established** for various checkpoints within the project's software life cycle • An **overall strategy** will be **developed to achieve** the defined **goals** • Identified **quality control and assurance activities** will be **performed** and their **performance confirmed**

	organisational level	• **Actual performance** against the quality goals will be **monitored** • Appropriate **action** will be **taken** when quality **goals** are **not achieved**
MAN.4 Risk management	Identify and mitigate the project risks continuously throughout the life-cycle of a project. The process involves establishing a focus on monitoring of risks at both the project and organisational levels	• The **scope** of the risk management to be performed for the project will be **determined** • Appropriate **risk management strategies** will be **defined and implemented** • **Risks** to the project will be **identified** in the **project strategy**, and **as** they **develop** during the conduct of the project • The **risks** will be **analysed** and the **priority** in which **to apply resources to monitor** these risks will be **determined** • **Risk metrics** will be **defined, applied, and assessed** to **determine** the **change** in the risk state and the progress of the monitoring activities • Appropriate **action** will be **taken to correct or avoid** the impact of **risk**

Table 8-14 Processes assessed in management

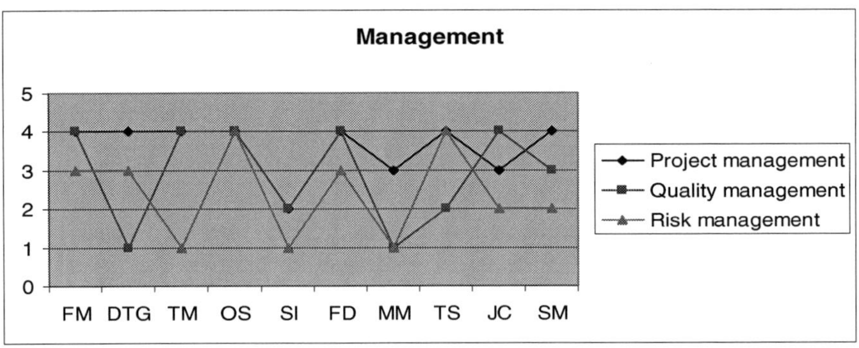

Figure 8-19 Scoring of processes assessed in management

Project management is widely followed but the broader quality management, which means planning and having goals for quality and risk management, are much more variable. Quality and risk management are frequently included as part of business planning and other management activities, rather than being specifically noted. Therefore, it is possible that some of these scores are actually lower than a more detailed and extensive assessment might show.

Operations (Human resources management, Measurement)

SPICE process	Purpose	Expected results
ORG.3 Human resources management	Provide the organisation and projects with individuals who possess skills and knowledge to perform their roles effectively and to work together as a cohesive group	• The **roles and skills** required for the operations of the organisation and the project will be **identified** through timely review of the organisational and project requirements • **Training** will be **identified and conducted** to ensure that all individuals have the skills required to perform their assignments, using mechanisms such as training strategies and materials • **Individuals with the required skills and competencies** will be **identified and recruited** using mechanisms such as procedures, or they will be trained as appropriate to perform the organisational and project roles • Effective **interaction** between individuals and groups will be **supported** • The **work force** will have the skills to **share information** and **coordinate** their **activities efficiently** • **Objective criteria** will be **defined** against which group and individual performance can be monitored **to provide performance feedback** and to enhance performance

ORG.5 Measurement	Collect and analyse data relating to the products developed and processes implemented within the organisational unit, to support effective management of the processes, and to objectively demonstrate the quality of the products.	• An appropriate **set of measurements**, driven by the project and organisational goals, will be **identified** • **Data** required will be **collected and analysed** • A collection of **historical data** relating to process implementation will be **established and maintained** • **Measurements** will be **used to support decisions** and **provide** an objective **basis for communication** between the interested parties

Table 8-15 Processes assessed in operations

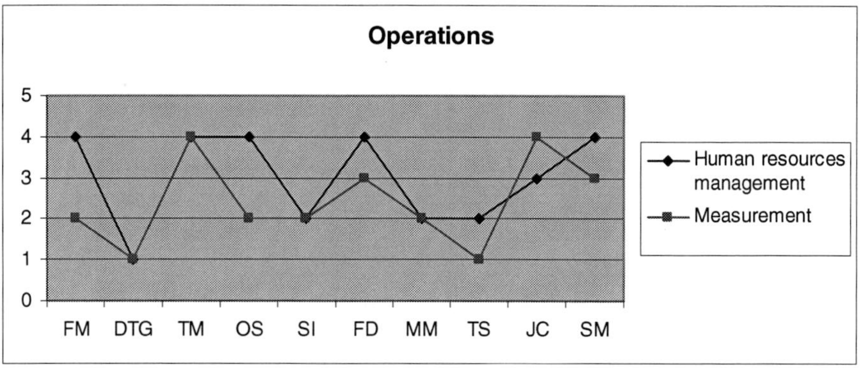

Figure 8-20 Scoring of processes assessed in operations

As has already been noted, measurement has been one of the two most abandoned SPI initiatives. Part of the reason for this has been stated as the fact that there is not enough of a return for the effort expended. However, another reason for this might be the increased use of tools which provide data as a secondary benefit, thereby rendering a separate measurement system unnecessary. Few companies even look at using data to examine trends and for the better management of their software.

Human resources management is quite variable because of the range of company sizes. FM, OS, FD and SM have strong human resources processes but they are all quite large companies (although the divisions represented in the interviews were much smaller) so this is to be expected.

8.4 Results of SPI assistance in Ireland

8.4.1 Results of data evaluation

One rather surprising finding was that five of the companies assessed had 30 employees or fewer and five were larger; therefore, this was not as much of a small company assessment as the author had initially anticipated. In spite of the findings by others that small companies are different from large companies (Cater-Steel and Rout 2006, Richardson and von Wangenheim 2007) many characteristics of the software environment evaluated in this research are the same for different sizes of organisations:

- Average project team sizes are usually six people or fewer.
- Development projects are usually six months in duration or shorter.
- Web-based distributed PC systems are the norm for most, either in current systems or planned migration from older centralised systems.
- Improvements were made in most companies, with size not appearing to be a factor. More importantly, most of these changes have been sustained in companies regardless of their size. Of the five companies with the highest average scores in process ratings, FD improved apparently without any influence from the SPI training, OS and SM are large companies, FM and TM are small companies; the last four show improvements related to the assistance programmes.
- Standardisation of software processes, whether following a specific standard or not, is one of the greatest benefit recorded by companies of all sizes. In companies with high staff turnover, the standardisation appeared to play a very supportive role. ISO 9001 is current in four companies, SI and TM have 11-20 employees, FM has 21-30 employees, and JC has 51-100 employees. FD at 31-50 employees in the department assessed was ISO 9001 certified for several years until the decision was made their processes were far advanced beyond the standard. ISO 9001 certification has proved valuable in organisations of varying sizes including all but the smallest surveyed.
- Most companies of any size indicated good senior management support.

- The link between understanding of company vision and goals and the success of SPI does not appear to have any connection to size of the organisation.

Another interesting comparison is with what the experts say is required for success in SPI and what this research showed. Many authors have written about the reasons for success and failure (Osorio *et al.* 2007, Groth 2004, Maxwell and Forselius 2000, Hutchings *et al.* 1993, Brodman and Hannigan 2003).

Perhaps it is sufficient here to look at a few of the documented basic principles for software process change that reflect questions asked in this survey (Humphrey 1990, Sanders 1998). These are compared against the responses from all companies in Table 8-16.

The scores of the process assessments are listed below in Table 8-17 along with various facts about each company as stated in the interview. Looking only at those companies which give credit to the SPI assistance for improvements (not FD or TS), the six that have the highest assessment scores all had consulting assistance, either with training (ISCP), or without (TRI-SPIN, PIEs, SPIRE).

SPI success factor (SSF)	Criteria for evaluation	Companies that have SSF	Companies that do not have SSF
Senior management leadership required to launch the change effort and to provide continuing resources and priority.	Answers to questions about senior management support for SPI in the past	Well or very well for all. JC fluctuated. SI very well locally, not at all with foreign owner.	TS reported no improvements because of lack of management support
Software process improvement involves continual learning and growth.	Past improvements, current SPI and plans for future SPI	All but TS show improvements at some level for all periods	TS shows no past improvements from SPI programmes, but current and future SPI exists
Software process changes will not be retained without conscious effort and periodic reinforcement.	Answers to questions about senior management support for SPI now	All companies at very well or well	
SPI goals must be well understood and related to business and technical goals.	How well groups understand link between SPI and business	Senior, middle, technical managers all very well or well; employees very well or well except SM and TM which are average	
SPI people must be well-respected	Do most senior and most respected SEs support SPI?	All always or often, except JC who said 50% of the time[15]	

Table 8-16 Compare research with success factors from literature

[15] JC could be in either column depending on if you see the cup as half empty or half full. In view of interviewee comments about being overworked and under time constraints, it is possible the situation is better than '50%' of the time might indicate.

Co. in order of process rating, out of 4.00	Type of knowledge transfer[16]	Standard followed	No. programmes	ISO or more?	No. emp?	Past S.M. support?[17]	Cur S.M. support?
FD (3.88)	T	CMM	1	yes	31-50	v.w.	v.w.
OS (3.80)	C	none	1	no	>100	v.w.	v.w.
SM (3.75)	C, T&C	ISO	2	no	>100	w.	w.
FM (3.58)	T&C, C	ISO	2	yes	21-30	v.w.	v.w.
TM (3.50)	C	ISO[18]	1	yes	11-20	v.w.	v.w.
TS (3.35)	T	CMM	1	no	>100	p.	w.
DTG (3.15)	C, C	none	2	no	21-30	v.w.	v.w.
JC (3.10)	T&C	ISO	1	yes	51-100	var.	w.
MM (2.76)	T	CMM	1	no	6-10	v.w.	v.w.
SI (2.39)	C, T, C	ISO[19], CMM, SPIRE	3	yes	11-20	v.w.	w.

Table 8-17 Selected information on companies

8.4.2 Conclusions about specific improvements

In this study, some processes have been more successfully implemented than others. Of particular interest is the careful attention to the interfaces with customers and suppliers. Those companies categorised as "not applicable" also had stable platforms. Any purchasing was done under long-term contract from known suppliers which was done at the

[16] T=training, C=consulting, T&C=training and consulting both

[17] S.M.=senior management support, v.w. = very well, w.=well, p.=poorly, f.=fluctuating

[18] Implemented ISO 9001 through TRI-SPIN consultant support

[19] Implemented independently from SPI programmes

corporate level above the assessed group, or there was no purchasing at all as part of the customer product. No attempt was made to correlate the score for human resource management with the size of the company, but the only large company that does not have a satisfactory score for this process is TS. Risk management and measurement scores are the lowest, but since risk management is often included as part of business management documentation and measurement can be part of the tools used for other purposes, the scores might actually have been higher if a detailed assessment had been done. Table 8-18 shows processes in order of rating

Process(s)	Rating score
Acquisition preparation (three 0's), supplier selection (four 0's)	4.00
Supply, validation	3.80
Configuration management	3.70
Documentation, quality assurance, project management	3.60
Customer acceptance (two 0's), software requirements analysis, software design	3.50
Verification	3.40
Joint review, audit, problem resolution	3.20
Human resource management	3.00
Software testing, quality management	2.90
Risk management, measurement	2.40

Table 8-18 Processes in order of rating

8.4.3 Comparison of literature and this research

The processes that show the most frequent improvements in the literature are project management, configuration management and testing (Batista and Figueiredo 2000, Cater-Steel 2001 and 2004, Daily and Dresner 2003, Richardson 1999, von Wangenheim *et al.* 2006). The processes most frequently described as having improved during the course of this research were project management, improved testing/quality and added measurement (Table 8-4). Scores from companies in this survey are high in configuration management although this fact was not described by interviewees, possibly because such processes have been in place for so long, that they are considered "business as usual".

Therefore, we can conclude that Irish companies involved in this research conform with available international data. However, the need for and attempt at using measurement is also noted, even though it is not received very well in some companies.

CHAPTER NINE

SUMMARY AND CONCLUSIONS

9.1 Introduction

This chapter summarises the entire research process. Conclusions about individual issues are discussed, along with the original objectives and the structured process used to achieve answers about them. Associated activities and publications arising from this research are described, as well as significant contributions to the software engineering and software business communities. Future activities connected with this research are reviewed, including a potential web-based tool to assist small software companies. Table 9-1 covers possible weaknesses in the research and balancing measures which the author used to counteract these.

9.2 Conclusions about the MMAI

The MMAI was developed as part of this research project and as a basic quality model which has two components: (A) questions about the company, its past, present and future plans involving software management and, (B) a more formal assessment instrument to evaluate the performance of processes common to the three most widely-used standards/models in software.

Based on the results of the interviews and assessments, the model fulfilled its purpose and forms a significant contribution to the literature. It enabled the author to get a rounded picture of the company within a relatively short time and its progression through software management changes within the context of other events in the company. The pattern of related questions enabled the interviewer to go back and discuss previous answers if there seemed to be any inconsistencies. The inclusion of purpose and expected results in the assessment instrument enabled the interviewer to clearly express what information was needed from the interviewee.

The assessment instrument also confirmed the value of using SPICE as a framework within which to fit other standards. It is important to note that this was not a SPICE assessment as defined in the standard. SPICE has more processes in it than would have been taught or used with these companies but using a tailored SPICE profile in an assessment of basic process performance suited the particular needs of this research.

The MMAI was used across a diverse set of organisations and proved that it works as desired in evaluating the status of software management. No tool has been documented previously in the literature which is able to cover such a wide variety of basic processes within the most commonly-used software standards and using a reasonable amount of time for early stage assessment. Furthermore:

- The analysis showed the relative effectiveness of different types of assistance programmes with the companies interviewed.
- Factors for success were identified, including the widely-accepted need for management support, but so too were other factors as less-widely discussed in the literature.
- The possible benefits of ISO 9001 were identified including regular visits by an auditor and the potential for a wider community using the standard.
- Future plans to take advantage of this and other related research have been identified in order to create an additional and potentially-useful tool for small organisations in Ireland and elsewhere.

9.3 Conclusions about company improvements

The original research question was to find out if there were long-term benefits in companies that received SPI assistance up to 14 years ago. In the case of those companies who took part in the survey, all but two demonstrated that there were indeed long-term benefits. Both of those two companies are highly process-oriented now but we cannot say for certain whether this had anything to do with the SPI assistance. MM, the company that shows the lowest scores today actually reported improvements at the time of training. It is now recovering from a major reduction in size which may also account for the low scores.

In addition, the fact that so many similarities were identified between companies, whether large or small, is interesting in itself given that the author is in agreement with other researchers concerning the differences between them[20]. One conclusion that may be drawn is the fact that the business requirements for standards and process management are more important than company size in determining what improvement takes place or becomes incorporated within the software management process. However, this is an area that is really beyond the scope of this research.

A range of original research objectives was defined, as were the required methods with which to respond to these issues and questions, as discussed below.

9.3.1 Objective 1

Determine if a culture of improvement exists in the organisation

Out of the original 80 organisations, 77 are in the Republic of Ireland, 23 are currently still operating and, apparently, continuing to develop software. Sixty-nine companies proved to be inaccessible, even when incorporating the methods followed by this author. It may be that some were still accessible and still "in business" but that more information was required to locate them. Of those companies which do still exist, there is no way to know if SPI assistance worked with them, albeit that it is possible different avenues of access would allow another researcher to investigate further. Ten companies were accessed, interviewed and assessed. Based on the data available, all but one organisation (TS) reported sustained improvements at some level (although one (FD) could not attribute it to the SPI assistance).

9.3.2 Objective 2

Determine if there is any difference in the long-term success rate for organisations following one model rather than another or none.

ISCP (training + mentoring)

Three organisations (FM, JC, SM) were trained in ISO 9001 through ISCP, one through TRI-SPIN (TM), and one (SI) gained certification by other means. Of these, four (FM, SI, TM and JC) have current ISO 9001 certifications; three (SI, TM and JC) have had continuous ISO 9001 certification since the SPI programme. Four of the five companies trained

[20] This includes the cost and effort needed to use standardised software process assessment models and the doubts about their usefulness in the smaller organisation (von Wangenheim *et al.* 2006b).

in ISO 9001 showed continued success. This figure is higher than for any other improvement programme but the numbers are not sufficient to state clearly whether all expectations were satisfied.

However, if we expand beyond ISCP to ISO 9001 itself and add FD, who was certified to ISO 9001 until they felt they had gone beyond it, ISO 9001 has proved to be far more useful and widely practiced than the author expected. It may continue to play an essential role in maintaining software process improvement for several reasons:

1. For those who participated in ISCP, perhaps there was extra value in doing both training and mentoring, as the original programme developers believed. The training sessions introduced each subject area and the mentors helped the attendees implement it in their companies.
2. It may be that evaluation and understanding of processes is just as important as the auditing of them and that may be a factor here since part of implementing ISO 9001 requires evaluation of current processes and implementation of new ones on a structured basis.
3. ISO 9001 is a very structured standard widely understood and practiced in Europe where the community that uses it is much larger than for either of the other standards. This implies the potential customer base, at least within Europe, is much larger than for the other standards.
4. Regular visits by an auditor may be the triggering factor. Assessments and appraisals to the CMM/CMMI and ISO/IEC 15504 have been done in Ireland but not nearly as widely or for the purpose of gaining customer recognition.
5. ISO 9001 is broader than just software so could mean more in manufacturing companies than the CMM or SPICE (the technical report), both of which concentrate on software. This would certainly apply to TM and SI.
6. Certification and its advertisement may be more of a factor in getting or sustaining business than is apparent to those of us outside of the business community, although both Enterprise Ireland and the Centre for Software Engineering, which *are* involved in business, did not believe it to be that important in anecdotal information.

SPIRE, TRI-SPIN and PIEs (mentoring only)

Two companies took part in SPIRE (FM and SI), consulting only but using a SPICE-based tool for assessments before and after the improvement. Both reported many improvements but both are also ISO

9001 certified so improvements would have become part of the documented process the company is required to follow. It would be difficult to say today how much improvement, if any, can be ascribed only to participation in SPIRE.

Three companies (DTG, SI and TM) took part in TRI-SPIN and two companies (DTG and OS) had PIEs, which were mentoring only and not based on any particular standard. All report tangible improvements which can be traced directly to these programmes through published case studies and reports, as well as results of the interview. With one exception, even where specific improvements were not maintained the improvements were credited with leading to a more maintainable, improved software environment. The interviewee at SI stated that code reviews, which were initiated as part of the TRI-SPIN improvements did not last, although other types of reviews are an integral part of their process.

SCATE (training only)

SCATE followed the same model of training as ISCP, with groups of companies sending up to two persons to each of nine sessions on specific topics, but had no mentoring within the companies. The three companies (FD, MM and TS) that took part in SCATE only, which had training in CMM Level 2 and introduction to CMM Level 3, showed improvements but none could specifically ascribe any to the training they received. Only in MM was the interviewee the one who took part in the training.

The interviewee at FD knew about the SCATE participant (who now works in a different part of the organisation) but did not know about SCATE. This company is highly process-oriented and has been for many years so one person trained in SCATE would have been a tiny part of a continuous improvement programme.

According to the former Quality Manager at TS, there was no support for any of the SCATE concepts at the time so he went back to software development. The current interviewee who is in charge of SPI reports many improvements but these are not known to be directly related to the training in SCATE.

There are indications that training in the CMM and other components of SCATE might have had some influence in all these companies but it is difficult to quantify.

9.3.3 Objective 3

Determine if there is any difference in long-term success rate for organisations depending on what form of knowledge transfer was a part of the programme(s) in which they participated.

No interviewee who had training (only) could tie any specific improvements to that programme. Therefore the conclusion can be reached that the particular type of knowledge transfer involved does matter. In the case of this research, it cannot be proved that training alone made a substantial difference in the companies which participated. The case study written by MM at the end of SCATE training did show improvements at the time, but no link with specific improvements today could be made.

9.3.4 Conclusions about individual issues

- Companies of varying sizes and types of business all agree that smaller teams are more effective than large teams in software projects.
- The preponderance of web-based systems in all types of businesses may lend some credence to future development of standards for web-based developers (Grünbacher *et al.* 2004)[21].
- Strong management support is defined by every author as important for sustainable process improvement, as noted in Chapter 6. This research confirms this, with the caveat that the support of ISO 9001 or other active standard can carry the company over variations in management support or employee turnover. This is indeed described by standards developers as one of the benefits of adopting a standard. This benefit may come from regular and continuous audits for ISO 9001.
- However, it must be noted that no matter how good the software processes are, they may be such a small component of the overall business model that other factors are more likely to influence the success or failure of the business. The European Foundation Quality Model (www.efqm.org) lists enablers (leadership, people, policy and strategy, partnerships and resources, processes), leading to results for people, customers, society and key performance. Processes,

---

[21] ISO/IEC 23026 (2006) defines recommended practices for World Wide Web page engineering for Intranet and Extranet environments, based on World Wide Web Consortium (W3C®) and related industry guidelines.

specifically software processes, are only part of the means to success for a company.

9.3.5 Review of the research process

According to Fink (1995), good systems for collecting information on a broad range of subjects have six features: specific, measurable objectives; sound research design; sound choice of population or sample; reliable and valid instruments; appropriate analysis; accurate reporting of survey results. This research has all those components:

- Measurable objectives of developing a model to find out long-term results following specific programmes
- Sound research design where the method used of interviewing with the MMAI provide a consistent and reliable result
- The population chosen served the purpose of enabling the answer to the research questions
- The analysis showed useful information about what companies trained in SPI are actually doing in Ireland and the links from interview to reporting are sound

9.4 Contributions of the author

This author has participated in three main research-generation activities in order to help small software companies in both Ireland and elsewhere:

- Creation of a software development guide for small companies, published at the request of Enterprise Ireland in 2004;
- Membership on the working group to create an international standard (ISO/IEC 29110) specifically designed for small companies;
- This research into how to determine what small companies in Ireland are doing in the areas of software management.

The results of this research and subjects covered in the software development guide both contributed to the development of the standard. This kind of linkage between research, development of standards and tools which all support each other should be a useful way of capitalising on the results of research.

Further areas are being explored, such as the development of a three-part web-based package:

1. Self-assessment starting with the MMAI used in this research, evolving to use of the standard for small companies (ISO/IEC 29110) once it is stabilised.
2. Prioritisation of improvements using Quality Function Deployment, as described by Richardson (1999), with customer and business requirements compared to assessment ratings in specific processes. As an example, this could be used to help a company decide if it is more important to increase the assessment score for project management, currently at 2.6 or the score for measurement, currently at 1.3. With scores available for 20 processes vs. perhaps a dozen customer preferences or business requirements, this could be very useful to analyse the more important improvements to make to satisfy customer and business requirements.
3. Small improvement packages to be applied in areas identified as lacking in the assessment and prioritised for improvement; this might be based in part on subjects included in the SCATE training programme developed by the author and described in Chapter Three. The format would be much different, geared to a web-based system instead of a training class where each subject was discussed.

Potential opportunities for Lero in this process might include:

1. Research into prioritisation of processes for greatest benefit to the organisation
2. Translation of this into a web-based tool
3. Work with one or more companies to implement SPI, possibly including usage of the tool as it evolves
4. Involvement in commercialisation of tool, possibly through spin-off company or work with existing company

The benefits to Lero extend from the potential for several possible graduate student research projects to another visible link with industry. Better software management in companies involved can lead to more competitive advantage, as well as a possible commercial product for exploitation. For software companies throughout Ireland, this may be the path to a standardisation which improves the global competitiveness of the country through the greater recognition of its software capabilities.

9.5 Publications arising from this research

"What happened after SPI assistance in Ireland?" was presented by the author at the 4th International SPICE Conference on Process Assessment and Improvement, Klagenfurt, Austria in 2005. This described the SPI assistance programmes and gave the broad outline of the research to follow.

Plans for the research described here were documented in 'Research into long-term improvements in small- to medium-sized organisations using SPICE as a framework for standards', *Software Process Improvement and Practice*, Wiley 12, 351-359. (Appendix 22)

"Finding out what happened after SPI assistance in Ireland" was presented at EuroSPI 2008. This describes the overall research and specifically the development of the MMAI.

9.6 Discussion and limitations of the research

Table 9-1 is an analysis of possible weaknesses in the research methodology, execution, data collection and analysis and conclusions drawn. All issues are described within the overall purpose of the research (in order to find out if the assessment model enables determination of a culture of improvement and if such a culture exists). The questions and answers, as they currently stand, may not be sufficient if a more rigorous assessment is required for contractual or regulatory reasons.

Possible weakness	Balancing measure
The most useful or insightful questions were not asked to determine if a culture of improvement really does exist.	The survey instruments were a combination of closed questions with encouragement for the interviewee to augment them as appropriate. This provides a balance between structure and the freedom to add useful information unique to the site. Questions are structured to cover a continuum from the time of the SPI programmes through plans for the future to look for any disconnects in an SPI environment.
The interviewer put "spin" on the answers to make her earlier work with companies look like she did a better job or that SPI is more important than it actually is.	The same questions are asked of all interviewees and failures are reported as well as successes. There is no attempt with this research to determine the importance of SPI to the success of the business; the second part of the research is concerned with determining if SPI has been maintained after initial training/consulting.

The interviewer is biased, wanting certain answers.	Interviews were conducted by sitting with each interviewee and reading questions exactly as they were printed, with no prompting for answers.
Interviewees are biased, wanting to make the organisation sound better than it really is.	The first part of the interview is to talk about the confidentiality agreement and how research is reported in the literature so that no company can be identified unless it wants to be, sometimes as a co-author. The next part of the interview is to discuss the flow of material: interviewee statements to be collated into a report which is returned for assurance of correctness to the interviewee only. The report goes to no other person so there is nobody else to comment on its contents unless the interviewee wants it to happen. At points that may sound questionable the interviewer can ask to see database screens or documentation or whatever is appropriate to look for concurrence on what interviewee stated. There is no real reason to believe any interviewee has reason to be other than truthful. No business decisions or promotions hinged on the results of the interview. All, even the most strongly managed, freely admitted to those activities they do not do or do poorly.
There was lack of understanding on the part of the interviewer on what the interviewee stated	Several questions are similar but asked in different ways or for different time periods or to support each other; wherever there appeared to be any discrepancies the earlier question and answer were reviewed to make sure that the answers were as intended. All interviewees were sent a summary of information along with recommendations for further improvement within two weeks of the interview; all interviewees were invited to make any changes if the answers were not correct.
There was lack of understanding on the part of the interviewee on what the interviewer stated.	In the few cases where clarifications were needed, an example would be supplied without actually answering the question. For example, "What does acquisition preparation mean?" might be answered by, "What happens when you decide to buy something?"
The interviewer did not remember correctly what was said in the interview.	All answers and comments were written down and read back to the interviewee as they were being written and agreement was asked that they were correct or corrections were made, as appropriate. As soon as possible after the interview, within 24 hours in most cases, the answers and comments were transcribed into the draft report that was then sent to the interviewee for concurrence.

The links between the questions asked, the answers given, the results noted and conclusions drawn are not strong	Every link is discussed and justification for it is given. The letter sent to the interviewee to gain consensus that the information is correct contains all answers, all scores and why the scoring was given. All conclusions have accompanying data and rationale given as part of the conclusion.
If another person did the same research, the results would not be the same	This is not the type of research that can be repeated by anyone, not even the original author and interviewee, with the same companies and expect to get the same answers; the very fact of having gone into companies and asked the questions, as well as having sent out a report on the interview and recommendations for the future has changed the environment.
If another person had done the research, the results would have been different	This is undoubtedly true. Any research which relies on two people, interviewer and interviewee, is unique. However, this by itself does not negate the value of the research. If this research were repeated in other circumstances with more data accumulated in the same way, there is no reason to believe the results would lead to different conclusions or be incorrect.
This is a research methodology which is limited to the target population used.	The research is repeatable in other circumstances, and is particularly helpful where a group of companies is trained in different standards/models; this is a useful set of basic processes which could be used in any environment. One example would be in other European countries which shared in multiple E.C.-sponsored SPI programmes.
The target population is too small to be able to draw any general conclusions.	The goal of the research was two-fold: to develop an assessment model which can be used in a heterogeneous environment and to validate the model using a specific set of companies; there is no attempt to generalise the responses beyond this population, but there are comparisons to other improvement programmes documented in the literature and suggestions for further activities.
The target population is biased towards SPI or they would not have been involved.	This is true to the extent that all companies at one time were involved in SPI. However, of the 11 companies involved in the research, 4 were contacted through cold calling at the door; the others responded to phone calls or e-mails to names known to the author. Of the 4 contacted cold, 3 are very process oriented and 1 is too small to have adopted more formal processes, but they did not come running to take part in this research specifically because they are biased towards SPI.

No electronic equipment was used for recording questions and answers or data from the process assessment. How was accuracy guaranteed?	The interviewer has experience with the use of equipment, its sometimes unreliability and possible tendency to get in the way of rather than enhance interviewing, particularly in once-off short interviews such as these. She decided that if written results are read back to the interviewee, a written report repeating them is sent to the interviewee, and the questions are structured so that they address different aspects of the same issue, that is just as accurate *for the purposes of this research.* Other purposes might require other tools.

Table 9-1 Possible weakness in the research and balancing measures

The ability to undertake this research with the target population was very dependent on the background, experiences and personal archives of the author, including final reports on the programmes, some of the case studies, reports from the European Commission and other materials that were in personal archives but not available publicly. Also, as stated earlier, this was a very unusual situation, with the European Commission funding multiple types of improvement programmes. Such a combination of circumstances is unlikely to be repeated, at least not in the author's lifetime and environment. Therefore, this was a unique research opportunity which promises to deliver further future benefits for the research and business communities.

9.7 Future research

The model that was developed for this research could be used by other researchers to expand the database about the capability of other companies as relating to a set of basic processes that are common to all of the major standards.

- Research in other countries taking part in these European Commission-sponsored programmes could be compared to the results in Ireland. Software PIEs are known to have taken place in most European countries. SCATE was taught in Belgium, Finland, France, Greece, Luxembourg, Sweden, Switzerland and The Netherlands, as well as Ireland. SPIRE was also followed in Austria, Italy, Sweden and the United Kingdom. TRI-SPIN improvements took place in Northern Ireland. These are all candidates for further research, given the time and resources. The European Commission may be interested in sponsoring such follow-on research in these other countries.

- Enterprise Ireland is very supportive of Irish companies and their improvement programmes. One possibility to develop a wider view of the status of Irish software companies is for Enterprise Ireland to sponsor use of the MMAI (or its evolution, ISO/IEC 29110) to expand a database of software practices throughout the business community. This would give a firm basis for improvement programmes. For example, if assessments show common areas where companies need improvement, the need for workshops and consultant support could be justified.
- Lero might consider performing such assessments at the beginning of any collaborative work with industry to develop a profile of where the industrial partner can contribute in areas where it is strong and where Lero personnel can help improve areas of weakness.

The MMAI is a significant model which can be used for many purposes as described above. Consequently, the results of the validation of the MMAI through this research could be the start of a database describing software company capabilities throughout Ireland or Europe.

APPENDIX

INTERVIEW GUIDE

Part A, organisation and SPI environment

Part I Organisation profile

I-1 Main business of the organisation

Aerospace	1	Education	8	Media	15
Automotive	2	Finance	9	Resources (petroleum/mining, wind, etc.)	16
Banking	3	Health/ pharmaceutical	10	Public administration	17
Construction	4	IT/software	11	Public utilities	18
Consumer goods	5	Insurance	12	Retail	19
Defence	6	Leisure/tourism	13	Telecommunications	20
Distribution/logistics	7	Manufacturing	14	Other	21

I-2 Type of organisation

Academic institution	1	Industrial producer-mass	5
Research institution	2	Service provider	6
Industrial innovation/inventor	3	Other	7
Industrial producer-niche	4		

I-3 Role(s) in the organisation?

Managing director/CEO	1	Quality specialist	9
Senior executive	2	Process specialist	10
CTO/CIO	3	Researcher	11
Middle manager	4	Student/apprentice/trainee	12
Line supervisor	5	Lecturer/teacher/trainer	13
Production worker	6	Product specialist	14
IT/software/systems developer	7	Pubic relations/marketing	15
Service staff	8	Other	16

I-4 Number of employees in the organisation

1-5	1	31-50	5
6-10	2	51-100	6
11-20	3	>100	7
21-30	4		

I-5 Number of software employees in the organisation

1-5	1	31-50	5
6-10	2	51-100	6
11-20	3	>100	7
21-30	4		

I-6 Average total team size on software projects, including all personnel

1-6	1	19-24	4
7-12	2	>24	5
13-18	3		

I-7 Average number of software personnel on software projects

1-4	1	13-16	4
5-8	2	>16	5
9-12	3		

I-8 Typical length of development projects in months

1-6	1	19-24	4
7-12	2	>24	5
13-18	3		

I-9 Typical type of development project

Web-based	1	Safety critical	5
Distributed	2	Transaction	6
Embedded	3		7
Real-time/time critical	4		

Part II Past culture for improvement

II-1 Your organisation took part in one or more process improvement programmes some years ago. Do you or anyone you know remember taking part in this?
Yes myself Yes other No

II-2 As far as you know, did change in the organisation take place as a result or this or other triggers for improvement in software processes?
Yes No Sometimes

II-3a If not, why do you think it didn't?

Not enough time
Not enough interest
Gone through massive changes

II-3b If yes, what kinds of changes took place in management of the organisation's software development and maintenance environment?

Adopt standards
New tools
Transform processes
Improved testing/quality
Better project management
New personnel positions
New business
Improved structure, approach

II-4 Senior management support is the single factor that all research has shown is absolutely necessary for sustained and systematic progress in adoption of change; to what extent have changes in software management had that senior management support?

Very well Well Average Poorly Not at all

II-5 Research has also shown that improvements must be linked to business goals to be successfully sustained. To what extent were employees informed about overall business objectives, vision and goals?
Very well Well Average Poorly Not at all

II-6 Was the organisation vision and mission lived by people in their daily work? For example, if the vision was to provide top quality service, did people work to provide this?
Always Often 50% of the time Seldom Never

II-7 Did the most senior, most experienced and most respected software engineers embrace this process of making improvement?
Always Often 50% of the time Seldom Never

II-8 We make changes to improve the business in some ways. When you made changes or improvements in the way you manage software, what improvements did you see?

Better products
Better scheduling
Better cost/revenue
Less rework
Slower delivery of better products

II-9 How much did this affect the everyday workings of the overall organisation?

Very well Well No change Slightly worse Much worse
II-10 How was the organisation affected?

Better morale
More efficient
Forced people to evaluate work
Lot more structure

II-11 Were any improvement initiatives started that tailed off or were not widely implemented? Particularly with tools, companies often see them fall into disuse once the 'toolmaster' leaves. Sometimes a methodology or standard is supported until the expert leaves, taking the real expertise away. Has anything like this happened here?

Measurement
Tools
Reviews
Documenting requirements, use cases
Formal standard
None

Part III Current culture for improvement

III-1 What level of senior management support exists today for change/improvement in software management?

Very good Good Average Poor Very poor

III-2 To what extent are today's employees informed about overall business objectives, vision and goals?

Very good Good Average Poor Very poor

III-3 Is the organisation vision/mission lived by people today in their daily work?

Always Often 50% of the time Seldom Never

III-4 Do the most senior, most experienced and most respected software engineers embrace this process of making change/improvement?

Always Often 50% of the time Seldom Never

III-5 Business objectives and goals should drive any improvement/change regime. How well would you say these groups of people understand the link between the needs of the business and changes in daily activities?

III-5a Senior management

Very well Well Average Poorly Not at all

III-5b Middle management
Very well Well Average Poorly Not at all

III-5c Technical management

Very well Well Average Poorly Not at all

III-5d Software developers and maintainers

Very well Well Average Poorly Not at all

III-6 Identify the factors that might inhibit a culture of improvement today. Some that other organisations have identified include:

Lack of senior management support
Lack of middle management support
Fear of openness
Loss of face or seniority
Daily pressure of work
Fear of light shown on work
None

III-7 What do you think is the most important need for your business today?

Higher quality products
Better schedule control
Better cost control
Faster time to market
Tighter security
Broadband
Better telephone services
Infrastructure/roads
More universal product
Need to export
More employees
Link between business and solutions
Higher market share

III-8 What are your greatest areas of concern? Staff turnover? Rising expenses? Other?

Staff turnover
Rising expenses
Currency issues
Keeping up with technology
High cost vs. low cost locations

III-9 Businesses try to satisfy customers. Do you understand how customers view your organisation?

High quality
Low cost
Speed
Innovation
Customer service
Plain speaking

III-10 Has their view changed and been expressed to you as you have made changes and improvements?

Yes, improved
Yes, worse
No
Don't know

III-11 How would you describe what a 'good' organisation looks and feels like?

Independent
More flexible
Innovative and efficient
Organised
Don't know

III-12 How would you describe your organisation today?

Disorganised
Hard to get work down
Improving
Need more people
Better communication of goals
Organised
Good organisation
Don't know

III-13 If these two sets of adjectives are different, why do you think this is?

No difference
Technology limitations
Don't know

Part IV Plans for the future

IV-1 What changes do you have planned for the future? Some possibilities include:

Change software development
Double productivity
Adopt formal process
Measurement system
New products
Buy another company

IV-2 Do you have an overall strategy in place to make these changes happen?

Yes No Working on it

IV-3 If you could change one thing—not your boss or your pay check—what would it be?

Better traffic management
Strong customer sales focus
Get engineering budget
More people
Optimise processes

Part B, Assessment instrument

The processes assessed are covered detail in Chapter 7, Data collection and analysis, 7.3.3 Process assessment

GLOSSARY

AIS	Advanced Information Services, Inc.
ALCAST	Automated Life-Cycle Approach to Software Testing in the Finance & Insurance Sector (PIE)
AUTO-DOC	The Introduction of an Automated Document Management System to automate recognised documentation practices in the software process (PIE)
CEO	Chief Executive Officer
CMM	Capability Maturity Model
CMM-SW	Capability Maturity Model-software
CMMI	Capability Maturity Model Integrated
CSE	Centre for Software Engineering
CTO	Chief Technical Officer
CUS	Customer-Supplier Process Category (in ISO/IEC 15504)
DCU	Dublin City University
DSDM	Dynamic Systems Development Method
E.C.	European Commission
ENG	Engineering Process Category (in ISO/IEC 15504)
ESPINODE	ESSI PIE Node
ESPITI	European Software Process Improvement Training Initiative
ESSI	European System and Software Initiative
GSD	Global Software Development
HRE	Humanity Relationships Executive (used in example)
ICSE	International Conference on Software Engineering
IEEE	Institute of Electrical and Electronic Engineers
IFM	Incremental Funding Method
ISCP	ISO 9001 for Small Companies Programme
ISEB	Information Systems Examination Board
ISO	International Organisation for Standardisation
IEC	International Electro-technical Commission
IT	Information Technology
JAVA-V&V	Verification & Validation Methodology for JAVA Development Environment (PIE)
KPA	Key Process Area
MAN	Management Process Category (in ISO/IEC 15504)

MASLYD	Metrics & Software Lifecycle Definition (PIE)
MMAI	Multi-Model Assessment Instrument
NPV	Net Present Value
NSAI	National Standards Authority of Ireland
OPF	Organisation Process Focus
ORG	Organisation Process Category (in ISO/IEC 15504)
OSS	Open Source Software
PCS	Project Management and Engineering Global Control System (PIE)
PE	Product Engineering (in CMM Level 3)
Phoenix	Mature Software Application Adaptation Project (PIE)
PIE	Process Improvement Experiment
PITA	Process Improvement Through Automation (PIE)
PROMM	Project Management and Metrication (PIE)
PP	Project Planning
PT&O	Project Tracking and Oversight
QA	Quality Assurance
QMS	Quality Management System (in ISO 9001, usually Quality Manual and associated procedures)
RAD	Rapid Application Development
RM	Requirements Management
ROI	Return On Investment
SCATE	Small Company Action Training and Enabling
SCM	Software Configuration Management
SEI	Software Engineering Institute (developers of the CMM, CMMI)
SEPIE	Software Engineering Process Improvement Experiment (PIE)
SPI	Software Process Improvement
SPICE	Software Process Improvement and Capability determination (ISO TR 15504)
SPIRE	Software Process Improvement for Regions of Europe
SQA	Software Quality Assurance
SSF	SPI Success Factors
STTF	Software Technology Transfer Finland
SUP	Support Process Category (in ISO/IEC 15504)
TQM	Total Quality Management
TR	Technical Report
TRI-SPIN	TRans-Ireland Software Process Improvement Network
XP	Extreme Programming

BIBLIOGRAPHY

Altman, D. (2006) "You like tomato and I like tomahto", *International Herald Tribune*, 4 October, 14.

Bagchi, T. (1997) "Competitiveness and TQM: is the synergy really a surprise?", paper presented at PICMET'97 Portland International Conference on Management of Engineering and Technology, Portland Oregon, 27-31 July 1997.

Batista, J. and Dias de Figueiredo, A. (2000) "SPI in a very small team: a case with CMM", *Software Process Improvement and Practice*, Wiley 5, 243-250.

Berry, D. (2008) "The software engineering silver bullet conundrum", *IEEE Software*, March/April, 18-19.

Biehl, R (2004) "Six sigma for software", *IEEE Software*, March/April, 68-70.

Boehm, B. and Huang, L. (2003) "Value-based software engineering: a case study", *IEEE Computer*, March/April, 33-41.

Boehm, B. and Turner, R. (2005) "Management challenges to implementing agile processes in traditional development organisations", *IEEE Software*, September/October, 30-39.

Börjesson, A. and Mathiassen, L. (2004) "Successful process implementation at Ericsson", *IEEE Software*, July/August, p. 36.

Brodman, J. and Johnson, D. (1994) "What small businesses and small organisations say about the CMM", *IEEE Software*, p 331.

Brodman, J. and Hannigan, S. (2003) "Achieving level 2 and beyond", paper presented at *Software Engineering Process Group Conference*, Boston, MA, February 24-27, 2003.

Brodnik, M., Plouse, R. and Leip, T. (2008) "Why do I need all that process? I'm only a small project" [online], available: http://www.stsc.hill.af.mil/crosstalk/2008/02/0802Brodnik.html [accessed 3 March 2008] ©Intel Corporation.

Brooks, F. (1995) *The Mythical Man-month*, Silver revised version of 1975 original), Reading, PA, Addison-Wesley.

Brown, L., ed. (1993) *Oxford English Dictionary, the new shorter, Oxford*: Clarendon Press.

Capability Maturity Model® Integration (CMMI^SM^), Version 1.1, CMMI^SM^ for Software Engineering, (CMMI-SW, V1.1), Staged Representation

(2002) CMU/SEI-2002-TR-029, ESC-TR-2002-029 [online], available at: http://www.sei.cmu .edu/cmmi/models/ sw-staged.doc [accessed 13 Sep 2007].

Caputo, K. and Hefner, R. (2004) "Strategies for transitioning from SW-CMM to CMMI", paper presented at *Software Engineering Process Group Conference*, Orlando, Florida, 11 March, 2004.

Card, D. (1991) "Understanding process improvement", *IEEE Software*, July, 102-103.

Casey, V. and Richardson, I. (2006) "Project management within virtual software teams", paper presented at the *International Conference on Global Software Engineering (ICGSE'06)*, Costão do Santinho, Florianópolis, Brazil, October 16-19.

Cater-Steel, A. (2001) "Process improvement in four small software companies", In: *13th Australian Software Engineering Conference*, IEEE Computer Society, 26-28 August, Canberra, Australia, 262-272.

—. (2004) "Low-rigour, rapid software process assessments for small software development firms", In: *15th Australian Software Engineering Conference*, IEEE Computer Society, 13-16 April, Melbourne, Australia, 368-377.

Cater-Steel, A. and Rout, T. (2006) "SPI program retrospective: evaluating long-term benefits for small firms", paper presented at *6th International SPICE Conference*, Luxembourg, 3-5 May

Cepeda, S., Garcia, S. and Langhout, J. (2008) "If CMMI useful and usable in small settings? One example" [online], available: http://www.stsc.hill.af.mil/crosstalk/2008/02/0802Cepeda.html [accessed 3 March 2008].

Charette, R. (2005) "Why software fails", *IEEE Spectrum*, September, 42-49.

Chen, J., Lee, T., Zhang, T. and Zhang, Y. (2003) "Systems requirements for organisational learning", *Communications of the ACM*, 46(12), 73-78.

Clements, P., Jones, L., Northrop, L. and McGregor, J. (2005) "Project management in a software product line organisation", *IEEE Software*, September/October, p. 54-62.

Conrow, E. (2005) "Risk management for systems of systems", *Crosstalk [online]*, available: http://www.stsc.hill.af.mil/crosstalk/2005/02/0502conrow.html [accessed 5 Feb 2008].

Corbett, T. (1995) *Report on CSE's first ISO 9001 cluster for Small companies*, Dublin, CSE, DCU.

Coulter, C. (2005) "Prison service computer system costing 500,000 Euros was abandoned", *The Irish Times C&AG's Report*, 28 September, p. 8.

Daily, K. and Dresner, D. (2003) "Towards software excellence—informal self-assessment for software developers", *Software Process Improvement and Practice*, Wiley 8, 157-168.

Damian, D. (2006) "Requirements engineering in distributed projects", panel description from the *International Conference on Global Software Engineering (ICGSE'06)*, Costão do Santinho, Florianópolis, Brazil, October 16-19.

Debou, C. and Kuntzmann-Combelles, A. (2000) "Linking software process improvement to business strategies: experiences from industry" *Software Process Improvement and Practice*, Wiley 5, 55-64.

Dedrick, J., Gurbaxani, V. and Kraemer, K. (2003) "Information technology and economic performance: a critical review of the empirical evidence", *ACM Computing Surveys*, 35(1), 1-28.

Dekkers, C. (2005) "Creating requirements-based estimates before requirements are complete", *Crosstalk* [online], available: http://www.stsc.hill.af.mil/crosstalk/2005/04/0504dekkers.html [accessed 24 March 2008].

Dellana, S and Wiebe, H. (1992), "Application of total quality management to research and development: an historical perspective", *IEEE Computer*, September, 327-331.

Demirörs, E., Demirörs, O., Dikenelli, O. and Keskin, B. (1998) "Process improvement towards ISO 9001 certification in a small software organisation", *IEEE* Proceedings of the 20th International Conference on Software Engineering, Kyoto, Japan, April 19-25.

Denne, M. and Cleland-Huang, J. (2004) "The incremental funding method: data-driven software development", *IEEE Software*, May/June, p. 39-47.

Devaraj, S. and Babu, S. (2004) "How to measure the relationship between training and job performance", *Communications of the ACM*, 47(5), 63-67.

Dieste, O., Juristo, N. and Shull, F. (2008) "Understanding the customer: what do we know about requirements elicitation?", *IEEE Software*, March/April, 11-13.

Donnellan, E. and Reid, L. (2005) "Millions overpaid to health staff under new pay system", *The Irish Times*, 5 October, p. 1.

Donzelli, P. (2006) "A decision support system for software project management", *IEEE Software*, July/August, 67-75.

Dreyfus, L., Ahire, S. and Ebrahimpour, M. (2004) "The impact of just-in-time implementation and ISO 9000 certification on total quality management", *IEEE transactions on engineering management*, 51(2), 125-141.

Drobka, J., Noftz, D. and Raghu, R. (2004) "Piloting XP on four mission-critical projects", *IEEE Software*, November/December, 70-75.

Ebert, C. (2006) "Road blocks and enablers for global software engineering projects", for panel at the *International Conference on Global Software Engineering (ICGSE'06)*, Costão do Santinho, Florianópolis, Brazil, October 16-19.

Erdogmus, H., Favaro, J. and Strigel, W. (2004) "Return on investment", *IEEE Software*, May/June, 18-22.

ESPINODE Executive Summary, http://www.atb-bremen.de/spinode-ng/ecr/ Executiv_Summary _s3.htm (2002).

ESPITI—The Complete European guide to the Initiative (1995) Forschungszentrum Karlsruhe GmbH and MARI Ltd, with contributions from ESPITI regional organisations.

European Foundation Quality Model accessible at: http://www.efqm.org/ [accessed 02 May 2010].

Feather, M., Cornford, S. and Hicks, K. (2008) "A broad, quantitative model for making early requirements decisions", *IEEE Software*, March/April, 49-56.

Ferguson, J. and Sheard, S. (1998) "Leveraging your CMM efforts for IEEE/EIA 12207", *IEEE Software*, September/October, 23-28.

Ferguson, P., Leman, G., Perini, P., Renner, S. and Seshagiri, G. (1999) "Software process improvement works!" *Advanced Information Services, Inc., Technical Report CMU/SEI-99-TR-027, ESC-TR-99-026*, Pittsburgh, PA, Carnegie Mellon University, Software Engineering Institute.

Fetzer, D. (2002) "Making investment decisions for software process improvement", The DOD Software Tech News, 5(4), 19-22 available at: www.softwaretechnews.com [accessed 30 August 2007].

Fink, A. (1995) *How to Design Surveys*, Thousand Oaks, CA: Sage Publications.

Fitzgerald, B. and Kenny, T. (2004) "Developing an information systems infrastructure with open source software", *IEEE Software*, January/February, 50-55.

Flowers, S. (1996) Software *failure: management failure*, Chichester, West Sussex, England: John Wiley and Sons.

Garcia, S. (2005) "How standards enable adoption of project management practice" *IEEE Software*, September/October, 22-29.

Gerlach, J., Neumann, B., Moldauer, E., Argo, M. and Frisby, D. (2002) "Determining the cost of IT services", *Communications of the ACM*, 45(9), 61-67.

Glinz, M. (2008) "A risk-based, value-oriented approach to quality requirements", *IEEE Software*, March/April, 34-41.

Grable, R., Jernigan, J., Pogue, C. and Davis, D. (1999) "Metrics for Small Projects: Experiences at the SED", *IEEE Software*, March/April, 21-29.

Grimstad, S and Jørgensen, M. (2007) "Inconsistency of expert judgment-based estimates of software development effort", to be published in *Journal of Systems and Software*.

Groth, R. (2004) "Is the software industry's productivity declining?", *IEEE Software*, November/December, 92-94.

Grünbacher, P., Ramler, R., Retschitzegger, W. and Schwinger, W. (2004) "Making quality a first-class citizen in web engineering" in Wong, B., ed. *Software Quality: Proceedings from the Second Workshop*, Edinburgh, Scotland, Monday 24th May 2004.

Gruschke, T. and Jørgensen, M. (2007) "Assessing uncertainty of software development effort estimates: learning from outcome feedback", to be published in *ACM Transactions on Software Engineering and Methodology*.

Guerrero, F. and Eterovic, Y. (2004) "Adopting the SW-CMM in a small IT organization", *IEEE Software*, July-August, p. 29.

Hantos, P. (2005) "Inherent risks in object-oriented development", *Crosstalk* [online], available: http://www.stsc.hill.af.mil/crosstalk/2005/02/0502Hantos.html [accessed 24 March 2008].

Herron, D and Gamus, D. (2005) "Identifying your organisation's best practices", *Crosstalk*, [online], available: http://www.stsc.hill.af.mil/crosstalk/2005/06/0506Herron.html [accessed 24 March 2008].

Holt, G. (2005) "Software risk management from a system perspective", *Crosstalk*, [online], available: http://www.stsc.hill.af.mil/crosstalk/2005/02/0502Holt.html [accessed 24 March 2008].

Horn, C. (2009) "Why has software been so difficult to write well?", *The Engineers Journal*, 63(9), 476-479.

Howard, A. (2001) "Software engineering project management", *Communications of the ACM*, 44(5), 23-24.

Howard, A. (2002) "Rapid application development: rough and dirty or value-for-Money Engineering?", *Communications of the ACM*, 45(10), 27-29.

Hsieh, Y. (2006) "Culture and shared understanding in distributed requirements engineering", paper presented at the *International Conference on Global Software Engineering (ICGSE"06)*, Costão do Santinho, Florianópolis, Brazil, October 16-19.

Humphrey, W. (1990) *Managing the Software Process*, 1989 ed. reprinted with corrections made, New York: Addison-Wesley.

Hunter, R. and Thayer, R., eds. (2001) *Software Process Improvement*, IEEE Computer Society.

Huo, M., Verner, J., Babar, M. and Zhu, L. (2004) "How does agility ensure quality?", in Wong, B., ed., *Software Quality: Proceedings from the Second Workshop*, Edinburgh, Scotland, Monday 24th May.

Hutchings, T., Hyde, M., Marca, D. and Cohen, L. (1993) "Process improvement that lasts: an integrated training and consulting method", *Communications of the ACM*, 36(10), 105-113.

Ibrahim, L. (2001) "For the FAA, software process improvement is not enough", The DOD Software Tech News, 4(3), 5-7 available at: www.softwaretechnews.com [accessed 30 August 2007].

ISEB foundation course in testing, version 2.0 (2002) Systeme Evolutif, Maidenhead UK.

ISO available at: www.iso.org. [accessed 19 May 2008].

ISO 9001 : Quality systems, model for quality assurance in design/ development, production and installation (1994) International Organisation for Standardization, Geneva, Switzerland.

ISO 9001 : 2000 Quality Management Systems – Requirements, (2000) Committee draft, ISO/TC 176/SC 2/N 434 International Organisation for Standardisation, Geneva, Switzerland.

ISO 9000-3 Guidelines for the Application of ISO 9001 to the Development, Supply and Maintenance of Software, International Organisation for Standardization, Geneva, Switzerland.

ISO/IEC 12207: Information technology – Software life cycle processes (1994) International Organisation for Standardisation, Geneva, Switzerland.

ISO/IEC PDTR 29110, WD2 Software Engineering – Lifecycle Profiles for Very Small Enterprises (VSE) (2008[22]) JTC1/SC7/WG10 International Organisation for Standardization, Geneva, Switzerland.

[22] Work in progress by JTC VSC 07/WG 24 to create a Technical Report that references other standards. Part 1 Overview; Part 2 Framework and taxonomy; Part

ISO/IEC TR 15504 Software Process Assessment, (1998) JTC1/SC7/WG10 International Organisation for Standardization, Geneva, Switzerland.

ISO/IEC 15939: Software Measurement Process (2001) JTC1/SC7/WG10 International Organisation for Standardization, Geneva, Switzerland.

ISO/IEC 23026: Software Engineering – recommended practice for the internet – web site engineering, web site management, and web site life cycle (2006) JTC1/SC7 International Organisation for Standardization, Geneva, Switzerland.

Jackson, M. (2004) "Seeing more of the world", *IEEE Software*, November/December, 83-85.

Jensen, B., Lyngshede, S. and Soendergaard, D. (2004) "A quality definition for open source software" in Wong, B., ed., Software Quality: *Proceedings from the Second Workshop*, Edinburgh, Scotland, Monday 24th May 2004.

Jones, C. (2008) "Development practices for small software applications" [online], available: http://www.stsc.hill.af.mil/crosstalk/2008/02/0802Jones.html [accessed 3 March 2008].

Jørgensen, M. (2005) "Practical guidelines for expert-judgement-based software effort estimation", *IEEE Software*, May/June, 57-63.

Jurison, J. (1999) "Software project management: the manager's view", *Communications of the Association for Information Systems*, 2(17), 1-41.

Juristo, N., Moreno, A. and Strigel, W. (2006) "Software testing practices in industry", *IEEE Software*, July/August, 19-21.

Karlsson, J. and Ryan, K. (1997) "A cost-value approach for prioritising requirements", *IEEE Software*, September/October, 67-74.

Kautz, K. (1999) "Making sense of measurement for small organisations", *IEEE Software*, March/April, 14-20.

Kautz, K. and Larsen, E (2003) "The dissemination of software process improvement innovations: the ESPITI project revisited", available: http://www.iris.informatik.gu.se/conference/iris20/8.htm [accessed 21 November 2003].

Kimmerly, P. (2005) "Process therapy", *Crosstalk*, [online], available: http://www.stsc.hill.af.mil/crosstalk/2005/06/0506Kimmerly.html [accessed 24 March 2008].

3 Assessment guide; Part 4 n Profile specifications; Part 5 n, Management and engineering guides, where n stands for each profile.

Kitson, D. (2005) "The CMMI® product suite and international Standards: an update" paper presented at the *4th International SPICE Conference on Process Assessment and Improvement*, Klagenfurt, Austria, 28-29 April.

Krasner, H. (2001) "Accumulating the body of evidence for the payoff of software process improvement", written in 1997, in Hunter, R. and R. Thayer, eds., *Software Process Improvement*, Piscataway, NJ: IEEE Computer Society, 519-529.

Labanyi, D. (2005) "Garda computer summonses thrown out", *The Irish Times Motors*, 28 September, p. 1.

Lee, S. and Roberts, P. (1997) "Quality management strategy evaluation using quality function deployment methodology under Chinese culture", paper presented at PICMET"97 Portland International Conference on Management of Engineering and Technology, Portland Oregon, 27-31 July 1997.

Lindvall, M., Muthig, D., Dagnino, A., Wallin, C., Stupperich, M., Kiefer, D., May, J. and Kähkönen, T. (2004) "Agile software development in large organisations", *IEEE Computer*, December, 26-34.

Little, T. (2004) "Value creation and capture: a model of the software development process", *IEEE Software*, May/June, 48-53.

Mahapatra, R. and Lai, V. (2005) "Evaluating end-user training", *Communications of the ACM*, 48(1), 67-70.

Maxwell, K. and Forselius, P. (2000) "Benchmarking software development productivity", *IEEE Software*, January/February, 80-88.

McGarry, J., Card, D., Jones, C., Layman, B., Clark, E., Dean, J. Hall, F. (2002) *Practical Software Measurement*, Boston: Addison-Wesley.

McGee, H. (2008) "Delays and overruns in State online projects highlighted", *The Irish Times*, 8 January, p. 5.

McGibbon, T. (1999) "A business case for software process improvement revised; measuring return on investment from software engineering and management", A DACS state-of-the-art report, prepared for Air Force Research Laboratory, Rome, NY.

McMahon, P., (2005) "Extending agile methods: a distributed project and organisational improvement perspective", [online], available: http://www.stsc.hill.af.mil/crosstalk/2005/05/0505McMahon.html [accessed 24 March 2008].

Menzies, T. and Cukic, B. (2000) "When to test less", *IEEE Software*, September/October, 107-112.

Messerschmitt, D. and Szyperski, C. (2004) "Marketplace issues in software planning and design", *IEEE Software*, May/June, 62-70.

Metzler, S. (1998) "SCATE, review Group Findings – Ireland", paper presented at the *SCATE Workshop*, Brussels, Belgium, June 19.

Mitev, N. (2000) "Toward social constructivist understandings of IS success and failure: introducing a new computerised reservation system", in: *Information Systems: The Twenty-first International Conference*, Brisbane, Queensland, Australia.

Morrison, C. (1996) *Trans Ireland – Software Process improvement Network v. 1.03*, Belfast, Northern Ireland, Software Industry Federation.

National Standards Authority of Ireland, available at http://www.nsai.ie [accessed 6 Feb 2008].

Nelson, R, E. Whitener, E. and H. Philcox, H. (1995) "The Assessment of End-User Training Needs", *Communications of the ACM*, 38(7), 27-39.

Nidiffer, K and Dolan, D. (2005) "Evolving distributed project management", *IEEE Software*, September/October, 63-72.

Nilson, C (1998) *How to manage training*, New York, American Management Association.

O'Connell, F. (1994) *How to run successful projects II – the silver bullet*, Hemel Hempstead, Hertfordshire, UK: Prentice Hall.

Oppenheim, A. (1966) *Questionnaire Design and Attitude Measurement*, London: Heinemann.

Osorio, S., Soto, D., Ramirez, P. and Toro, D. (2007*) A study of the critical success and failure factors for small and medium enterprises of software development, Parquesoft case*, San Buenaventura University Engineering Faculty, System Engineering Program, Santiago de Cali.

O'Sullivan, P. and Fitzpatrick, J. (2004) "Choosing a software engineering process model", *The Engineers Journal*, 58 (05), 338-341.

Paasivaara, M. and Lassenius, C. (2006), paper presented at the *International Conference on Global Software Engineering (ICGSE'06),* Costão do Santinho, Florianópolis, Brazil, October 16-19.

Paulk, M., Weber, C., Garcia, S., Chrissis, M. and Bush, M. (1993) *Key Practices of the Capability Maturity Model SEI-93-TR-025*, Pittsburgh, PA, Software Engineering Institute.

Paulk, M. (1994) *A Comparison of ISO 9001 and the Capability Maturity Model for Software, CMU/SEI-94-TR-12; ESC-TR-94-12*, Pittsburgh, PA, Carnegie Mellon University, Software Engineering Institute.

—. (1999) "Analysing the conceptual relationship between ISO/IEC 15504 (software process assessment) and Capability Maturity Model for software", presented at *1999 International Conference on Software Quality*, Cambridge MA.

Premraj, R., Twala, B., Mair, C. and Forselius, P. (2004) "Productivity of software projects by business sector: an empirical analysis of trends", Software Engineer.org Newsletter, 5 September, available at: [accessed 24 March 2008].

Pulford, K., Kuntzmann-Combelles, A. and Shirlaw, S. (1996) *A quantitative approach to Software Management: the ami Handbook*, Wokingham, England: Addison-Wesley.

Putnam, L., Putnam, D. and Beckett, D. (2005) "A method for improving developers' software size estimates", *Crosstalk* [online], available: http://www.stsc.hill.af.mil/crosstalk/2005/04/0504Putnam.html [accessed 24 March 2008].

Reid, L. (2005) "HSE to suspend second computer project", *The Irish Times*, 6 October, p. 1.

Richardson, I. (1999) *Improving the software process in small indigenous software development companies using a model based on quality function deployment*, PhD thesis, University of Limerick.

—. (2001) "Software process matrix: a small company SPI model", *Software Process Improvement and Practice*, Wiley 6, 157-165.

Richardson, I. and von Wangenheim, C. (2007) "Why are small software organisations different?", *IEEE Software*, January/February, 18-22.

Rifkin, S. (2000) "When the project absolutely must get done: marrying the organisation chart with the precedence diagram", *IT Metrics Strategies*, VI (5), 1, 8-16.

Rifkin, S. (2001) "Why software process innovations are not adopted", *IEEE Software,* July/August, 110-112.

Rising, L. and Janoff, N. (2000) "The scrum software development process for small teams", *IEEE Software*, July/August, 2-8.

Roetzheim, W. (2005) "Estimating and managing project scope for new development", *Crosstalk*, [online], available: http://www.stsc.hill.af.mil/crosstalk/2005/04/0504Roetzheim.html [accessed 24 March 2008].

Rost, J. (2004) "Political reasons for failed software projects", *IEEE Software*, November/December, 102-104.

—. (2005) "Software engineering theory in practice", *IEEE Software*, March/April, 96,94.

Rout, T. (2005) "SPICE tutorial", tutorial presented at the *4th International SPICE Conference on Process Assessment and Improvement*, Klagenfurt, Austria, 27 April.

Rout, T. and Tuffley, A. (2007) "Harmonising ISO/IEC 15504 and CMMI", *Software Process Improvement and Practice*, Wiley 12, 367-371.

Runeson, P. (2006) "A survey of unit testing practices", *IEEE Software*, July/August, 22-29.

Sanders, J. (1996) ESPITI *PPR_M18T, version 1.1*, Dublin, CSE, DCU 14 June.

Sanders, M. (1997) "SCATE—managing your software before it manages you", ESSI P24 291. Catalyst Software, Dublin.

Sanders, M. ed. (1998) *The SPIRE handbook—Better Faster Cheaper Software Development in Small Companies*, Dublin, CSE, DCU.

Sanders, M. and Richardson, I. (2008) "Finding out what happened after SPI assistance in Ireland", In: EuroSPI'2008, 3-5 September, Dublin, Ireland, 1.23-1.32.

Sarma, A. and van der Hoek, A. (2006) "Towards awareness in the large", paper presented at the *International Conference on Global Software Engineering (ICGSE"06)*, Costão do Santinho, Florianópolis, Brazil, October 16-19.

Scannell, T. (1996) *ESPITI User Survey, Results and Analysis*, CSE, DCU, Dublin, 16 May.

Sheard, S. and Miller, C. (2000) "The Shangri-La of ROI", *Technical report for INCOSE members of Software Productivity Consortium*, Herndon VA, USA.

Sliger, M. (2004) "Fooling around with XP", *Better Software*, May/June, p. 16.

Small Company Action Training and Enabling, Report on Results of SCATE Threads French-English-Greek (1998) SCATE project Consortium Members, 25 September.

Software Engineering Institute (2007) *Process maturity profile CMMI® SCAMPI℠ class A appraisal results, 2007 mid-year update September 2007* [online], available: http://www.sei.cmu.edu [12 March 2008].

Spinellis D. and Szyperski, C. (2004) "How Is open source affecting software development?", *IEEE Software*, January/February, 28-33.

SPIRE Case Studies (1998) September-December, Dublin, DCU.

Stallman, R. (2004) "Against software patents", *25th International Conference on Software Engineering (ICSE"03)*, Edinburgh, Scotland, 25-28 May.

TickIT Guide to Software Quality Management System Construction and Certification using EN29001/BS 5750 Part 1, Issue 2.0 (1992) London, DISC TickIT Office, 28 February.

Tiwana, A. and Keil, M. (2004) "The one-minute risk assessment tool", *Communications of the ACM*, 47 (11), 73-77.

TRI-SPIN Case Studies (1996) Dublin, DCU.

Verner, J., and Evanco, W. (2005) "In-house software development: what project management practices lead to success?", *IEEE Software*, January/February, 86-93.

Vidakovich, J (2000) *Trainers in motion*, New York, American Management Association.

Voas, J. and Laplante, P. (2007) "Standards confusion and harmonisation", *IEEE Computer*, 40(7), 94-96.

von Wangenheim, C., Anacleto, A. and Salviano, C. (2006) "Helping small companies assess software processes", *IEEE Software*, January/February, 91-98.

Zhiying, Z. (2003) "CMM in uncertain environments", *Communications of the ACM*, 46(8), 115-119.